ON THE EDGE

AMERICA'S MIDDLE NEIGHBORHOODS

Paul C. Brophy, Editor

The American Assembly
New York City

First Edition, September 2016.
© 2016 The American Assembly and The Federal Reserve Bank of San Francisco.
ISBN: 978-0-936904-14-6
All rights reserved. No part of this publication may be reproduced or transmitted
in any form or by any means without permission in writing from:
The American Assembly, 475 Riverside Drive, Suite 456, New York, NY 10015
www.americanassembly.org

THE AMERICAN ASSEMBLY
COLUMBIA UNIVERSITY

Library of Congress Cataloging-in-Publication Data has been applied for.
First published in report form by the Federal Reserve Bank of San Francisco.

Book and cover designed by Elizabeth Nebiolo

ACKNOWLEDGMENTS

As editor, I have many people to thank for their energy, scholarship, and commitment to this book and to middle neighborhoods.

David Erickson, head of the Community Development Department at the Federal Reserve Bank of San Francisco, showed immediate interest in middle neighborhoods as soon as I presented the idea to him. He committed much time and effort to produce this volume in report form for the bank's *Community Development Investment Review*—and this book would not have been possible without his early interest and support.

David Mortimer and his colleagues at The American Assembly, publisher of this book, were quick to see the value of a discussion of middle neighborhoods in the context of Legacy Cities—a lead initiative at The American Assembly.

Of course, thanks goes to all of the authors who, due to their commitment to middle neighborhoods, found the time to produce the thoughtful essays in this volume. All of the chapters in the book display deep thought, years of experience, and intellectual curiosity about neighborhoods and middle neighborhoods.

We had an excellent production staff that made the book as reader-friendly as possible: Mark Leneker, Elizabeth Nebiolo, Michelle Olson, and Sarah Roggio.

Finally, thanks to the many dedicated residents and community leaders working in cities across the nation to improve their neighborhoods. Their everyday commitments and concerns inspired every author in this volume and many others who believe in the importance of middle neighborhoods.

TABLE OF CONTENTS

TABLE OF CONTENTS

FOREWORD

By David J. Erickson, Director, Community Development
Department, Federal Reserve Bank of San Francisco
and David H. Mortimer, President, The American Assembly

A younger colleague asked a profound question the other day: "Could community development be more like a vitamin instead of an aspirin?"[1] Of course, we need medicine to help heal communities in deep need—the aspirin. But what tools do we have to keep neighborhoods healthy in the first place? We need vitamins, too.

Millions of homes in this country provide shelter in communities that are mostly intact; they are in communities that may be struggling in some ways but have many existing strengths and assets. This housing stock—which is larger than all the government subsidized housing stock ever built—should be used in a strategic way to improve the lives of low-income and lower-middle income Americans.[2] These communities, often referred to as "middle neighborhoods," require some strategic investments—but at a much smaller scale than is required to provide affordable housing in a hot real estate market, or to revitalize neighborhoods that have fallen into deep distress and are full of vacant structures, high crime, and poorly performing schools. In many instances, a whole middle neighborhood might require less in government and philanthropic subsidy to keep it viable than it costs to build a single apartment in New York or San Francisco. And keeping these communities from sliding into neglect and disinvestment is also a long-term savings, since the cost of turning communities around once they have lost their confidence and their amenities have decayed is astronomical.

We must continue to have focused and energetic conversations about income and wealth inequality and how inequality can play out over geographic space—including gentrification, displacement, and neighborhood decline.[3] These problems are significant and require a robust response if we are to try to preserve a society in which everyone has the opportunity to lead a healthy, productive, and satisfying life. To that end, we need more tools to address these problems.

---

[1]   This idea came from William Dowling at the Federal Reserve Bank of San Francisco.

[2]   David J. Erickson, *Housing Policy Revolution: Networks and Neighborhoods* (Washington, DC: Urban Institute Press, 2009), p xvi.

[3]   Gentrification and displacement are significant problems in strong market cities where low-income renters and home owners are being displaced from their communities. It is worth noting, however, that this problem is isolated in a few places. An analysis in *Governing* magazine indicated that only 8 percent of census tracts experienced gentrification pressure between 2000 and 2010. For more information on methodology and their results, see Mike Maciag, "Gentrification in America Report," *Governing* (2015), available at http://www.governing.com/gov-data/census/gentrification-in-cities-governing-report.html.

But we also must have another conversation. We need to assess how middle neighborhoods can help create the opportunities we want for everyone in our society. Every middle neighborhood should be viewed as a potential to create an "opportunity neighborhood." A neighborhood that encourages work and achievement in school. A safe neighborhood where children can play and exercise. A neighborhood that builds social connections and community. A neighborhood where homeowners can expect homeownership to be a sound investment. A neighborhood that improves overall population health and helps check our runaway growth in avoidable chronic disease.

The essays in this volume tackle strategies to do just that. They do so from many angles and perspectives in communities across the country. The experts writing here are exploring new ways we can use middle neighborhoods as one of the most powerful tools we have to create opportunity neighborhoods and push back on the many headwinds that are leading to increased economic segregation in the United States. They show us how to produce more vitamins.

This volume represents a collaboration between the Federal Reserve Bank of San Francisco and The American Assembly of Columbia University, which was initiated by the book's editor Paul Brophy. It extends and complements the work and interests of The Assembly's Legacy Cities Partnership and the bank's well-known work in our nation's communities. The chapters were initially published in Volume 11, Issue 1 of the *Community Development Investment Review*.

We are grateful for the generous support of the Muriel F. Siebert Foundation, which helped make this volume possible.

David H. Mortimer
President
The American Assembly

David J. Erickson
Director, Community Development
Federal Reserve Bank of San Francisco

PREFACE
MIDDLE NEIGHBORHOODS IN AMERICA'S CITIES AND SUBURBS: REDISCOVERING A PRECIOUS ASSET

By Paul C. Brophy, Principal
and Brophy & Reilly, LLC

Policymakers in America have long understood that the quality of life in neighborhoods—or the absence of it—matters a great deal to the social and economic vitality of larger cities and surrounding metropolitan regions. This understanding translated into clearing slums in the 1950s and 1960s, improving distressed neighborhoods via community development corporations later in the twentieth century, and seeking communities of opportunity in today's policy environment.

Largely absent from these policy and redevelopment efforts is the consideration of neighborhoods in the middle. These are neighborhoods that are not in deep distress, but are not thriving either.

These "middle neighborhoods" exist in almost all cities and some larger suburbs. They are especially important in places where the overall population of a city is declining. Population fragility in these areas is much more of a concern than the phenomenon of gentrification—which is prevalent in hot-market cities. As Henry S. Webber describes in his chapter, the decline of these cities' middle neighborhoods has had more negative consequences for their residents than rapidly rising prices.

These cities—which are struggling to hold their population and move their economies into the twenty-first century—have been labeled "legacy cities." Much of the material in this volume focuses on these cities.

Legacy cities have experienced profound economic decline and population loss because of fundamental shifts in the global economy and policy decisions made at the local, state, and federal levels. Legacy Cities Partnership[1] defines these cities—which are primarily located in the Great Lakes and Northeast regions—as metropolitan areas with over 50,000 residents that have lost 20 percent or more of their population since the mid-century. The future trajectory of these categorized 48 legacy cities will have major consequences for neighborhood vitality. It also will impact public finances and housing markets throughout the country.

The middle neighborhoods described in this volume usually have a functioning housing market, which is one indicator of any neighborhood's well-being. But it is not at all clear to existing

---

[1] More information is available at http://www.legacycities.org/.

residents and prospective movers-in whether the trajectory of housing values is going up or down. Often these neighborhoods are situated near or adjoin distressed neighborhoods—and there is an active worry that the nearby distress could spread to the middle neighborhoods. One way to think about middle neighborhoods is that they are on the edge of transition.

These are also neighborhoods where housing is often quite affordable. In addition, quality of life—measured by employment rates, crime rates, and public school performance—is sufficiently good that new residents are still willing to play the odds and choose these neighborhoods while knowing that they may decline rather than improve. In fact, in cities where rising prices are resulting in displacement of modest-income households, these middle neighborhoods can be areas that provide good housing and neighborhood environments for those needing more modestly priced housing.

The well-being of these neighborhoods is essential for the families and individuals living in them. It is also critical for the overall financial stability of many cities and suburbs that rely on the property tax base of these neighborhoods. Should these middle neighborhoods decline in value by slipping into distress, local governments will have even fewer dollars to provide needed city services in these and other neighborhoods.

As Ira Goldstein, William Schrecker, and Jacob Rosch describe in this volume, these middle neighborhoods house a substantial portion of the residents of many older cities—with the overall percentage of residents living in middle neighborhoods of the cities studied ranging from 37 percent to 51 percent.

Given the importance of these neighborhoods to America's cities and suburbs, it is unsettling how little attention is being paid to ensuring that these neighborhoods transition into greater health rather than lapse into decline. This volume is an effort to add middle neighborhoods as a focal point for the nation's urban and suburban agenda, with special emphasis on legacy cities.

The authors in this volume think of attention to middle neighborhoods as "an ounce of prevention being worth a pound of cure," as Benjamin Franklin said long ago. Strengthening middle neighborhoods is very inexpensive and relatively simple when compared with the great costs and complexities of remediating the deep challenges of distressed communities or covering the costs of producing affordable housing in very hot markets.

On the Edge aims to stimulate a national dialogue about middle neighborhoods.

Joseph McNeely and I begin the book by tracing earlier efforts to stabilize these neighborhoods. Ira Goldstein and his colleagues at The Reinvestment Fund then describe the demographics and characteristics of this category of neighborhoods in select cities. George Galster continues this overview and makes the case for why middle neighborhoods matter in America's cities and suburbs. Bob Weissbourd then places these neighborhoods in their economic context regionally.

Alan Mallach next describes the many challenges that face middle neighborhoods and the importance of homeownership in them.

Other *On the Edge* authors provide important case studies of promising approaches underway to strengthen middle neighborhoods, with a particular focus on Detroit, Milwaukee, Baltimore, and cities in Ohio. These chapters are very close to the ground and offer sound practical examples and advice for strengthening middle neighborhoods.

The final chapter focuses on the policy changes needed at the local level to support those working to improve middle neighborhoods. This work covers general policy changes and particular ways to balance physical improvements with historic preservation.

All of these esteemed authors believe that increasing our understanding of middle neighborhoods will enhance the discussions underway nationally and locally about improving distressed neighborhoods or coping with gentrification. We hope *On the Edge* sparks new discussions, research, and policies as well as innovative programs that will strengthen and secure the social and economic vitality of middle neighborhoods in all of America's cities and suburbs.

I. THE MIDDLE NEIGHBORHOOD MOVEMENT, 1970–2000

By Joeseph McNeely, Community Development Consultant
and Paul C. Brophy, Brophy & Reilly, LLC

Since the turn of the twentieth century, a broad range of people and institutions has been concerned with improving neighborhoods in America's cities. Whether efforts were led by the reformers during the Progressive era fighting for building and safety codes or business leaders figuring out how to revitalize cities[1] in the 1950s and 1960s, these efforts sometimes included actions to strengthen urban neighborhoods were sometimes part of those efforts.

During the 1970s, there was a remarkable surge in grassroots activity in moderate-income (i.e., working-class and lower middle-income) neighborhoods across the country. It was well documented in the media and literature.[2] The National Commission on Neighborhoods (1977–1979) produced two volumes of case studies about these remarkable organizations.[3] National centers provided training and support to local groups.

Groups often sprang up in reaction to public projects like highway construction or school demolition. They turned their energy toward keeping the population they had and attracting new residents to neighborhoods that had been losing population. The phenomenon blanketed the country: Jamaica Plains, Boston; the Hill, Providence; North Ward, Newark; Southeast Baltimore; Manchester, Pittsburgh; Detroit Shoreway, Cleveland; North Toledo; Hamtramak, Detroit; Southwest Chicago; Blue Hills, Kansas City; Santa Fe Dr., Denver; and Chinatown, San Francisco, to name but a few of thousands.

The national convergence of local groups led to significant federal policy changes, including passage of the Community Reinvestment Act. For the last 20 years, however, the national recognition and support of this local energy, and attention to appropriate national policies for neighborhood revitalization, has largely disappeared. Where did that surge in national activity, funding, media attention, research and policy come from and where did it go? What remains and how do we use it to build critical attention to the plight of middle neighborhoods at this moment?

---

1   See https://www.youtube.com/watch?v=RUmECXiB_RU for an interesting period piece on how ACTION tried to generate support for improving neighborhoods.
2   See Henry Boyte, *The Backyard Revolution: Understanding the New Citizen Movement* (Philadelphia: Temple University Press, 1981).
3   The case studies were appendices to the commission's final report, all of which are at http://catalog.hathitrust.org/Record/000303116?type%5B%5D=all&lookfor%5B%5D=national%20commission%20on%20neighborhoods&ft=

WHERE DID THE ENERGY TO REVITALIZE MIDDLE NEIGHBORHOODS COME FROM?

The major upsurge of activity in middle neighborhoods in cities began as community organizing efforts. The success of that organizing led to enormous policy change for public and private institutions. The subsequent self-help neighborhood revitalization programs led to a new set of strategies for neighborhood revitalization, many of which are standard practice today. The growth ranged from organizing to policy impact programs to strategies.

THE ORGANIZING WAS THE RESULT OF A CONVERGENCE OF THREE FORCES.

The first force was progressive organizing by religious institutions and religious institution-funded community organizations oriented to reducing white flight from cities and building organizations that could form effective coalitions with inner-city minority and civil rights groups. The thesis was that cities would not survive if they became "black, brown and broke,"[4] nor would there be effective political will for the resource allocations needed for inner-city development without a coalition across the whole city.

The second force was a backlash in blue-collar, white communities resentful of the public attention and government resources devoted to minority, inner-city communities when their blue-collar neighborhoods in the same cities were suffering their own problems.

A final force was the emergence of white ethnic identity organizing, partially in response to the emergence of black identity, but also from the efforts of third-generation descendants of southern and Eastern European immigrants to reclaim the values and ethnic strength of the first generation of immigrants.

While it began in community organizing, the movement turned to revitalization projects and programs to implement its aspirations. National foundations and support groups, longtime advocates of revitalization approaches to community development, encouraged the expansion of the neighborhood organizations' agenda and capabilities. The Ford Foundation, for example, had pioneered such an approaches in "the gray areas program" of the 1950s and the Community Development Corporation (CDC) program of the 1960s. The movement also had intellectual and academic underpinnings and advocates, ranging from Herbert Gans' study of Italian neighborhoods in Boston[5] to Jane Jacobs' advocacy of revitalizing walkable communities rather than demolishing and starting over with modernistic high-rises.[6] The concepts of neighborhood and the strategies of organizing communities, mobilizing assets, revitalizing before dilapidation sets in, and finding ways to compete in the market to attract new residents with assets have antecedents in earlier efforts that include the settlement house movement of the early twentieth century, 1950s and 1960s civil rights opposition to urban renewal, and modifications

---

[4]　Msgr. Geno Baroni used this phrase in a speech at a conference on Minority Business Development sponsored by the Federal Reserve Bank of Boston in 1976. Proceedings are at http://www.bostonfed.org/economic/conf/conf17/conf17.pdf.

[5]　Herb Gans, *The Urban Villagers: Group and Class in the Life of Italian-Americans* (London: The Free Press, 1981).

[6]　Jane Jacobs, *The Death and Life of Great American Cities* (New York: Random House, 1961).

to the federal urban renewal program in the Neighborhood Development Program and the Federally Assisted Code Enforcement program.[7]

As the middle neighborhood organizations with origins in fighting public projects and programs turned their attention to community development projects and programs, they were grouped with earlier Community Development Corporation (CDC) efforts in more distressed neighborhoods under the broad term of neighborhood development organizations. While the Ford Foundation and federal support continued for an early group of CDCs sponsored by the Ford Foundation, new federal initiatives were more broadly defined to fit the new universe of neighborhood development organizations. The Carter administration, for example, initiated programs at in many departments, including Housing and Urban Development (HUD), the Economic Development Administration, the Department of Labor, and Health and Human Services.

Some examples may help illustrate the evolving agendas and the enormous energy at the grassroots level:

- While fighting blockbusting and white flight in her Austin neighborhood in Chicago in the early 1970s, Gail Cincotta encountered—and her organization documented— the disappearance of lending for home mortgages and home improvement loans. This withdrawal of bank involvement occurred in spite of the fact, as documented in a study by Northwestern University, that her community had assets on deposit in banks and savings and loan associations sufficient to completely revitalize itself. The disinvestment and discriminatory lending against racially mixed and middle-city neighborhoods came to be called "redlining," after the red line the Federal Housing Administration drew on a map of the city around neighborhoods it considered too risky to insure. Cincotta and her organizers contacted similar middle-neighborhood community organizations across the country that soon documented similar behavior. Cincotta and Shel Trapp, a leading Chicago organizer, created National People's Action to fight redlining in cities across the nation. This group fought redlining wherever it was occurring, in distressed neighborhoods or middle neighborhoods that lenders judged would lapse into distress and were not deserving of mortgage loans. Of course, the inability of buyers to get a mortgage created a self-fulfilling prophecy, causing neighborhoods to fall into distress. National People's Action won support from a national organization—the National Center for Urban Ethnic Affairs, led by Msgr. Geno Baroni—that was encouraging local organizing in blue-collar neighborhoods across the country. Baroni's researchers and the staff of Sen. William Proxmire's Senate Banking Committee helped further document redlining and created a policy framework to address it. Baroni used his extensive contacts in the

---

[7] This chapter provides only a cursory history of a very complex set of activities that focused on neighborhoods in American cities in the twentieth century. For a far more complete history, see Robert Halpern, *Rebuilding the Inner City: A History of Neighborhood Initiatives to Address Poverty in the United States* (New York: Columbia University Press, 1995); and Steven D. Soifer, Joseph B. McNeely, Cathy L. Costa, and Nancy Pickering-Bernheim, *Community Economic Development and Social Work* (New York: Columbia University Press, 2014). See esp. chaps. 4–5, "History of Community Economic Development."

civil rights movement to build a genuine coalition of white ethnic, black, and Latino organizations to press for the end of redlining. This movement led to the passage of the Home Mortgage Disclosure Act (1975) and the Community Reinvestment Act (1977), both of which have been instrumental in increasing bank lending in neighborhoods in cities and suburbs.

• In 1968, a neighborhood leader in Pittsburgh, Dorothy Richardson, quietly began a program that combined energies from neighborhood residents, banks and savings and loan associations, and city government to increase lending in transition neighborhoods. The Neighborhood Services Program (NHS) combined three critical elements, and was aimed at middle neighborhoods. The three elements were (1) active organizing at the neighborhood level to engage residents in neighborhood improvement, (2) a commitment from lenders to provide mortgage loans and home improvement and marketing loans in the neighborhood to qualified buyers and owners, with a high risk loan pool for those not bankable, and (3) investments from city government in infrastructure in the neighborhoods and the use of code enforcement to get landlords and homeowners to improve their properties. This middle neighborhoods program soon caught on, and with enthusiastic support from the Federal Home Loan Bank Board [FHLBB], other NHS programs were started in other cities. By 1979, there were 13 operational NHS programs and another 10 in the development stage. This successful program to preserve middle neighborhoods was adopted by the FHLBB and HUD, and became housed in the Neighborhood Reinvestment Corporation, which is now NeighborWorks America, a congressionally charted corporation.

• In Baltimore, the South East Community Organization (SECO)—which had its origin in stopping plans for an interstate highway—and similar groups in five other cities engaged in a demonstration program funded by the federal Economic Development Administration to spread the revitalization work from housing to commercial areas. Going beyond architecturally driven models of the time (parking, brick sidewalks, and public space improvements), SECO adapted the commercial real estate techniques of suburban malls, with which the older neighborhood commercials strips competed. Its successful model added a central organization combining merchants and community leaders, the discipline of coordinated marketing and events, careful market capture analysis to determine the right mix of businesses to fill vacancies, and technical assistance and funding for business expansion. That model was later adapted to rural areas by the National Trust for Historic Preservation under the banner of "main streets." Ironically, Main Streets later reintroduced the concepts in urban commercial districts.

The middle neighborhoods also adopted other proven tools and incentives for revitalization: historic preservation; pre-purchase housing counseling; creative financing and appraisal techniques to promote housing rehabilitation and homeownership; and targeted workforce training directly linked to businesses in the neighborhood. Bankers and community activists worked together to meet the requirements of the Community Reinvestment Act, which led to a whole new domestic field of community development banking: leveraged lending techniques by which banks could help revitalize neighborhoods while still making safe investments and earning a profit.

WHERE DID ALL THIS ENERGY GO?

There are many reasons that the middle neighborhoods energy and agenda diminished in importance in urban policy and practice.

First, the presidential administrations of Ronald Reagan and George Bush turned their focus away from neighborhoods and "the urban crisis" and the role of government in saving cities to dealing with housing and homelessness. For example, Jack Kemp's focus as HUD Secretary under President Bush was on reforming public housing. The effect was so lasting that even the subsequent Democratic administration of President Clinton only marginally increased resources to neighborhoods through his Empowerment and Enterprise Zones programs and some increase in appropriations for federal programs like the Community Development Block Grant Program.

As federal support shifted in the Reagan-Ford administrations, local philanthropy expanded dramatically to provide support for neighborhood development organizations. A new set of private, national support organizations grew up: the Local Initiative Support Corporation (LISC); the Enterprise Foundation; and the Development Training Institute. Working with local funders, these national organizations created a local infrastructure for technical assistance, funding, and project development that helped stabilize the industry of neighborhood development organizations across dozens of cities. While some of the original national apparatus has disappeared—like the National Congress for Community Economic Development (NCCED) and the National Neighborhood Coalition—today there are city and state associations of these neighborhood development organizations as well as a National Association of Community Economic Development Associations (NACEDA), and other constituency groups of and for community development.

However, national attention, particularly in the philanthropic community, shifted from the middle neighborhoods and community development generally to the issues of homelessness and poverty. The impact of the Reagan-Bush cuts in cities increased and made especially visible the number of homeless people. As the plight of the homeless became a constant front-page story, public support grew for government housing programs to address it; and finally in the late 1980s, led to new funding. That funding, however, was most targeted to the homeless and those deeply in need, not the neighborhood revitalization strategies of the middle neighborhoods. Similarly, as housing prices rose in strong market cities and suburbs, it became clear that housing affordability was becoming its own crisis in America, and considerable energy was appropriately focused on dealing with the housing affordability crisis.

At the same time, policymakers were becoming acutely aware of the emergence of a new phenomenon of persistent poverty in concentrated, isolated, mostly minority census tracts of the hundred largest cities. The phenomenon was amply revealed in the census reports in 1970-1990 and extensively studied by leading researchers such as William Julius Wilson.[8] With President Clinton announcing "the end of welfare as we know it," the plight of so many desperately poor people garnered the interest of leading foundations that had been supporting the neighborhood movement. With the focus on poverty alleviation, there was a growing disaffection with place -based strategies for their failure to eradicate poverty—symbolized by the controversial but influential front-page New York Times Magazine article by Nicholas Lehman, "The Myth of Community Development"(January 9, 1994). Resources began to shift from neighborhood revitalization to strategies directly targeted to helping individual poor people get out of areas of concentrated, isolated poverty and into the mainstream economy through employment and other personal financial enhancement programs.

WHAT DID THE NEIGHBORHOOD MOVEMENT LEAVE BEHIND?

If national attention and national policy innovation is what led to calling the outpouring of local energy regarding neighborhoods a "movement," that spotlight moved on to other movements. Nonetheless, a high level of neighborhood-based activity continues in major cities across the country. The policies created by the neighborhood movement, like the Community Reinvestment Act, remain in force. The strategies and programs for neighborhood revitalization invented or refined in the 1970s and 1980s, like early intervention and reversal of disinvestment in the housing market and neighborhood commercial revitalization, have become standard practice. Some of the national framework, like the national NeighborWorks America and the Local Initiative Support Corporation (LISC), continue robust programs of support and training. Many universities have incorporated some form of community economic development into their curriculum, even offering specializations or degrees.

Moreover, many of the core principles of the middle-neighborhood revitalization strategies are permanently ingrained in community development practice locally and nationally. These include:

- the focus on a specific defined geographic area;
- a strategy of energizing revitalization when the disinvestment and deterioration has only begun rather than waiting until the neighborhood has been virtually abandoned and then initiating a process of clearance and redevelopment;
- a partnership of public, community, and private sectors to design and implement neighborhood improvement actions;
- an emphasis on assets in the neighborhood as the driver rather than deficits as has often been the emphasis in government programs;
- a market orientation toward restoring conventional economics and reinvestment in a neighborhood;
- the use of private-sector investment and project development techniques applied with social values derived from a genuine community process, including market analysis and complex financial structuring; and,

---

[8]   William Julius Wilson, *The Truly Disadvantaged: The Inner City, the Underclass, and Public Policy*, (Chicago: University of Chicago Press, 1990).

- a comprehensive approach that integrates residential, commercial, and human resource development.

While the strategies have been incorporated in best practices, there has been little national dialogue or discussion of the value and needs of the middle neighborhoods since the early 1990s. Some cities have experimented with new configurations of the strategies for a new set of neighborhoods—like Battle Creek's, Milwaukee's and Baltimore's, Healthy Neighborhoods— but there has been almost no discussion of a federal government role or support except in the trade associations of those organizations and the national networks to which they belong.

In 1979, James F. Timilty, the chairman of the National Commission on Neighborhoods, ended his letter transmitting the commission's report to President Carter by saying, "Now is the time for a national policy that works in, for, and through the neighborhoods for the people who live there." As others have written in this volume, it is still timely to take these words seriously to build from the energies within America's middle neighborhoods and to brighten their future.

Joseph McNeely is a nationally known expert and consultant on community development and a veteran community organizer. He is currently president of Metroscape Development, a real estate development firm focused on Baltimore City. From 2006–2015, he served as the initial organizer and first Executive Director of the Central Baltimore Partnership. In the early 1970s, he was the founding executive of Baltimore's South East Community Organization (SECO) and Southeast Community Development Corporation before serving at the national level in the Carter administration. He then was the president of the national Development Training Institute for 20 years. From 2006–2012, he also served as co-facilitator of the Weinberg Fellows program for nonprofit executives at the University of Baltimore's Schaefer Center. He has written extensively on community development, including a textbook in the field published by Columbia University Press, Community Economic Development and Social Work *(2014). He has taught graduate courses on community development at several universities in Maryland, New York, and Ohio. Mr. McNeely, an attorney, lives in Baltimore, is the father of twin daughters, and is married to Patricia Massey, a successful real estate developer in Baltimore City.*

Paul C. Brophy is a principal with Brophy & Reilly, LLC, a consulting firm specializing in economic development, and neighborhood improvement in legacy cities; the management of complex urban redevelopment projects; and the development of mixed-income housing communities. Brophy has been a senior advisor to the Center for Community Progress, a senior scholar at the George Warren Brown School at Washington University in St. Louis; a senior advisor to Enterprise Community Partners; and the chair of the Legacy Cities Partnership. Prior to the formation of Brophy and Reilly, LLC, Brophy was the co-CEO of Enterprise Community Partners. Prior to that, he held executive positions in Pittsburgh city government working on economic development, and downtown and neighborhood improvement. Mr. Brophy holds degrees from LaSalle University and the University of Pennsylvania. He is co-author of three books: Neighborhood Revitalization: Theory and Practice *(1975);* Housing and Local Government *(1982), and* A Guide to Careers in Community Development *(2001).*

II. THE CASE FOR INTERVENTION IN MIDDLE NEIGHBORHOODS

By George Galster, Hilberry Professor of Urban Affairs, Wayne State University

For several decades, America has been acting out a national drama that might be called "A Tale of Two (Types of) Cities." One archetypical city is growing in population, employment, and real income per capita; it has successfully managed a transition to the postindustrial economy and has tight housing markets. The other archetypical city is struggling to find its place in the twenty-first century economy, and its housing markets are considerably weaker on balance. This essay focuses on the latter type of cities, which has recently been termed "legacy cities."[1]

Within legacy cities' neighborhoods we see the same drama played out on a smaller scale. On the one hand, some neighborhoods offer high-quality residential life in all dimensions. Some of these neighborhoods have traditionally been strong and attractive, others have recently been constructed, and still other older neighborhoods have blossomed with renovations of their housing, revitalized retail sectors, and an influx of well-educated households. On the other hand, some neighborhoods continue to decay, empty out, and be inhabited by impoverished people who increasingly experience an erosion of public safety as well as quality of public and private services and facilities. Both of these extremes have been analyzed by those studying gentrification (e.g. Hyra, 2018; Freeman, 2011) and the concentration of poverty.[2]

There is a third type of neighborhood in legacy cities as well—a "middle neighborhood," which is situated between the two extremes above. Compared with places that are gentrifying or concentrating disadvantage, middle neighborhoods have been largely ignored by urban scholars and planners.[3] This oversight must be rectified because middle neighborhoods play a vital role in the overall health of a city and, I will argue, in the well-being of its poorest citizens, even if they do not live in them.

[1] The American Assembly, *Reinventing America's Legacy Cities* (New York: author, 2011).

[2] D. Hyra, *The New Urban Renewal: The Economic Transformation of Harlem and Bronzeville* (Chicago: University of Chicago Press, 2008); L. Freeman, *There Goes the Hood: Views of Gentrification from the Ground Up.* (Philadelphia: Temple University Press, 2011). For concentrated poverty, see W. J. Wilson, *The Truly Disadvantaged.* (Chicago: University of Chicago Press, 1987); Paul Jargowsky, *Concentration of Poverty in the New Millennium: Changes in the Prevalence, Composition, and Location of High-Poverty Neighborhoods* (New York: The Century Fund, 2014).

[3] For an exception, see A. Mallach, *Managing Neighborhood Change: A Framework for Sustainable and Equitable Revitalization* (Montclair: National Housing Institute, 2008).

My goal in this essay is to establish a rationale for why scholars and policymakers should seriously consider middle neighborhoods as a locus of potential policy innovation and intervention. I first provide an overview of the theory of metropolitan housing submarkets, which provides the foundation for understanding neighborhood dynamics. Within this framework, I explain downward "filtering," the primary dynamic hurting neighborhoods in legacy cities. Second, I explain how the filtering process often involves complex adjustments in lower-quality neighborhoods. Third, I explain the various inefficiencies and inequities associated with filtering. It is the tempering of the negative consequences of filtering that provides the core justification of interventions aimed at stabilizing middle neighborhoods. Finally, I discuss the equity and efficiency aspects of such potential interventions in middle neighborhoods.

THE DRIVERS OF NEIGHBORHOOD CHANGE AND FILTERING

Neighborhoods change is based on the decisions by property owners and prospective and current residents. These decisions will influence the ongoing flow of resources—money, people, time, and social and political capital—to a neighborhood that over time will influence its myriad characteristics.[4] These decisions are based on uncertain expectations about what will occur both in the neighborhood in question and in others with which this neighborhood competes.

As a foundation, I draw on the model of the metropolitan housing market developed by Rothenberg, Galster, Butler, and Pitkin.[5] This model begins by classifying the housing stock into "quality submarkets," or sets of homes and apartments that households perceive as closely substitutable, considering all the myriad attributes of the housing bundle—including place-based attributes associated with its neighborhood, such as public services, natural endowments, environmental quality, etc. Each submarket has its own supply and demand characteristics and relationship to other submarkets. Supply into one submarket (through new construction and net conversion of existing dwellings) will be influenced, among other things, by the relative rate of return that owners and developers can reap in this submarket compared with others. Demand by households in one submarket will be influenced, among other things, by the market valuations (sales prices or equivalent capitalized rents) in close-substitute submarkets that are competing for these households. Changes in the rents or sales prices in any one submarket are transmitted sequentially to other submarkets by housing owners and developers altering their supply decisions in response to a new submarket pattern of rates of return, and by households altering their occupancy decisions in response to new relative market valuations across substitute submarkets from which they can choose.

---

[4]   George Galster, *Homeowners and Neighborhood Reinvestment* (Durham: Duke University Press, 1987). See esp. chap. 14; W. Grigsby, G. Baratz, G. Galster, and D. MaClennan, *The Dynamics of Neighborhood Change and Decline, Progress in Planning series # 28* (London: Pergamon, 1987); K. Temkin and W. Rohe, "Neighborhood Change and Urban Policy," *Journal of Planning Education and Research* 15 (1996): 159-170; G. Galster, "On the Nature of Neighborhood," *Urban Studies* 38, no. 12 (2001): 2111–24.

[5]   J. Rothenberg, G. Galster, R. Butler, and J. Pitkin, *The Maze of Urban Housing Markets: Theory, Practice and Evidence* (Chicago: University of Chicago Press, 1991).

This model of housing dynamics can be useful in understanding neighborhood dynamics.[6] The connection between metropolitan housing submarkets and neighborhoods is straightforward. Most neighborhoods in the market-based systems consist primarily of residences classified (by households, owners, and developers) as close substitutes in the same quality submarket. This is so for three reasons.[7] First, economies of scale in construction lead private developers to build homes in a subdivision that typically have similar physical characteristics. Second, developers often find it most profitable to build homogeneously high-quality subdivisions because many well-off households are willing to pay a premium for neighbors of high socioeconomic status. Third, because spatially based attributes contribute to a dwelling's quality and, hence, submarket designation, dwellings in close proximity will share many common attributes and thus tend to be classified in the same quality submarket tautologically.

Any forces affecting a particular housing submarket will also affect the neighborhoods where such a dwelling is located; the greater the representation of the given housing submarket type in a neighborhood, the greater the spatial impact there. In addition, it suggests that forces originally having an impact anywhere (either in terms of quality submarket or geographic location) in the metropolitan area will eventually have some impact everywhere, as the shock is transmitted (in progressively weaker magnitudes) across submarkets of increasingly dissimilar substitutability.

A classic illustration of these neighborhood dynamics is the process of filtering.[8] Filtering is a situation in which the market valuations (sales prices and rents) of a submarket are systematically lowered, permitting some households to gain occupancy who previously were unwilling or unable to occupy this submarket for financial reasons. Moreover, some residential property owners in such deflated submarkets choose to convert their dwellings to a lower-quality submarket designation. Filtering thus has defining elements of change on both demand (household) and supply (property owner).

Filtering is typically triggered in a region containing a legacy central city as follows: Developers may speculate and build a number of high-quality submarket homes on exurban, undeveloped tracts on the metropolitan fringe. Should this increase in overall housing supply exceed the increase in demand for the high-quality submarket (say, owing to smaller growth of high-income households) in aggregate, there will be a net decline in the market valuations and rate of return associated with such dwellings. Some households that previously chose not to occupy the high-quality submarket now do so, as prices have fallen and become affordable. Concurrently, some owners of pre-existing dwellings in the high-quality submarket may now choose to downgrade the quality of their units to take advantage of comparatively superior rates of return in the somewhat lesser-quality submarkets. They typically accomplish this by passive under-maintenance: investing insufficient upkeep to maintain the dwelling in its original submarket.

---

[6]   Ibid.
[7]   K. Vandell, "Market Factors Affecting Spatial Heterogeneity Among Urban Neighborhoods," *Housing Policy Debate* (1995): 103–109.
[8]   G. Galster and J. Rothenberg, "Filtering in Urban Housing: A Graphical Analysis of a Quality-Segmented Market," *Journal of Planning Education and Research* 11 (1991): 37–50.

These dual adjustments jointly restore equilibrium in the high-quality submarket but sequentially upset it in the next lower-quality submarkets. There, demand has fallen (from some erstwhile occupants choosing a superior quality submarket) and supply has risen (from some owners downgrading from higher-quality submarkets into the given submarket). Both adjustments on demand and supply drive down market valuations. As a result, adjustment processes to both supply and demand ensue analogous to the above, but in the process they generate forces that are transmitted still farther down the submarket quality array.

By the time system-wide equilibrium is restored, there have been a series of changes in demographic and physical attributes of neighborhoods constituting submarkets. In every submarket, the least competitive neighborhoods have witnessed: (1) an influx of households of somewhat lower financial means than the typical residents who left (often manifested as a switch from owner-occupants to renters), and (2) a decline in the physical quality of the dwellings, particularly in lower-quality submarkets. In the extreme, they experience dilapidation and even abandonment. The metropolitan aggregate new construction of high-quality dwellings in excess of household demand rendered the array of lower-quality neighborhoods relatively less attractive and less expensive. This generated altered flows of resources (occupancy patterns by households, financial resources by owners) that ultimately changed absolutely the attributes of these neighborhoods in ways that eroded the quality of life of residents and the financial returns of property owners there.

THE COMPLEX NATURE OF NEIGHBORHOOD FILTERING

Once begun in a neighborhood, the filtering process at some point is likely to cross a threshold: a critical point past which change accelerates. As explained in the next sections below, the nature of filtering holds at least two crucial practical implications. First, it suggests that the filtering process will lead to large social inefficiencies. Second, it suggests that scarce public resources may be applied most effectively before filtering is allowed to runs its course.

There are four distinct, not mutually exclusive, mechanisms through which thresholds may be produced: collective socialization, contagion, gaming, and preference models.[9] The first two rely on collective actions and social interaction to create thresholds; the other two involve more individual attitudes and behaviors. One can analyze behavior of households to move out of the declining neighborhood through collective socialization, gaming, and preference models; behavior of households who move in to such neighborhoods through gaming models; and behavior of households, dwelling owners, and business people who remain in the neighborhood through collective socialization, gaming, and contagion models.

Collective socialization theories focus on the role that social groups exert on shaping an individual's attitudes, values, and behaviors.[10] Such an effect can occur to the degree that: (1)

---

[9]   For a review, see G. Galster, "Nonlinear and Threshold Aspects of Neighborhood Effects." In *Soziale Kontexte und soziale Mechanismen [Social Contexts and Social Mechanisms]*, eds. Jurgen Friedrichs and Alexandra Nonnenmacher (Wiesbaden: Springer, 2014): 117–133; for evidence, see G. Galster, R. Quercia, and A. Cortes, "Identifying Neighborhood Thresholds: An Empirical Exploration," *Housing Policy Debate* 11, no. 3 (2000): 701–732.

[10]   George Simmel, *George Simmel on Individuality and Social Forms* (Chicago: University of Chicago Press, 1971); M. Weber, *Economy and Society*. 2 volumes (Berkeley: University of California Press, 1978).

the individual comes in social contact with the group, and (2) the group can exert more powerful threats or inducement to conform to its positions than competing groups. Given the importance of interpersonal contact in enforcing conformity, if the individuals constituting a group were scattered randomly over urban space, they would be less able either to convey their positions effectively to others with whom they might come in contact or exert much pressure to conform. It is only when a group reaches a certain critical mass of density or power over a predefined area that it is likely to become effective in shaping the behaviors of others. Past this threshold, as more members join the group, the group's power to sanction nonconformists grows. This growth in power is particularly dramatic when the position of the group becomes so dominant as to become normative in the area.[11] The reverse is also true: What previously constituted civil behaviors in a neighborhood, enforced by collective norms, may rapidly erode as the previously dominant group moves out, eventually falling below its threshold of normative dominance and being replaced by those who do not share the erstwhile norms.

The basic tenet of contagion models is that if decision makers live in a community where some of their neighbors exhibit non-normative behaviors, they will be more likely to adopt these behaviors themselves. In this form of "social learning," neighborhood problems are believed to be contagious, spread through peer influence. Crane proposes a formal contagion model to explain the incidence and spread of social problems within a neighborhood.[12] The key implication of his contagion model is that there may be critical levels of social problems in neighborhoods. He states that if "the incidence of problems stays below a critical point, the frequency or prevalence of the problem tends to gravitate toward some relatively low-level equilibrium. But if the incidence surpasses a critical point, the process will spread explosively. In other words, an epidemic may occur, raising the incidence to an equilibrium at a much higher level."[13] From our perspective, we would observe attributes such as crime and social incivilities rise disproportionately in a neighborhood undergoing filtering when it reaches a point where concentrations of disadvantaged populations exceed a threshold. Several empirical studies suggest that this threshold is in the range of 15–20 percent poverty rates in a census tract.[14]

Gaming models assume that, in many decisions involving neighborhoods, the costs and benefits of alternative courses of action are uncertain, depending on how many other actors choose various

[11] More modern sociological treatises closely related to collective socialization also suggest thresholds, such as Wilson's (1987) contention that as a critical mass of middle class families leave the inner city, low-income blacks left behind become isolated from the positive role models that the erstwhile dominant class offered. Economists also have developed several mathematical treatises involving collective socialization effects in which thresholds often emerge as solutions to complex decision problems under certain assumptions (G. Akerlof, "A Theory of Social Custom, of Which Unemployment May Be One Consequence," *Quarterly Journal of Economics* 94 (1980): 749-775; Galster, 1987: ch. 3; W. Brock and S. Durlauf, "Interactions-based Models." In *Handbook of Econometrics*, vol. 5 (Amsterdam: North-Holland, (2000)).

[12] Jonathan Crane, "The Epidemic Theory of Ghettos and Neighborhood Effects on Dropping Out and Teenage Childbearing," *American Journal of Sociology* 96 (1991): 1226–1259.

[13] Ibid.

[14] George Galster, "An economic efficiency analysis of deconcentrating poverty populations," *Journal of Housing Economics* 11, (2002): 303-329.; George Galster, Jackie Cutsinger, and Ron Malega, "The Social Costs of Concentrated Poverty: Externalities to Neighboring Households and Property Owners and the Dynamics of Decline," *Revisiting Rental Housing: Policies, Programs, and Priorities* (Washington, DC: Brookings Institution Press, 2008), 93–113.

alternatives. The individual's expected payoff of an alternative varies, however, depending on the number or proportion of neighbors who make a decision before the given actor does. Thus, the concept of a threshold amount of observed prior action is central in this type of model. The well-known prisoners' dilemma is the simplest form of gaming model,[15] but more sophisticated variants have been developed and applied to neighborhood change.[16] As illustration, consider the situation of potential filtering of a neighborhood but the potential losses in property values might be forestalled were all its owners to improve their properties as a group. However, individual owners may believe that they will not earn back the value of their investment if they were to reinvest when no others followed suit. A conservative gaming strategy of behaving to minimize prospective loss, regardless of what others may do, will lead many owners to refrain from reinvesting first. Only if a threshold proportion of owners were to reinvest would these skeptics be convinced to follow suit.[17]

Preference models claim that actors in a residential environment will respond if the aggregate behavior of others (or, an outside event) raises an undesirable neighborhood attribute above the level they find tolerable. A process internal to the neighborhood can be triggered once the attribute reaches the critical threshold. The trigger occurs because actors in a neighborhood are assumed to have different tolerance levels, with the least tolerant responding first. If an additional change in the neighborhood attribute results from the course of action taken in response to the initial event by those with the lowest tolerance level, the new level of the neighborhood attribute may now be above the tolerance level of some of the less tolerant remaining actors. The process may continue with new rounds of attribute change and actor adjustment until the process is completed. At the extreme, the process may end when all the original actors in a neighborhood have responded. The theoretical development of preference models has focused on changes in a neighborhood's racial composition from white to non-white occupancy, though extensions to preferences for other sorts of neighborhood attributes are straightforward. For example, if some "undesirable" household type were to move into a neighborhood as part of the filtering process, the original residents least tolerant of the new residents may leave. If more members of the undesirable group filled their vacant dwellings disproportionately, still more of the original residents may find the now-higher proportion of undesirables intolerable, and move out. And so it continues. Seminal theoretical work in this vein has been produced by Schelling;[18] Schnare and MacRae;[19] and Taub, Taylor and Dunham.[20]

NEIGHBORHOOD FILTERING PROCESSES ARE SOCIALLY INEFFICIENT

The discussion so far implies that changes in the altered flows of resources into neighborhoods as they filter are not likely to produce socially efficient outcomes. By "socially efficient," I mean outcomes that provide the greatest aggregate well-being to society as a whole by getting the most

15   T. Schelling, *Micromotives and Macrobehavior* (New York: Norton, 1978).
16   M. Granovetter, "Threshold Models of Collective Behavior," *American Journal of Sociology* 83 (1978): 1420–1443; M. Granovetter and R. Soong, "Threshold Models of Diversity: Chinese Restaurants, Residential Segregation, and the Spiral of Silence," *The Journal of Sociology* 18 (1986): 69–104.
17   R. Taub, G. Taylor, and J. Dunham, *Paths of Neighborhood Change* (Chicago: University of Chicago Press, 1984).
18   T. Schelling, "Dynamic Models of Segregation," *Journal of Mathematical Sociology* 1 (1971): 143–186; T. Schelling, *Micromotives and Macrobehavior*.
19   A. Schnare and C. MacRae, *A Model of Neighborhood Change*, Urban Institute report no 225–4 (Washington, DC: The Urban Institute, 1975).
20   R. Taub, G. Taylor, and J. Dunham, *Paths of Neighborhood Change*.

out of our finite human, natural, and financial resources. At least four reasons make filtering socially inefficient: externalities, gaming, expectations, and flawed pricing of attributes owing to information asymmetries.

One individual's act can be thought of as generating externalities for several reasons: (1) the act of one property owner toward dwelling maintenance may change the neighborhood's aggregate upkeep profile and quality of life; (2) because the act of one household to move into or out of a neighborhood may marginally change its aggregate population attributes, and (3) all such changes affect the decision making of other current and prospective residents and property owners in that place, the individual's act can be thought of as generating externalities. Externalities are indirect costs or benefits imposed on others by an individual's action. For example, the choice of a property owner in a filtering neighborhood to allow the facade of the home to fall into disrepair generates external costs to neighbors. The choice of an owner to abandon the property represents an even more severe example of a negative externality generator. When a low-income household moves into a neighborhood already at its threshold of concentrated disadvantage, it imposes negative externalities on those living there via the upsurge in induced negative social behaviors, as explained above. Because in all such cases, external costs do not accrue to the decision-maker, a suboptimal amount of the activity is chosen in aggregate: the classic economic inefficiency. That is, filtering is a process that produces too much dwelling decay and abandonment and too much concentrated disadvantage compared with what would be best for society as a whole.

The earlier reference to gaming also serves as a reference here. Individual neighborhood households and property owners lack certainty about the decisions of a myriad other households and owners in the neighborhood or those who are considering investing in the neighborhood. Yet, the payoffs from their alternative choices depend on such decisions of others. Thus, autonomous decision makers are likely to adopt strategies that do not produce the greatest good for the collective. The unwillingness to maintain buildings adequately in an area until other investors do so first is a classic example of a gaming-induced social inefficiency.

Expectations are, of course, imperfect and prone to major errors. But this in itself does not imply a systematic bias toward inefficient choices. Rather, expectations about the future may prove to be so "certain" in the view of the decision-maker that the resulting choice encourages the expectation to transpire. This is the famous "self-fulfilling prophecy." An illustration is panic selling of homes often associated with filtering. Because of some anticipated negative neighborhood change, several homeowners become convinced that property values will fall rapidly. They therefore try to sell their homes quickly at a discount. The rash of "For Sale" signs and the rumors that these homes are selling cheaply convince other owners in the neighborhood that, indeed, neighborhood quality and property values are on the way down. As they too try to unload their properties, panic ensues and prices do, as some prophesied, drop precipitously. The sorts of prices produced by these self-fulfilling prophecies are unlikely to allocate resources efficiently. Instead of accurately capitalizing the underlying quality (and replacement cost of the dwellings) in the neighborhood, these artificially deflated prices encourage owners with less personal financial means to purchase property. These owners are likely to invest less in home maintenance and repair than their higher-income forebears,[21] thereby shortening the useful lifetimes of these valuable assets and inefficiently encouraging more filtering.

Finally, certain attributes of a particular neighborhood, especially those associated with the sentimental and social-interactive dimensions, cannot be evaluated well by potential residents or property buyers who are not yet located there compared with those who have lived there for some time. For example, one can only guess how attached one might become to prospective neighbors and a neighborhood before having the experience of living there. This divergence in information can also lead to inefficient transactions. As illustration, consider a viable neighborhood that enjoys strong social capital among its residents and owners. Unfortunately, such valuable social interchanges will be difficult for the market to understand and value, dependent as this social capital is on the idiosyncrasies of personal interrelationships that have been built among current residents. The sales prices and rents of this neighborhood are thus too low; they do not reflect fully the quality of life. This means that many prospective buyers with less financial means will make inefficient choices: They will be more willing and able to buy or move into this neighborhood than if it had been fully evaluated by the market. Thus, there is excessive filtering from the perspective of social efficiency.

NEIGHBORHOOD FILTERING PROCESSES ARE SOCIALLY INEQUITABLE

Analogous to the efficiency analysis is equity. By "equity," I mean that those who are most disadvantaged generally, especially low-income households and those of color, should reap disproportionately greater benefits from any process or policy or suffer disproportionately smaller costs from such.

I believe it reasonable to hypothesize that neighborhood filtering processes disproportionately impose personal and financial costs on lower-income households and property owners in lower-quality neighborhoods. Theory suggests, for example, that the filtering process in declining metro areas ultimately produces residential abandonment, the financial and quality of life externalities associated with which undoubtedly primarily affect the low-income households and those of color. The well-documented problems associated with concentrated poverty neighborhoods (Wilson, 1987; Friedrichs, Galster and Musterd, 2005) are similarly suggestive that the distress produced when neighborhoods surpass multiple physical, financial, and sociological thresholds are borne disproportionately by disadvantaged households.[22]

Several recent studies have found that home appreciation rates vary by low-income and high-income market segments and by race in ways that support this assertion about inequities. Flippen found dramatic geographic differences in home appreciation rates across neighborhoods delineated by racial-ethnic composition.[23] From 1970 to 1990, U.S. census data showed that homes in

[21]   George Galster, *Homeowners and Neighborhood Reinvestment.*

[22]   W. J. Wilson, *The Truly Disadvantaged*; J. Friedrichs, G. Galster, and S. Musterd, eds. *Life in Poverty Neighbourhoods* (London & New York: Routledge, 2005).

[23]   C. Flippen, "Unequal Returns To Housing Investment? A Study of Real Housing Appreciation among Black, White and Hispanic Households," *Social Forces* 82 (2004): 1523–51.

neighborhoods with less than 2 percent black residents appreciated by more than 22 percent, whereas those in neighborhoods with 2 percent to 30 percent black residents appreciated 10 percent, and those with more than 30 percent black residents appreciated less than 8 percent, on average.[24] Among loans to low-income borrowers originated between 1998 and 2002, blacks experienced 10 percent lower annual equity appreciation than whites.[25] Even larger black-white gaps were apparent in home appreciation rates for low-income buyers graduating from a Denver public housing-run asset-building/counseling program; Hispanics evinced even lower appreciation rates than blacks.[26]

Beyond the direct negative impacts of filtering on low-income residents and property owners of lower-quality neighborhoods, negative indirect impacts ensue through fiscal consequences for the political jurisdictions encompassing such neighborhoods. Filtering means that higher-income residents are eventually supplanted by somewhat lower-income residents—and in the extreme, producing concentrations of poverty. This process reduces the aggregate local income tax revenues that the jurisdiction can collect. Associated reductions in geographic density of disposable income will reduce the aggregate sales of local retailers serving these neighborhoods, thereby lowering the sales tax revenues that the jurisdiction can collect. Declines in local residential and retail establishment property values will erode the property tax revenues that the jurisdiction can collect. Thus, if filtering becomes a dominant dynamic in a jurisdiction, it will seriously degrade its various tax bases, forcing it into the unenviable dilemma of either reducing the quality and quantity of public services or raising the rates or expanding the types of taxation. The burdens of both options fall most heavily on the lower-income residents of the jurisdiction.

Some might argue that filtering actually benefits lower-income renter households who are willing and able to occupy somewhat better quality dwellings than they would otherwise because filtering lowers rents. Although there is some merit in this argument, the number of such "winners" in the filtering process and the degree of their benefit are subject to a number of critical parameters related to the structure of submarkets in the given metropolitan area.[27] More fundamentally, the supposed benefit of getting better housing quality for the money is ephemeral in legacy cities, especially for the poorest of renters. If there is an inadequate flow of net rental income (in combination with property appreciation) to justify continued investment in maintenance and repairs required to keep the dwelling at its current quality, over time its condition will erode. Moreover, as this process spreads across the affected neighborhood, it degrades the quality of the larger residential environment for all residents. This degradation becomes most extreme when filtering leads to abandonment of some structures. Indeed, the surviving housing may be "cheap," but this reflects the lack of residential and neighborhood quality that is being capitalized.

---

24   During the same period, the patterns were less monotonic for Hispanic composition, however. Homes in neighborhoods with less than 2 percent Hispanic residents appreciated more than 14 percent, those with 2–5 percent Hispanic residents appreciated 27 percent, those with 5–10 percent appreciated 23 percent, and those with more than 10 percent appreciated 15 percent.

25   M. Stegman, R. Quercia, and W. Davis, "The Wealth-Creating Potential of Homeownership: A Preliminary Assessment of Price Appreciation among Low-Income Home Buyers," in *Chasing the American Dream: New Perspectives on Affordable Homeownership* (Ithaca: Cornell University Press, 2007), 271–92.

26   A. Santiago, G. Galster, and A. Kaiser, "The Financial Consequences of Low-Income Homeownership" (unpublished paper, Wayne State University, 2008).

27   These issue are too technical for this essay, but see Galster and Rothenberg (1991).

RATIONALE FOR INTERVENTION IN MIDDLE NEIGHBORHOODS

Thus far, I have established that filtering imposes large costs on legacy cities that are disproportionately borne by its most vulnerable citizens. It hastens the flight of a neighborhood's better-off residents and the deterioration and eventual abandonment of its residential and nonresidential properties. If it becomes widespread, filtering erodes the jurisdiction's tax base and its ability to supply a range of good-quality public services. Filtering as a dominant dynamic in legacy cities must be thwarted. This, in essence, is the rationale for intervening in middle neighborhoods.

I propose that interventions designed to stem filtering-induced decline should be targeted to middle neighborhoods. Even though these places are not where the most vulnerable citizens live, nor where the evils of filtering wreak the most havoc of blight and abandonment, they are the places where interventions may plausibly head off these worst-case situations in the future. Local governments should target financial incentives, regulations, and investments of infrastructure and public services to neighborhoods at crucial threshold points of decline. In concert, these actions could help alter perceptions of key neighborhood investors, provide compensatory resource flows, minimize destructive gaming behaviors, internalize externalities, and moderate expectations, thereby defusing self-fulfilling prophecies.[28]

Consider two hypothetical scenarios of neighborhood dynamics (Figure 1). The horizontal axes in Figure 1 portray time passing as a neighborhood transitions from stability to the point of decline spawned by filtering. The vertical axes portray the dollar amounts of private and public resources flowing into the neighborhoods as investments in the residential and nonresidential properties and in the public infrastructure. I propose an aggressive strategy of intervention at the stage of neighborhood incipient decline, when the filtering forces have just started to induce property owners to withhold some of their erstwhile investments (shown as the declining solid line in Figure 1, Scenario A). It is at this point when only a modest amount of public investment (shown as the increasing dashed line in Figure 1, Scenario A) would be required to booster the confidence of private investors and convince them to reassess their investment strategies. Once the private flows of investments have been reestablished, the public sector can once again withdraw until filtering threatens again. This could be termed a "catch it before it falls too far" strategy.

---

[28]   It is beyond the scope of this essay to delve into the particulars of what form this intervention might take. For an evaluation of alternative strategies, see Galster (1987).

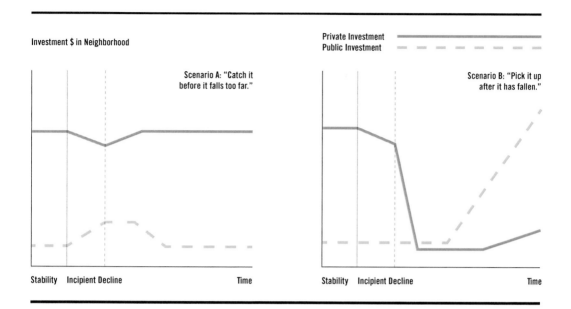

Figure 1: Alternative Scenarios for Public Interventions Into the Filtering Process

Compare the proposed strategy in Scenario A to that in Scenario B, which is often pursued today in legacy cities. This strategy might be termed a "pick it up after it has fallen" approach. Scenario B represents a strategy of trying to revitalize a neighborhood after filtering has run its course and the place is littered with blighted and abandoned structures and perhaps vacant lots where now-demolished structures once stood. These are areas that have suffered massive private disinvestment (shown by the steeply falling solid line in Figure 1, Scenario B). Such neighborhoods clearly require massive infusions of public monies (shown by the steeply rising dashed line in Figure 1, Scenario B) to trigger any complementary response by the private sector. Compared to Scenario B, Scenario A suggests a more efficient, better-leveraged use of public resources available for neighborhood reinvestment, which in the typical legacy city are all too scarce. By preserving the place of middle neighborhoods in the metropolitan quality hierarchy, my proposed strategy would forestall (and hopefully, avoid entirely) their slide into low-quality neighborhoods. This, in turn, would forestall the destruction and abandonment of current low-quality but viable neighborhoods and all the pernicious efficiency and equity problems noted above.

SUMMARY AND CONCLUSION

The stock of attributes composing a neighborhood at any moment is the result of past and current flows of households and resources—financial, social-psychological, and time—into and out of the space in question. To understand the factors and processes that influence the decisions governing these flows is to uncover the roots of neighborhood change. One such dynamic in legacy cities is filtering, wherein an excess of high-quality housing supply deflates property values and erodes investment incentives in successively lower-quality submarkets.

The attributes of a neighborhood, including the composition of its households, likely influence the behavior of those residing and owning property there. This means that uncoordinated actions by households, property owners, and institutions that alter the package of neighborhood attributes will have unintended consequences as an inherent part of the filtering process. These consequences will be particularly severe if processes exceed threshold points. Behaviors ruled by gaming and self-fulfilling prophecies also are rampant as part of filtering. All of this suggests that filtering yields socially inefficient and inequitable outcomes in legacy cities, spawning fiscal distress as a side effect. There is thus a prima facie case on efficiency and equity grounds for local policy intervention to counter this clear case of market failure.

Middle neighborhoods should be the locus of such intervention. Defusing the filtering process in this category of neighborhoods, it avoids subsequent filtering in the lower-quality submarkets of the city and its associated worst-case inefficiencies and inequities. Compared with an common approach that tries to reclaim neighborhoods only after filtering has run its devastating course, the approach recommended here would prove a much more effective, leverage-inducing use of public funds.

George Galster earned his Ph.D. in economics from M.I.T. and now serves as Clarence Hilberry Professor of Urban Affairs at Wayne State University. He has published 145 peer-reviewed articles, eight books, and 34 book chapters on a wide range of urban topics. He has been a consultant to the U.S. Departments of Housing and Urban Development and Justice, and served on the Consumer Advisory Council of the Federal Reserve's Board of Governors. The Urban Affairs Association placed him on their "Service Honor Roll" in 2014 and awarded him the "Contributions to the Field of Urban Affairs" prize in 2016.

III. DEMOGRAPHICS AND CHARACTERISTICS OF MIDDLE NEIGHBORHOODS IN SELECT LEGACY CITIES

By Ira Goldstein, William Schrecker & Jacob L. Rosch, Reinvestment Fund

Legend goes that when notorious bank robber Willie Sutton was asked why he robbed banks, he said, "because that's where the money is." When asked why we should be concerned with the middle neighborhoods of our legacy cities, one practitioner said, "because that's where the people are."

Legacy cities represent a unique subset of American cities because they struggled to manage a severe loss of manufacturing jobs and experienced significant population loss.[1] Legacy cities like Detroit and St. Louis have declined in population by nearly 62 percent since their peak in the 1950s. Others like Pittsburgh, Baltimore, and Philadelphia lost 55 percent, 34 percent, and 26 percent of their 1950 populations, respectively.

Across legacy cities, middle neighborhoods generally are home to a large share of the people and households that remain. Although protecting the population that remains in legacy cities is a strategic priority for city leaders, they typically have not focused on middle neighborhoods. Instead, with some exceptions, they are now more focused on high-profile downtowns that they believe will build the local tax base and create jobs. Middle neighborhoods generally do not get the attention of nonprofits and community development corporations (CDCs) either. Such organizations usually focus on the most distressed areas, and because middle neighborhoods are not the most blighted or highest poverty areas, they typically do not receive the benefit of federal community development funds. Notwithstanding the customary lack of attention, middle neighborhoods represent a significant part of the tax base that supports critical municipal functions.

The decline of federal resources to support community and economic development has motivated policymakers to use evidence when allocating their increasingly scarce housing and community development resources. In an environment of limited resources, community development leaders are challenged to rediscover the value and the importance of middle neighborhoods.

Our core argument here is that middle neighborhoods in legacy cities are vital because they are home to a substantial segment of a city's population and therefore provide the tax base on which so many city services rely. Further, despite the population decline and job losses in legacy cities, middle neighborhoods have relatively stable populations. These areas are generally racially mixed,

[1]   See, for example, http://www.legacycities.org.

and residents are reasonably well educated, employed, and in households with modest (or higher) incomes. Moreover, middle neighborhoods tend to be relatively affordable and, therefore, are generally opportune places for an important segment of a city's population. Attention to these places is critical because, we believe, residents of middle neighborhoods possess the economic wherewithal to have choices—and should the value proposition for their communities begin to fail, they could exercise those choices and leave. Underscoring the importance of this notion, Philadelphia's former mayor John Street called these neighborhoods the "key battlegrounds"— lose them and you lose the city.[2]

To explore our argument, this chapter offers a data-based description of the middle neighborhoods of several legacy cities: Baltimore, Detroit, Milwaukee, Philadelphia, Pittsburgh, and St. Louis. This is not a random selection of legacy cities; they are cities for which Reinvestment Fund has completed its Market Value Analyses (MVAs), described below, within the last five years.[3] It is through brief case studies of each of these cities that we can systematically understand what the middle neighborhoods look like demographically, socially, and economically. Further, through insights gained from interviews with practitioners in each of these cities, we explore the strengths, challenges, and opportunities for middle neighborhoods.

A CHANGING FUNDING ENVIRONMENT IN LEGACY CITIES

An obvious place to begin a brief review of the historical funding context of these markets is with the federal Community Development Block Grant (CDBG) program. The CDBG program has historically been a, if not the, critical source of funds for communities across the United States to address housing, community and economic development, infrastructure, and related needs. As Figure 1 shows, between 1975 and 2014, annual federal allocations have fluctuated substantially, but overall are down 72 percent in inflation-adjusted terms. Although other sources of funds now support affordable housing (e.g., the Low Income Housing Tax Credit, which began in 1986), the loss of CDBG is crucial because of the flexibility in its potential uses.

---

[2] City of Philadelphia, *Neighborhood Transformation: A Strategy for Investment and Growth* (2001).

[3] Alan Mallach and Lavea Brachman rank legacy cities from 1 to 18 based on a variety of demographic, social, and economic characteristics (with 1 being the strongest rank). Using their scale, the cities in this chapter represent the wide range of conditions among legacy cities. Philadelphia is ranked 1; Pittsburgh, 2; Baltimore, 3; Milwaukee, 5; St. Louis, 8; and Detroit, 17. See A. Mallach and L. Brachman, *Regenerating America's Legacy Cities* (Cambridge, MA: Lincoln Institute of Land Policy, 2013).

Figure 1: Annual CDBG Allocations (Raw and Inflation-Adjusted), 1975–2014 (Raw and Constant Dollars)

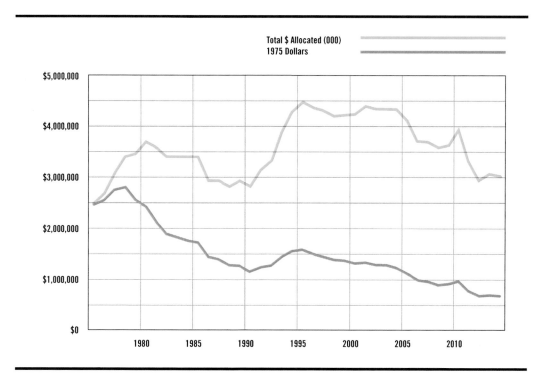

Table 1 presents data on the annual CDBG allocation in the six legacy cities we focus on here. Between 1975 and 2014, every city except for St. Louis and Milwaukee experienced a nominal loss in its CDBG allocation. In real terms, although the national average CDBG allocation declined by 72 percent, the allocations in these selected legacy cities declined from 75 percent in St. Louis to 86.9 percent in Baltimore (in real dollars).[4] The implication for cities is manifest: less federal funding to address critical community and economic development needs.

These cuts may not have had as direct an impact on middle neighborhoods, because, as more than one interviewee noted, the CDBG regulations and guidance historically made it difficult to direct CDBG funds to these areas. At the same time, however, the loss of CDBG funds has meant that more areas are competing for the same shrinking pool of resources. The relative scarcity of public funds in today's world of public investment and development has served to further emphasize the importance of middle neighborhoods when considering strategic deployment and return on investment of public dollars.

---

[4]   When the federal government consolidated existing categorical grants into the CDBG program, cities were held harmless against a loss of funding. The expiration of the hold harmless program and the introduction of new census data in 1980 led to a number of large funding fluctuations apparent in the 1975 and 1980 allocations. Personal communication with Todd M. Richardson, associate deputy assistant secretary, Office of Policy Development and Research, U.S. Department of Housing and Urban Development, 2015.

Table 1: CDBG Allocations (million $) 1975–2014

Historic CDBG Allocation												
	1975	1980	1985	1990	1995	2000	2005	2010	2014	($ 1975) 2014	Change	Change (Adj.)
Baltimore	32.75	33.81	26.81	21.63	30.72	29.71	27.00	25.18	18.81	4.28	-42.6%	-86.9%
Detroit	34.19	64.14	49.72	40.14	56.58	51.21	45.83	40.14	32.11	7.03	-6.1%	-78.6%
Milwaukee	13.38	22.79	17.68	14.68	23.30	22.22	19.62	18.27	14.99	2.57	12.0%	-80.8%
Philadelphia	60.83	71.96	60.92	48.56	72.93	69.09	59.72	55.33	39.31	8.93	-35.4%	-85.3%
Pittsburgh	16.43	26.04	19.59	15.87	23.11	21.24	19.14	18.04	13.01	2.96	-20.8%	-82.0%
St. Louis	15.19	35.18	26.00	20.30	29.94	27.49	23.51	21.36	16.18	3.79	6.5%	-75.0%
U.S. Total	2,473	3,704	3,411	2,818	4,485	4,236	4,110	3,941	3,023	687	22.2%	-72.2%

ECONOMIC AND DEMOGRAPHIC CHANGES IN LEGACY CITIES

In addition to changes in the funding environment, the population and the economy also changed in legacy cities.[5] Others have chronicled the national decline in manufacturing, and the experience of legacy cities is generally more severe because legacy cities had historically relied more heavily on manufacturing as the bedrock of their local economies. As Table 2 shows, with the exception of Milwaukee, the magnitude of the decline in manufacturing in legacy cities between 1967 and 2012 is more than double the national average (31 percent).

Table 2: Change in Manufacturing Employment, 1967–2012[6]

Manufacturing Employment				
	1967	2012	Raw Change	Percent Change
Baltimore	209,700	53,494	-156,206	-74%
Detroit	599,900	199,394	-400,506	-67%
Milwaukee	216,500	114,114	-102,386	-47%
Philadelphia	573,800	172,790	-401,010	-70%
Pittsburgh	299,600	90,107	-209,493	-70%
St. Louis	296,000	99,727	-196,273	-66%

The loss of population in these legacy cities was also severe. When city residents move, they frequently move from the urban core to the suburban counties in the region, and the movers are typically those who earn higher incomes and have higher educational attainment.

---

[5]   See, for example, http://www.legacycities.org. See American Fact Finder, *Manufacturing: Geographic Area Series: Industry Statistics for the States, Metropolitan and Micropolitan Statistical Areas, Counties, and Places: 2012 & 2012 Economic Census of the United States.* (Washington, DC: U.S. Census), at. xhtml?pid=ECN_2012_US_31A1&prodType=table. See also http://factfinder.census.gov/faces/tableservices/jsf/pages/productview.xhtml?pid=ECN_2012_US_31A1&prodType=table.

[6]   ftp://ftp2.census.gov/econ1977/Graphic_Summary_of_the_1977_Economic_Censuses.pdf.

Table 3 presents population data for the six legacy cities from 1950 to 2013. All except Milwaukee have lost population from their peaks in 1950 (Milwaukee peaked in 1960). Far and away, Detroit saw the most severe population loss at more than 1.1 million people, representing 62.3 percent of the 1950 population. St. Louis lost 538,000 people, or 62.8 percent of the 1950 population. Philadelphia experienced a comparable raw population loss (524,000), which represented 25.8 percent of its 1950 population.

Table 3: Population of Selected Legacy Cities, 1950–2013

Total Population								
	1950	1960	1970	1980	1990	2000	2010	2013
Baltimore	949,708	939,024	905,759	786,775	736,014	651,154	620,961	621,445
	Peak Year: 1950			Change; 2013–1950: (328,263)			Change; 2013–1950: -34.6%	
Detroit	1,849.568	1,670,144	1,511,482	1,203,339	1,027,974	951,270	713,777	706,663
	Peak Year: 1950			Change; 2013–1950: (1,142,905)			Change; 2013–1950: -61.8%	
Milwaukee	637,392	741,324	717,099	636,212	628,088	596,956	594,833	596,459
	Peak Year: 1960			Change; 2013–1950: (40,993)			Change; 2013–1950: -6.4%	
Philadelphia	2,071,605	2,002,512	1,948,609	1,688,210	1,585,577	1,517,550	1,526,006	1,536,704
	Peak Year: 1950			Change; 2013–1950: (534,901)			Change; 2013–1950: -25.8%	
Pittsburgh	676,806	604,332	520,117	423,938	369,879	334,563	305,704	306,062
	Peak Year: 1950			Change; 2013–1950: (370,744)			Change; 2013–1950: -54.8%	
St. Louis	856,796	750,026	622,236	453,085	396,685	348,189	319,924	318,995
	Peak Year: 1950			Change; 2013–1950: (537,841)			Change; 2013–1950: -62.8%	

Except for Pittsburgh, each of the legacy cities experienced substantial growth in the number and percentage of minority (especially African American) residents (Tables 4 and 5). The African American population in Pittsburgh declined, but as a percentage of the total population, it increased.[7]

---

[7]   Thomas notes that this is not an uncommon pattern observed in legacy cities. She argues that understanding this trend is critical to developing proactive strategies in these cities that are attentive to fundamental social justice issues. J. M. Thomas, "Addressing the Racial, Ethnic, and Class Implications of Legacy Cities," in *Rebuilding America's Legacy Cities: New Directions for the Industrial Heartland* (New York: American Assembly, Columbia University, 2012).

Table 4: Black Population of Legacy Cities, 1950–2013

Black Population										
	1950	1960	1970	1980	1990	2000	2010	2013	Change; 2013–1950	
Baltimore	225,099	325,589	420,210	431,151	435,768	417,231	395,781	392,749	167,650	74.5%
Detroit	300,506	482,223	660,428	758,939	777,916	774,175	590,226	577,224	276,718	92.1%
Milwaukee	21,772	62,458	105,088	146,940	191,255	220,770	237,796	234,849	213,077	978.7%
Philadelphia	376,041	529,240	653,791	638,878	631,936	653,364	661,839	665,332	289,291	76.9%
Pittsburgh	82,453	100,692	104,904	101,813	95,362	89,517	79,710	77,400	(5,053)	-6.1%
St. Louis	153,766	214,377	254,191	206,386	188,408	177,627	157,160	154,888	1,122	0.7%

Table 6 shows that middle neighborhoods are generally more representative of the citywide racial composition than either stronger or weaker MVA market areas. Moreover, these areas are generally equally or more racially integrated than the city as a whole.[8]

Table 5: Percentage Black Population in Legacy Cities, 1950–2013

Black Population									
	1950	1960	1970	1980	1990	2000	2010	2013	Change; 2013–1950
Baltimore	23.7%	34.7%	46.4%	54.8%	59.2%	64.1%	63.7%	63.2%	166.6%
Detroit	16.2%	28.9%	43.7%	63.1%	75.7%	81.4%	82.7%	81.7%	402.7%
Milwaukee	3.4%	8.4%	14.7%	23.1%	30.5%	37.0%	40.0%	39.4%	1,052.7%
Philadelphia	18.2%	26.4%	33.6%	37.8%	39.9%	43.1%	43.4%	43.3%	138.5%
Pittsburgh	12.2%	16.7%	20.2%	24.0%	25.8%	26.8%	26.1%	25.3%	107.6%
St. Louis	17.9%	28.6%	40.9%	45.6%	47.5%	51.0%	49.1%	48.6%	170.6%

---

[8]   The Index of Dissimilarity ("D") measures how evenly two groups are distributed across a geographic area, with lower values representing higher levels of integration. D values literally translate into the percent of a population (e.g., African American) that would need to move to achieve a uniform (i.e., integrated) area. In every city but Detroit, the index is lower in middle market areas than a city's total score. See: O. Duncan and B. Duncan, "A Methodological Analysis of Segregation Indices," *American Sociological Review* 20 (1955): 210–17.

Table 6: Racial Composition and Segregation in Legacy Cities (Lower scores on the
Index of Dissimilarity mean greater integration; see footnote 8.)

	White	Index of Dissimilarity		White	Index of Dissimilarity
Baltimore City	29.6%	0.67	Mid-Markets	24.3%	0.59
Low-Markets	6.4%	—	High-Markets	70.4%	—
Detroit City	12.4%	0.61	Mid-Markets	17.4%	0.62
Low-Markets	7.4%	—	High-Markets	10.0%	—
Milwaukee City	44.7%	0.58	Mid-Markets	34.7%	0.44
Low-Markets	15.5%	—	High-Markets	76.1%	—
Philadelphia City	41.1%	0.62	Mid-Markets	56.7%	0.57
Low-Markets	15.6%	—	High-Markets	73.8%	—
Pittsburgh City	66.3%	0.49	Mid-Markets	77.0%	0.43
Low-Markets	59.3%	—	High-Markets	79.5%	—
St. Louis City	43.9%	0.61	Mid-Markets	65.9%	0.47
Low-Markets	11.5%	—	High-Markets	62.3%	—

USING THE MARKET VALUE ANALYSIS TO IDENTIFY MIDDLE NEIGHBORHOODS AND TARGET INVESTMENT

Although this chapter focuses on middle neighborhoods, it is important to point out that there is no bright-line definition of a middle neighborhood. One tool cities have used to identify their middle neighborhoods is Reinvestment Fund's Market Value Analysis.

Reinvestment Fund first created the MVA in 2001 in support of former Philadelphia Mayor John Street's Neighborhood Transformation Initiative.[9] The MVA summarizes a set of market indicators to measure the strength or weakness of the real estate market in individual areas of a city, ordinarily at a jurisdiction's census block groups.

Typically, the MVA relies on a set of indicators obtained from the local jurisdictions (i.e., administrative data). Usual indicators include median residential sale prices; foreclosures as a percentage of housing units (or residential sales); variation in sale prices; percentage of all housing units that are vacant; percentage of all parcels that are vacant; percentage of (occupied) housing units occupied by the owner; percentage of properties with building permits representing new construction or substantial rehabilitation; and mixture of land uses. Although this group of indicators may vary to a degree from city to city, the MVA uses a common set of indicators that reflects the market conditions that an investor or developer might observe when evaluating areas for investment or intervention.

---

[9]   For a more thorough description of the MVA's history and applications, see I. Goldstein, "Making Sense of Markets: Using Data to Guide Reinvestment Strategies," in *What Counts: Harnessing Data for America's Communities* (San Francisco: Federal Reserve Bank of San Francisco and the Urban Institute, 2014).

Most of these indicators are acquired at an individual address level and then aggregated to the census block group. Based on experience, the census block group is large enough to ensure that the data are reasonably stable yet small enough to ensure that the natural mosaic of a community is revealed.

Although the MVA is not designed to identify middle neighborhoods per se, the results make clear which areas of a city are strongest, which are most distressed, and which fall in the middle. We identified MVA markets that, across the spectrum of all local markets, generally reflect the typical levels of each MVA component indicator.[10] Next, we conferred with local experts in each legacy city to test the appropriateness of our designation of market types as middle neighborhoods. Although not every expert defined middle market areas exactly as we did, we achieved a reasonable consensus in most cities. From both of those processes, we identified the typically three or four MVA market categories that we designated middle markets, which we will then describe as middle neighborhoods.[11]

Each of the other market types were then categorized as low if they were in MVA categories that represented more market stress, and high if they were in categories with less stress. We caution that because of the subjectivity in the designation of middle markets, small differences between middle markets and the other categories should not be emphasized. Each of the MVAs presented in this chapter was created within the last five years.[12]

DATA AND METHODS

The data sources for this chapter are many. As part of the MVA process in each city, we gathered data from the respective housing or planning department, redevelopment authority, property assessor, and/or sheriff. Occasionally, we obtain data from propriety data sources (e.g., Valassis Lists, First American Real Estate Solutions) when administrative data do not exist. We also occasionally use census and American Community Survey (ACS) data, but for a variety of reasons, these are not favored as market indicators for use in the MVA.[13]

Prior to data aggregation for each MVA indicator, the data components are cleaned and validated with local subject matter experts and then through fieldwork (researchers review the data by systematically driving through the streets of the MVA city). Often the researchers are accompanied by local practitioners who have specific knowledge of an issue (e.g., abandonment and vacant land) or a neighborhood(s).

---

[10]   The general approach for designating middle markets for this analysis was to include markets that had characteristics that, taken together, were within about 50 percent to 200 percent of the citywide average.

[11]   In our experience, established neighborhood boundaries are typically composed of more than one MVA market type.

[12]   Data were most recently collected in the following years: Baltimore (2012–14); Detroit (2010-11); Milwaukee (2011–12); Philadelphia (2010–11); Pittsburgh (2011–13); and St. Louis (2010–12). It is frequently not possible to obtain each MVA data element entirely coincident in time. Moreover, for several indicators (e.g., residential sales or mortgage foreclosures) we will oftentimes aggregate across multiple years in an effort to obtain a sufficiency of activity upon which a stable estimate can be made. The years noted for each city therefore are presented as an indicator of the period for which the MVA is most representative.

[13]   ACS data are generally not preferred for MVAs because the margins of error are often quite large and the five-year aggregation makes the data less contemporary than other critical indicators.

Finally, researchers use a statistical cluster analysis to combine cases (i.e., block groups)—based on all of the measured indicators—into categories so that each group shares a common pattern of characteristics. The groupings are designed to maximize the similarity of areas within groups and maximize the differences between groups. The cluster analysis results are mapped and validated using a similar field validation process. Additional social, economic, and demographic characteristics in this chapter are gathered from the decennial censuses of 2000 and 2010 as well as the ACS, 2009–2013 five-year sample estimates.

MIDDLE NEIGHBORHOODS[14]

Across each of the studied cities, the middle neighborhoods are home to the largest segment of the population. In Detroit and Baltimore, more than one-half of the population resides in the MVA middle neighborhoods as defined by the MVA; Philadelphia's and St. Louis' middle neighborhoods are home to more than 40 percent, while Milwaukee and Pittsburgh house approximately 37 percent (Table 7).

Table 7: Population Distribution by Market Type

Percent of Total Population by MVA Market Type (ACS 2009–2013; 5-Year Estimates)						
Market Type	Philadelphia	Detroit	Baltimore	Milwaukee	Pittsburgh	St. Louis
High-Markets	11.6%	8.1%	20.6%	35.3%	22.1%	18.7%
Mid-Markets	42.9%	51.6%	51.2%	36.8%	37.1%	41.0%
Low-Markets	40.2%	38.3%	19.4%	24.7%	31.5%	33.7%
No MVA Market Type*	5.3%	2.0%	8.8%	3.2%	9.3%	6.6%

Block group areas with fewer than 5 sales are typically removed from MVA market designations.

Baltimore: Reinvestment Fund created multiple MVAs dating to 2005 in Baltimore. The most current MVA (Table 8) presents a more similar but not identical portrayal of Baltimore's housing market than previous MVAs. Aside from pockets of market stabilization and improvement (e.g., the Fells Point and Canton sections on the Patapsco River or Patterson Park to the north of Canton) and entrenched distress (e.g., Sandtown/Winchester and Park Heights), much of Baltimore shows modest strength or modest decline.

Baltimore's middle neighborhoods are home to 318,000 residents, equal to 51.2 percent of Baltimore's total population. Seventy-seven percent of residents are non-white in middle neighborhoods. Notwithstanding the relatively reasonable price of housing in Baltimore and modest income levels, owner—and especially renter—cost burdens are elevated. In fact, cost-burden levels for Baltimore's middle neighborhoods look more like their distressed counterparts than they do the stronger areas where incomes are substantially higher and the level of poverty is well below

---

[14] Tables 14, 15, and 16 contain the demographic data for all cities.

the citywide average. Residents of Baltimore's middle neighborhoods tend to be reasonably well educated, certainly when compared with residents of the more distressed market areas.

Sales prices in Baltimore's middle neighborhoods range between $40,000 and $115,000—a wide range, but still affordable for households earning a modest annual income. These middle neighborhoods face significant pressure from foreclosures and are not undergoing significant maintenance or upgrading, as evidenced by low levels of permitting. Middle neighborhoods in Baltimore are where renters with subsidies are finding homes, although they tend to be in the lower-priced areas of the markets. We note also that these areas run the full range of owner occupancy.

Driving through Baltimore's middle neighborhoods, one sees a full array of Baltimore's housing style, quality, level of maintenance, tenure, price points, and general curb appeal. But mostly, they represent places where modest-income families can find a home to meet their basic needs. At the same time, it is clear that maintenance is deferred in some of the market areas—conditions that most certainly undermine housing values and community stability.

Table 8: Characteristics of Baltimore's Markets

Baltimore 2014					
MVA Market Types	Number of Block Groups	Median Sales Price, 2012–2014 Q2	Variance Sales Price, 2012–2014 Q2	Foreclosure as Res. Lots, 2012–2014 Q2	Vacant Housing Units, 2014
A	48	$340,685	0.43	1.4%	0.3%
B	74	$192,635	0.47	2.8%	1.3%
C	97	$115,482	0.48	5.6%	1.1%
D	88	$72,714	0.61	5.6%	3.2%
E	89	$39,485	0.73	6.4%	6.1%
F	35	$37,858	0.71	5.9%	4.9%
G	98	$19,517	0.86	4.7%	16.7%
H	60	$11,775	0.97	2.9%	33.7%

MVA Market Types	Owner Occupied, 2014	Permits (>$10k) as Res. Lots, 2012–2014 Q2	Commercial & Industrial Land, 2014	Vacant Residential Lots, 2014	Rental Units Subsidized, 2014	Housing Units/ Square Mile, 2014
A	68.1%	6.9%	14.0%	1.3%	2.2%	6,228
B	40.6%	6.3%	20.0%	2.2%	4.5%	10,536
C	68.9%	2.4%	8.9%	0.6%	9.0%	4,712
D	46.7%	3.7%	13.1%	1.8%	8.5%	5,460
E	49.5%	2.2%	6.2%	1.8%	15.2%	7,308
F	41.0%	2.1%	54.6%	3.4%	11.2%	3,752
G	34.1%	1.9%	15.8%	2.6%	8.6%	8,816
H	21.4%	1.6%	15.1%	9.7%	5.4%	9,969

Detroit: Detroit's MVA (Table 9) was completed at a time when a state takeover and the potential bankruptcy of Detroit was becoming increasingly likely. Home prices in Detroit are substantially lower than in any of the other legacy cities. Even at the strongest end of the market, homes were selling for prices averaging under $125,000. Homes in Detroit's most distressed areas averaged under $5,000.

Like Baltimore, Detroit's middle neighborhoods are home to more than 50 percent of its population. There is no substantial difference in racial composition across the Detroit market categories. Although Detroit lost a significant percentage of its population, the losses in middle neighborhoods were substantially less severe, even compared with its strongest markets. Middle neighborhoods have a higher proportion of owner-occupied housing than even Detroit's strongest markets. This is a function of the relatively recent conversion and rehabilitation of housing stock in the downtown and midtown areas, much of which is now renter-occupied. Owner cost burdens (including the extremely cost burdened) for those residing in the middle neighborhoods of Detroit are relatively low compared with other parts of the city. Adult residents of Detroit's middle neighborhoods have reasonably similar levels of education as their counterparts in the stronger market areas. Although Detroit's poverty rate is generally higher than other legacy cities, the city's poverty rate in middle neighborhoods is relatively low.

The high level of real-estate owned (REO) homes (those held in the inventory of investors after foreclosure) and homes pending mortgage foreclosure actions—as well as the amount of vacant land (created through demolition)—are an obvious drag on the value and desirability of Detroit's middle neighborhoods. But, consistent with other legacy cities, several of the middle areas are highly owner-occupied. Further, middle neighborhoods have a higher proportion of the rental stock occupied by renters with a subsidy. Subsidized renters who live in middle neighborhoods are fortunate because these areas are some of the most stable places in Detroit.

Compared with other legacy cities for which we have completed MVAs, Detroit is unique in that the physical distance between areas of market strength and distress is extremely small, sometimes the width of a single street. It is clear that the city's middle neighborhoods (e.g., East English Village, Grandmont, Rosedale, Sherwood Forest) are places where families dedicate significant effort to maintaining their communities, despite everything going on around them. A home in pristine condition with a perfectly manicured lawn next to a burned-out structure is a common sight. It is here that signs frequently notify passers-by that a town watch is active. Many of the communities also appear to have worked to maintain their historic identity. However, more than in the other legacy cities, vacancy and abandonment (and apparent vacancy caused by fire or demolition) and properties warehoused in a lender or investor's REO portfolio are manifest.

Table 9: Characteristics of Detroit's Markets

Detroit 2011					
MVA Market Types	Number of Block Groups	Median Sales Price, 2009–2010	Variance Sales Price	Residential Properties Currently in REO	Residential Properties w/ Foreclosure Filing, 2009–2010
A	4	$124,500	0.80	3.2%	1.1%
B	10	$68,583	0.55	3.0%	3.1%
C	17	$31,500	0.76	1.9%	1.1%
D	60	$21,000	0.74	6.7%	4.9%
E	167	$11,888	0.90	7.0%	4.6%
F	127	$10,150	0.87	5.1%	3.8%
G	181	$6,050	1.17	7.3%	4.0%
H	77	$5,000	1.13	5.9%	2.9%
I	55	$4,100	1.16	4.3%	2.5%
MVA Market Types	Owner Occupied	Commercial/ Residential Land Use Ratio	Housing Units with Section 8	All Parcels Classified as Unimproved Vacant Lots	All Housing Units Classified as Vacant, Open & Dangerous
A	48.1%	0.12	0.2%	6.5%	0.5%
B	67.2%	0.07	1.0%	7.5%	0.0%
C	28.9%	0.13	1.6%	18.0%	1.0%
D	90.1%	0.04	2.1%	0.0%	0.0%
E	79.3%	0.05	3.2%	1.0%	0.0%
F	50.5%	0.08	2.4%	5.0%	2.0%
G	66.4%	0.05	3.3%	4.0%	2.0%
H	38.6	0.09	2.6	16.0	7.0
I	65.7	0.04	1.8	21.0	8.0

Milwaukee: Milwaukee's middle neighborhoods are home to approximately 37 percent of the city's population, generally lower than other legacy cities. However, a substantially larger share of the Milwaukee population resides in stronger markets and a smaller population is in distressed market areas. Milwaukee's middle neighborhoods are places with modest levels of owner occupancy and a substantial percentage of sales of duplexes and other small multifamily units (Table 10). Middle neighborhoods are still being affected by foreclosures; although, unlike other legacy cities, Milwaukee's more distressed markets are now being hit harder.

Milwaukee's population was stable between 2000 and 2013, with the middle neighborhoods growing by 1.7 percent. The largest proportionate loss was found in the more distressed market areas of the city. Milwaukee is similar to the other legacy cities in that a substantial share of the city's non-white population lives in middle neighborhoods. Though sales prices are relatively low, Milwaukee's middle neighborhoods are not particularly affordable for owners or renters. A relatively high percentage of residents are cost burdened.

Milwaukee's middle neighborhoods are split: markets with homes prices ranging from $90,000 to $120,000 and those, albeit often similar in appearance, with home prices from $50,000 to $70,000. Some of this bifurcation may be related to Milwaukee's legacy of racial segregation. However, some of the price difference can also be accounted for by the much higher levels of foreclosure activity in the less expensive neighborhoods. History tells us though that segregation and foreclosures are not unrelated phenomena.

Table 10: Characteristics of Milwaukee's Markets

Milwaukee 2012					
MVA Market Types	Median Sales Price, 2011–2012	Average Sales Price, 2011–2012	Variance Sales Price, 2011–2012	Foreclosures as a Percent of Sales	Duplex/ Multifamily Sales
A	$214,780	$234,429	0.46	14%	62%
B	$121,403	$121,067	0.38	21%	11%
C	$117,397	$113,297	0.43	24%	24%
D	$91,462	$99,228	0.55	31%	53%
E	$55,001	$64,723	0.65	47%	13%
F	$51,658	$63,400	0.73	49%	61%
G	$30,705	$44,611	0.85	51%	74%
H	$29,335	$44,001	0.91	51%	29%
I	$15,607	$29,497	1.09	65%	57%
MVA Market Types	Water Shut Off	New/>$10k Rehab	Owner Occupied	Publicly Subsidized Rental	Non-Residential Area
A	2	3	33	2	16
B	1%	4%	69%	3%	13%
C	2%	3%	43%	4%	62%
D	3%	3%	44%	6%	13%
E	3%	2%	49%	12%	24%
F	6%	2%	34%	6%	27%
G	9%	2%	29%	7%	20%
H	9%	3%	33%	9%	20%
I	16%	4%	26%	7%	24%

Philadelphia: Overall, 42.9 percent of Philadelphia's residents (663,000) live in the middle neighborhoods, a 4.6 percent rise over the decade. The non-white population of Philadelphia is over-represented in the more challenged market areas of Philadelphia. Although 47.8 percent of the residents in middle neighborhoods are non-white, disproportionately fewer (32.3 percent) of non-whites live in middle neighborhoods.

Philadelphia stands out among the group of legacy cities in a number of ways. First, it has the largest population. Second, a considerable share of Philadelphia's residential population resides in the strong market areas in the downtown. Third, Philadelphia's residential downtown—along with a few communities, particularly in the northwest section—have sale prices well over $600,000 (price points not frequently observed in the other cities). The middle neighborhoods, however, are relatively affordable and are unmistakably Philadelphia's owner-occupied communities (Table 11). New construction is rare in these areas; however, that which is new will be found largely in the northwest and the far northeast sections of the city. Mortgage foreclosures continue to affect these areas; a second wave related to the recession came on the heels of a significant number of foreclosures in the early 2000s due to subprime mortgages and abusive lending practices. Unlike some of the other legacy cities, middle neighborhoods in Philadelphia are largely absent renters with subsidies. Those renters are generally clustered in the most distressed markets.

Philadelphia's middle neighborhoods are home to 50 percent of all owners, and these areas have the highest typical owner-occupancy rate at 62.1 percent. Notwithstanding the prices in Philadelphia's strongest markets, the city's middle neighborhoods are relatively affordable compared with the other legacy cities, as evidenced by the relatively low levels of owner and renter cost burdens (among the cities examined, only Pittsburgh and St. Louis have lower levels of cost burdens). It is interesting to note just how different residents of Philadelphia's middle neighborhoods are from their stronger market counterparts. Of adults in middle areas, 23.2 percent have a college degree compared with 62.2 percent of those in the stronger markets. Such a stark difference is found only in Baltimore.

Philadelphia's middle neighborhoods are staunchly middle class communities. Many of the residents earn a modest income. The most recent wave of foreclosures has visibly affected many of these communities, which can be seen in the presence of REOs, especially in the more challenged parts of the middle areas. The poor quality of Philadelphia's schools hits these communities particularly hard. Unlike residents of the stronger markets, residents of middle neighborhoods generally cannot afford private schools, and public charter schools generally admit through lottery, not residence. The tenuousness of these communities is manifest, especially in the lower end of the middle areas.

Table 11: Characteristics of Philadelphia's Markets

Philadelphia 2011					
MVA Market Types	Number of Block Groups	Median Sale Price	Mean Sale Price	Variance Sales Price	Owner Occupied
A	9	$624,122	$707,042	0.58	39.8%
B	19	$435,249	$502,392	0.50	48.8%
C	50	$325,897	$354,545	0.46	49.3%
D	68	$245,930	$267,304	0.50	51.2%
E	125	$194,459	$196,960	0.39	63.9%
F	150	$148,066	$148,958	0.39	66.4%
G	247	$97,860	$100,361	0.48	62.4%
H	227	$51,190	$64,001	0.66	61.4%
I	358	$19,649	$31,094	0.94	48.1%

MVA Market Types	Vacant (L&I)	New Construction	Commercial	Foreclosures as a Percent of Sales	Public/Assisted Housing
A	1.6%	11.5%	5.7%	6.3%	0.0%
B	0.7%	7.0%	7.3%	5.9%	0.0%
C	1.4%	9.7%	6.6%	9.0%	0.8%
D	2.1%	6.5%	5.9%	17.7%	2.1%
E	1.0%	2.8%	3.3%	24.1%	0.5%
F	1.6%	1.9%	4.0%	33.5%	0.4%
G	2.7%	1.5%	3.9%	38.4%	3.8%
H	4.2%	0.6%	3.9%	45.9%	2.3%
I	8.1%	1.1%	5.1%	33.5%	10.3%

Pittsburgh: Of all legacy cities, Pittsburgh's middle neighborhoods are home to the lowest percentage of the city's population (37.1 percent). In some ways, this is a manifestation of the even distribution of the city's populations across all markets. Although Pittsburgh's population declined by almost 10 percent between 2000 and 2013, the middle neighborhoods fared reasonably well, losing only 5.3 percent of their population. We find a disproportionately large percentage of Pittsburgh's white population in these areas (43 percent) and a disproportionately smaller percentage of its non-white population in middle neighborhoods (26.2 percent).

Pittsburgh's middle neighborhoods have home sale prices that are affordable even for those of fairly modest means (Table 12). In general, the city's middle neighborhoods have the highest levels of owner occupancy—higher even than the stronger market areas. One MVA middle market type is home to a significant group of subsidized rental properties. Foreclosures in Pittsburgh are elevated in the middle neighborhoods, and like some of the other legacy cities, the REO inventory is readily visible to the casual observer.

Owing to the very low home sale prices, the cost burden in Pittsburgh's middle areas is relatively low compared with the other legacy cities. Cost burdens are also relatively low among renters living in middle neighborhoods.

The educational profile of Pittsburgh's adult population residing in middle neighborhoods is the most advantageous among these legacy cities. Approximately one-third of middle area residents have bachelor's degrees and fewer than 9 percent lack a high school diploma. The poverty rate for residents of middle neighborhoods is notably lower than the other legacy cities.

In validating Pittsburgh's MVA, we were struck by how stable and advantageous the city's middle areas were, and how few residents have fully exploited the many extraordinary physical elevations and view sheds the city has to offer. Homes on a hill with an unobstructed view of the rivers that in other cities might be million dollar tear-downs sell for under $35,000, for example. Several of the communities along the Allegheny River have market momentum, and the East Liberty section is showing substantial market strength. Like some of the other legacy cities, the impact of the universities and medical centers is readily apparent in the surrounding real estate markets.

Table 12: Characteristics of Pittsburgh's Markets

Pittsburgh 2013					
MVA Market Types	Number of Block Groups	Median Sales Price, 2011–2013	Variance Sales Price, 2011–2013	Foreclosures as a Percent of Sales 2011–2012	Commercial & Industrial, 2013
A	31	$33,578	0.50	4.70%	21.29%
B	34	$191,998	0.49	11.39%	39.31%
C	39	$119,922	0.55	17.95%	12.50%
D	33	$84,342	0.64	14.08%	45.72%
E	49	$69,816	0.52	28.20%	11.54%
F	18	$45,819	0.79	28.47%	18.58%
G	38	$40,787	0.79	30.92%	13.13%
H	42	$19,282	0.89	32.64%	25.53%
I	35	$8,790	0.92	32.46%	16.17%
MVA Market Types	Owner Occupied, 2010	Vacant Residential Land, 2013	Public Housing 2013	Violations, 2011–2012	All Permits 2011–2012
A	58.12%	3.06%	0.61%	7.65%	4.28%
B	23.90%	3.04%	3.09%	13.84%	3.53%
C	60.70%	11.53%	2.50%	14.79%	1.37%
D	35.88%	10.51%	9.93%	19.17%	2.08%
E	72.89%	9.75%	2.33%	15.79%	0.60%
F	47.88%	16.90%	59.53%	26.65%	1.59%
G	59.93%	18.22%	5.15%	23.25%	1.08%
H	51.66%	23.49%	21.81%	29.89%	1.50%
I	48.75%	36.42%	11.84%	34.07%	0.45%

St. Louis: St. Louis's middle neighborhoods are home to 41 percent of its population. These areas lost 8.2 percent of their population during the last decade, while the stronger market areas gained 10.7 percent. However, the city's most distressed markets—home to one-third of the population—lost 18.4 percent. The racial segregation in St. Louis is manifest in these markets. For example, although 60.7 percent of the white population lives in middle neighborhoods, only 36.8 percent of the non-white population lives in these areas.

The middle neighborhoods of St. Louis are largely in the southern part of the city, south of Dr. Martin Luther King Blvd. Like the other legacy cities, St. Louis's middle areas have comparatively low sale prices, making them reasonably affordable to both owners and renters. These are markets with high levels of foreclosures and a substantial level of investor activity (Table 13). As observed in other legacy cities, owner occupancy is generally highest in the middle neighborhoods. Like Detroit, vacant housing and land are common and have an obvious impact on community life. Subsidized rental housing, like other legacy cities, is more common in some of the middle neighborhoods—although there is a significant concentration in the city's most challenged market areas.

The adult population is relatively well educated in these middle neighborhoods compared with other legacy cities. One-third have bachelor's degrees, second only to Pittsburgh. Further, fewer than 15 percent failed to graduate from high school, again second only to Pittsburgh. St. Louis's middle areas have a poverty rate of 15 percent, a rate slightly above the city's stronger markets (13.5 percent).

Rehabilitation and redevelopment are consistent with the historic character of the city. Moreover, the quality of public facilities (i.e., parks and libraries) is amazingly high and consistent across the city, regardless of the challenges or strengths of the real estate markets. Although some of the most expensive real estate in St. Louis is adjacent to the city's Forest Park, there are several middle neighborhoods ringing the southern border of that same park. Even on the north side where the residential market is weaker, middle neighborhoods are adjacent to several of the city's parks. At the same time, like the other legacy cities, many of the middle areas in St. Louis are hanging on, apparently challenged by the elevated levels of investor-owned property.

Table 13: Characteristics of St. Louis' Markets

St. Louis 2013					
MVA Market Types	Number of Block Groups	Median Sales Price, 2010–2012	Variance Sales Price, 2010–2012	Foreclosure by Sales, 2010–2012	Bank and Investor Sales, 2010–2012
A	31	$205,311	0.55	13.08%	6.74%
B	26	$147,016	0.56	31.21%	9.26%
C	46	$122,314	0.44	20.69%	14.40%
D	53	$82,614	0.60	30.01%	19.07%
E	46	$48,766	0.74	34.99%	27.54%
F	51	$27,940	0.92	40.84%	28.40%
G	11	$21,578	1.04	38.77%	27.04%
H	38	$14,053	1.08	35.96%	34.58%
I	40	$8,036	1.27	33.55%	38.21%
MVA Market Types	Nonresidential, 2013	Owner Occupied, 2010	Vacant Housing Units, 2010	Subsidized Rental Housing, 2013	Permits of Housing Units, 2010–2013	Vacant Residential Land, 2013
A	25.83%	44.95%	12.96%	1.58%	8.58%	4.77%
B	68.80%	29.48%	15.16%	13.68%	12.18%	12.80%
C	10.55%	66.99%	9.15%	1.24%	3.57%	1.50%
D	31.59%	54.03%	15.49%	4.21%	5.92%	7.59%
E	25.90%	46.87%	18.16%	5.91%	3.03%	4.28%
F	19.13%	43.00%	23.96%	10.44%	2.23%	12.28%
G	81.72%	47.92%	22.07%	15.63%	7.35%	16.26%
H	18.29%	49.51%	27.17%	9.73%	2.21%	18.48%
I	33.30%	42.95%	32.14%	15.47%	3.15%	35.00%

Table 14: Demographic Characteristics of MVA Market Types

		2013 Population Counts						
Project	Market Type	Total Population	Non-White Population	White Population	Non-White	Total	Non-White	White
Baltimore 2014	Low-Markets	120,470 19.4%	113,216 25.3%	7,254 4.2%	94.0%	-18.2%	-16.8%	-35.1%
	Mid-Markets	317,930 51.2%	244,745 54.8%	73,185 41.9%	77.0%	-1.7%	7.2%	-23.0%
	High-Markets	128,142 20.6%	43,383 9.7%	84,759 48.5%	33.9%	8.2%	19.2%	3.3%
	No MVA Market Type	54,903 8.8%	45,511 10.2%	9,392 5.4%	82.9%	-11.6%	-6.2%	30.7%
Detroit 2012	Low-Markets	270,490 38.3%	257,429 39.7%	13,061 22.5%	95.2%	-34.8%	-33.4%	-54.1%
	Mid-Markets	364,980 51.6%	328,570 50.7%	36,410 62.7%	90.0%	-15.5	-11.3	-40.7%
	High-Markets	57,054 8.1%	51,469 7.9%	5,585 9.6%	90.2%	-33.2%	-34.0%	-25.1%
	No MVA Market Type	14,123 2.0%	11,135 1.7%	2,987 5.1%	78.8%	-25.7%	-30.1%	-2.7%
Milwaukee 2012	Low-Markets	149,533 24.7%	138,109 36.2%	11,424 5.1%	92.4%	-10.5%	-5.2%	-46.6%
	Mid-Markets	223,365 36.8%	165,979 43.5%	57,386 25.5%	74.3%	1.7%	22.6%	-31.8%
	High-Markets	213,895 35.3%	66,273 17.4%	147,622 65.7%	31.0%	7.6%	80.6%	-9.0%
	No MVA Market Type	19,606 3.2%	11,421 3.0%	8,185 3.6%	58.3%	-4.1%	5.5%	-14.9%
Philadelphia 2011	Low-Markets	621,548 40.2%	558,136 57.0%	63,412 11.2%	89.8%	-3.3%	3.4%	-38.4%
	Mid-Markets	662,758 42.9%	316,637 32.3%	346,121 61.1%	47.8%	4.6%	38.3%	-14.5%
	High-Markets	179,384 11.6%	53,708 5.5%	125,676 22.2%	29.9%	9.0%	-0.5%	13.7%
	No MVA Market Type	81,931 5.3%	50,958 5.2%	30,973 5.5%	62.2%	-3.9%	-3.5%	-4.4%
Pittsburgh 2013	Low-Markets	98,233 31.5%	49,344 45.2%	48,889 24.1%	50.2%	-17.1%	-8.4%	-24.4%
	Mid-Markets	115,667 37.1%	28,586 26.2%	87,081 43.0%	24.7%	-5.3%	20.5%	-11.5%
	High-Markets	68,927 22.1%	15,509 14.2%	53,418 26.3%	22.5%	8.7%	23.8%	4.9%
	No MVA Market Type	29,021 9.3%	15,677 14.4%	13,344 6.6%	54.0%	-19.4%	-24.3%	-12.8%
St. Louis 2013	Low-Markets	107,549 33.7%	95,598 52.3%	11,951 8.8%	88.9%	-18.4%	-16.3%	-31.8%
	Mid-Markets	130,682 41.0%	48,026 26.3%	82,656 60.7%	36.8%	-8.2%	2.0%	-13.3%
	High-Markets	59,603 18.7%	23,401 12.8%	36,202 26.6%	39.3%	10.7%	8.3%	12.3%
	No MVA Market Type	21,121 6.6%	15,842 8.7%	5,279 3.9%	75.0%	4.8%	1.3%	17.2%

Table 15: Housing Characteristics of MVA Market Types

Project	Market Type	Total Occupied Households	Owners	Renters	Owner Occupied	Owners Cost-Burdened	Renters Cost-Burdened	Owners Extremely Cost-Burdened	Renters Extremely Cost-Burdened
				2013 Households and Cost Burdens					
Baltimore 2014	Low-Markets	40,820	16,302 14.0%	24,518 19.6%	39.9%	36.4%	57.8%	17.8%	34.0%
	Mid-Markets	121,684	68,695 58.9%	52,989 42.5%	56.5%	37.5%	54.8%	15.7%	30.2%
	High-Markets	57,304	28,639 24.5%	28,665 23.0%	50.0%	27.5%	45.0%	10.7%	21.4%
	No MVA Market Type	21,647	3,037 2.6%	18,610 14.9%	14.0%	37.9%	52.9%	15.8%	28.2%
Detroit 2012	Low-Markets	93,591	51,048 38.3%	42,543 34.5%	54.5%	39.9%	62.8%	21.2%	45.0%
	Mid-Markets	133,970	71,295 53.6%	62,675 50.8%	53.2%	37.1%	59.0%	18.8%	37.2%
	High-Markets	22,850	10,078 7.6%	12,772 10.3%	44.1%	40.8%	55.3%	22.3%	33.3%
	No MVA Market Type	6,178	691 0.5%	5,487 4.4%	11.2%	39.3%	50.1%	18.4%	26.9%
Milwaukee 2012	Low-Markets	49,685	16,115 15.8%	33,570 25.6%	32.4%	46.8%	64.7%	22.2%	40.5%
	Mid-Markets	82,396	36,150 35.5%	46,246 35.5%	43.9%	40.2%	58.3%	16.3%	32.3%
	High-Markets	94,287	49,103 48.3%	45,184 34.5%	52.1%	30.4%	45.7%	10.8%	24.7%
	No MVA Market Type	6,448	370 0.4%	6.078 4.6%	5.7%	55.9%	60.1%	19.2%	31.6%
Philadelphia 2011	Low-Markets	216,621	109,418 35.2%	107,203 39.3%	50.5%	35.7%	57.5%	17.4%	36.2%
	Mid-Markets	249,943	155,309 50.0%	94,634 34.7%	62.1%	30.8%	51.6%	13.4%	29.8%
	High-Markets	86,498	40,602 13.1%	45,896 16.8%	46.9%	26.8%	43.0%	11.4%	23.0%
	No MVA Market Type	30,143	5,217 1.7%	24,926 9.1%	17.3%	34.6%	48.8%	12.8%	27.4%
Pittsburgh 2013	Low-Markets	42,150	22,367 33.6%	19,783 28.6%	53.1%	24.1%	51.8%	9.8%	28.9%
	Mid-Markets	53,358	30,222 45.4%	23,136 33.5%	56.6%	21.0%	44.9%	8.1%	24.6%
	High-Markets	32,671	12,675 19.0%	19,996 28.9%	38.8%	21.2%	44.8%	10.0%	26.8%
	No MVA Market Type	7,524	1,306 2.0%	6,218 9.0%	17.4%	26.2%	45.4%	9.3%	25.5%

St. Louis 2013	Low-Markets	40,952	18,043 28.8%	22,909 29.4%	44.1%	37.4%	61.8%	17.3%	38.0%
	Mid-Markets	60,108	32,792 52.3%	27,316 35.0%	54.6%	24.5%	48.6%	9.3%	25.3%
	High-Markets	30,825	10,561 16.8%	20,264 26.0%	34.3%	27.5%	43.7%	12.4%	23.6%
	No MVA Market Type	8,767	1,320 2.1%	7,447 9.6%	15.1%	24.7%	52.9%	11.6%	30.3%

Table 16: Education, Income, and Poverty of MVA Market Types

2013 Education, Income, and Poverty (vs. 2013 Households and Cost Burdens)						
Project	Market Type	Less Than High School	High School or Equivalent	Bachelor's Degree	Median Household Income*	Familes Below Poverty
Baltimore 2014	Low-Markets	29.9%	38.4%	6.5%	$29,206	31.1%
	Mid-Markets	19.3%	32.8%	21.0%	$44,609	16.0%
	High-Markets	10.3%	14.0%	59.6%	$75,971	8.8%
	No MVA Market Type	26.8%	32.2%	19.0%	$22,489	36.2%
Detroit 2012	Low-Markets	23.0%	35.9%	8.1%	†	38.4%
	Mid-Markets	22.0%	30.0%	15.1%	†	30.4%
	High-Markets	22.9%	31.1%	17.9%	†	36.4%
	No MVA Market Type	19.8%	28.4%	17.5%	†	30.5%
Milwaukee 2012	Low-Markets	31.3%	34.6%	7.8%	$24,868	41.1%
	Mid-Markets	21.6%	32.5%	16.3%	$35,271	26.3%
	High-Markets	9.2%	26.9%	35.6%	$52,152	10.9%
	No MVA Market Type	20.2%	29.3%	20.1%	$31,400	42.4%
Philadelphia 2011	Low-Markets	26.6%	40.0%	9.6%	$26,976	33.4%
	Mid-Markets	16.1%	36.3%	23.2%	$46,113	13.6%
	High-Markets	7.1%	15.4%	62.2%	$69,257	5.9%
	No MVA Market Type	18.0%	29.3%	32.2%	$27,249	24.0%

Pittsburgh 2013	Low-Markets	12.4%	38.6%	18.0%	$33,012	22.6%
	Mid-Markets	8.9%	30.8%	34.2%	$45,203	11.5%
	High-Markets	3.3%	13.1%	68.7%	$61,740	5.9%
	No MVA Market Type	20.5%	40.5%	15.5%	$14,564	38.1%
St. Louis 2013	Low-Markets	25.1%	33.4%	10.5%	$25,416	31.5%
	Mid-Markets	14.8%	23.3%	33.6%	$43,529	15.0%
	High-Markets	8.3%	14.4%	53.5%	$48,691	13.5%
	No MVA Market Type	22.8%	26.4%	17.6%	$18,990	46.4%

Note: Education counts only include individuals >25 years of age.

DISCUSSION

Economist Charles Tiebout is credited with popularizing the concept of the value proposition.[15] For policymakers and elected officials in legacy cities, it is a vital proposition for the middle neighborhoods. To reverse the loss of population, legacy cities must nurture the conditions and amenities that attract and retain residents.

In many ways, middle neighborhoods have the strongest value proposition for residents, at least for now. Middle neighborhoods contain an attractive housing stock and their homes are reasonably affordable for middle- and modest-income families.

Middle neighborhoods in each of the legacy cities manifest both market strengths and challenges. In many of the legacy cities, the middle neighborhoods are where racial-ethnic diversity is strong and modest-income families can live in a relatively opportune area. But, residents of middle neighborhoods

VALUE PROPOSITION

Attracting new residents and retaining those who currently live in the city requires an effective "value proposition." For Detroit, this proposition is firmly based on offering a high quality of life that is well within each resident's grasp. This is arguably a proposition the city has not been able to effectively make. People make decisions about cities based on what their neighborhoods offer, including access to employment opportunities, quality schools, efficient and effective public services, housing options, safety and security, and affordability. Detroit must deliver on these to make itself truly regionally competitive—where area residents, city residents, and those coming to the region for the first time can truly see themselves, and in many cases their families, living in Detroit.

Reinventing America's Legacy Cities. Strategies for Cities Losing Population. Report of the 110th American Assembly (New York: American Assembly, 2012), 13.

[15]   C.M. Tiebout, "A Pure Theory of Local Expenditures," *Journal of Political Economy*, 64, no. 5 (1956): 416–424.

also have relatively advantageous levels of education and income, which means they may have other options for where to live.

Accordingly, middle neighborhoods are also, in many ways, in the most precarious position. Local experts and practitioners pointed out that middle neighborhoods are the areas with the most to lose, and the farthest to fall when confronted with continued strain on residential markets.

One of the complications of working in middle neighborhoods is that cities are forced to simultaneously play offense and defense. A public official in one city noted the dual role that middle neighborhoods play as both nodes of strength for their surrounding neighborhoods and as fragile areas on the verge of decline. "If your neighborhood is close to strength, then you're really hoping to have positive bleed over. Where your neighborhood is surrounded by weaker areas, I could see folks thinking, 'Now might be the time to get out.'"

Middle neighborhoods are areas where, in the words of one interviewee, "One or two boarded up houses on a block" can be the difference between a neighborhood on the rise or one falling into distress. This means that for cities with limited resources, investing in the middle neighborhoods can often produce the largest returns. In the words of a community development expert, "If you ignore these places, then you'll continue to see declines."

Stated differently, middle neighborhoods are where the real estate market continues to operate within market expectations while also providing homes within reach for low- and middle-income families. In contrast, distressed market areas have experienced market fallout and collapse, signaled by very few home sales or residential property turnover.

"Areas with relatively strong market activity should be targeted for investment, with the goal of increasing demand, strengthening property values, and rebuilding confidence in the community. Focusing resources on these places, which may include residential neighborhoods, commercial districts, and/or downtowns, can motivate existing property owners to reinvest in their properties, and encourage people to buy in the area."

A. Mallach, *Rebuilding America's Legacy Cities. Report of the 110th American Assembly* (New York: The American Assembly, Columbia University, 2012), p. 329

One of Reinvestment Fund's operating assumptions, developed over the 15-year history of the MVA, is that, owing in part to the scarcity of available housing subsidies, what subsidy does exist cannot alone create a market. Rather, subsidies should be used strategically to leverage private market forces, clearing barriers to private actors, and thereby multiplying the impact of public dollars in a given neighborhood. One interviewee noted, "These are places where your neighborhood is not so far gone that it takes decades or millions of dollars to see something change." Middle neighborhoods provide an opportunity to make targeted and focused investments, the result of which will be readily apparent. As another interviewee noted, focusing on middle neighborhoods is the nexus of bringing private-sector discipline to public-sector practice: "Of course these [middle markets] are the places that you want to invest."

For legacy cities, the health of middle neighborhoods is more important than ever. In his address to the 2013 Federal Reserve Bank of Richmond Community Development Conference, Jeremy Nowak pointed to the dangers middle neighborhoods face. "Demographics, economics potentially, and cultural factors have given some advantages to cities," he said, "including cities that are relatively distressed and have been quite distressed for 40 or 50 years." Residents, he said, "are now willing to pay more if they have access to certain things." Nowak warned, "If the relationship between quality and cost does not work, then they will opt out."[16]

These words speak to the importance of supporting middle neighborhoods in our legacy cities, and are echoed by a recent Pew Research study of Millennials in Philadelphia.[17] Pew's research suggests that this younger generation was more likely than older generations to leave Philadelphia because of quality of life and opportunity issues (i.e., public safety, career opportunity, public education). At some point in the future, as Millennials age, get married, and have children, the importance of safe streets and good schools will increase and these "consumer-voters" (in Tiebout's parlance) will leave. For middle neighborhoods, the failure to address these core issues may leave residents with few reasons to stay. For legacy cities, losing the battle in these places will have systemic and long-lasting effects.[18]

In describing the condition in Youngstown, OH, Mallach and Brachman write: "Youngstown Neighborhood Development Corporation focused its resources on neighborhoods that, although troubled, were still vital and potentially capable of regeneration… There are strong arguments to prioritize such areas over attempts to pursue the large-scale reconfiguration of mostly abandoned areas. Legacy cities like Youngstown are now seeing extensive and often rapid destabilization of traditional neighborhoods like Idora; absent concerted efforts to reverse this trend, some cities may be left with few viable neighborhoods outside their downtown and near-downtown cores. This is a matter of far more urgency for the future viability of legacy cities than repurposing land in largely vacant areas…"

A. Mallach and L. Brachman, *Regenerating America's Legacy Cities* (Cambridge, MA: Lincoln Institute of Land Policy, 2013), p.52.

We return to the initial premise. Federal funds for neighborhood improvement have declined significantly during the past 40 years, and many of our public institutions and systems (e.g., public safety, public education, local government service, and infrastructure) are not where they need to be. Our officials are overly focused on the downtowns, and they are competing vigorously for high-profile, but spatially compact, revitalization opportunities for distressed neighborhoods (e.g., CHOICE Neighborhoods and Promise Zones). Middle neighborhoods are not a priority.

[16] Jeremy Nowak, "Redefining 'Rust Belt': An Exchange of Strategies by the Cities of Baltimore, Cleveland, Detroit and Philadelphia," presentation at the Federal Reserve Bank of Richmond, Community Development Conference, June 2013, Baltimore, MD. Available at http://jnowakassociates.com/publications/.

[17] Pew Research, "Millennials in Philadelphia: A Promising but Fragile Boom" (Washington, DC: Pew Research, 2014), at http://www.pewtrusts.org/en/research-and-analysis/reports/2014/01/21/millennials-in-philadelphia-a-promising-but-fragile-boom.

[18] Brophy's analysis of Baltimore's neighborhoods concludes with a set of recommendations that both prioritize the city's middle markets and offer a promising programmatic approach to working in these areas. Specifically, the multifaceted Baltimore's Healthy Neighborhoods initiative exemplifies a demonstrably impactful and "cost-effective approach to strengthening middle neighborhoods." Paul Brophy, *Great Neighborhoods Great City: Strategies for the 2010s*, 2012 update, (Baltimore, MD: Goldseker Foundation, 2012), p. 24, at http://www.mdarts.org/images/uploads/great_cities_2012.pdf

The fundamentals that support stability, opportunity, and quality of life are important to all city residents. But they are uniquely important to residents of middle neighborhoods.

Lastly, middle neighborhoods in these legacy cities are most representative of citywide racial composition and generally more integrated than the city itself or the other market types. Although we have argued that it is good public policy to use public funds to invest in middle neighborhoods from a community development or neighborhood improvement perspective, middle neighborhoods may also be important targets for public investment because they are places where opportunity is high and racial integration greatest.

Without a clear space in the public policy and investment conversations, the future of middle neighborhoods as areas of opportunity is in doubt. If Tiebout is correct, cities ignore their middle neighborhoods at their own peril. Unless policymakers recognize and act to maintain the quality of life and stability of these areas, residents may well leave because their economic wherewithal allows them to find those qualities elsewhere.

Ira Goldstein is the president of Policy Solutions at Reinvestment Fund. His research focuses on various aspects of housing and economic development in America's cities. Prior to joining Reinvestment Fund, Goldstein was Mid-Atlantic regional director of fair housing and equal opportunity at the U.S. Department of Housing and Urban Development. For more than 25 years, Goldstein has been a lecturer at the University of Pennsylvania, teaching courses focused on housing policy and social science research methods and statistics. Goldstein holds a Ph.D., M.A., and B.A. from Temple University.

Jacob L. Rosch is a research associate at Reinvestment Fund. His research focuses on residential housing markets, intersections between health and housing, and education. Prior to joining Reinvestment Fund, Mr. Rosch spent six years as a researcher and consultant advising educational institutions in K–12 and higher education. He holds a B.A. with honors from the University of North Carolina at Chapel Hill and an M.P.P. from the University of Chicago's Harris School of Public Policy.

William Schrecker has been a research analyst at Reinvestment Fund since 2013, with much of his work focused on residential real estate analyses. His recent MVA projects include Baltimore, New Orleans, and Wilmington, DE, with past research including Houston, Pittsburgh, and St. Louis. Mr. Schrecker holds an M.B.A. from the Fox School of Business at Temple University and an M.S.W. from the University of Pennsylvania.

APPENDIX 1: MVA MAPS

Appendix 1, Figure 1: Baltimore MVA

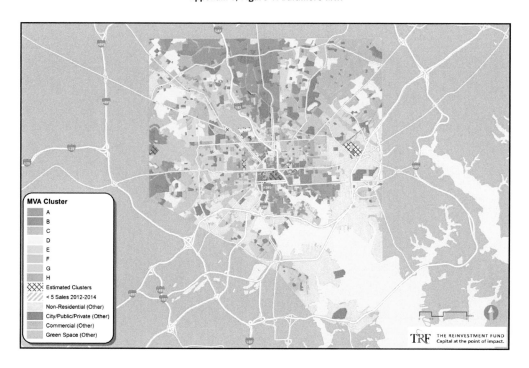

Appendix 1, Figure 2: Detroit MVA

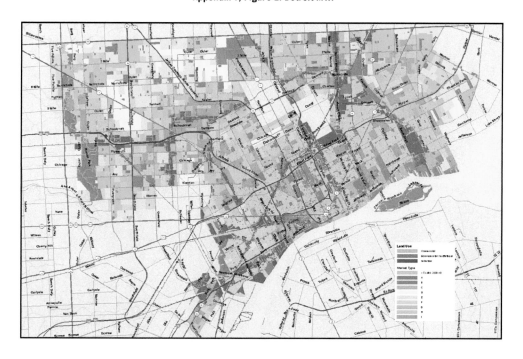

Appendix 1, Figure 3: Milwaukee MVA

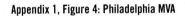

Appendix 1, Figure 4: Philadelphia MVA

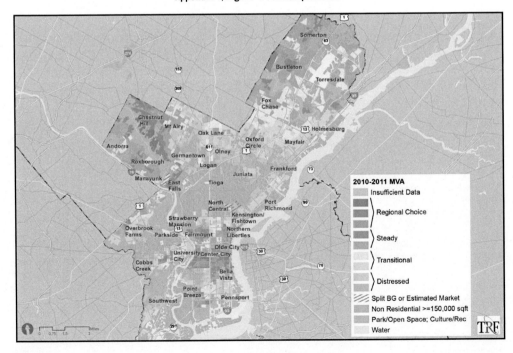

Appendix 1, Figure 5: Pittsburgh MVA

Appendix 1, Figure 6: St. Louis MVA

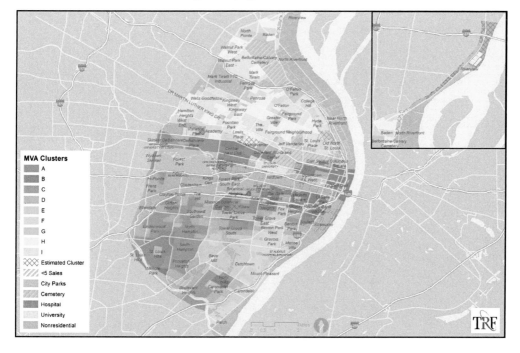

APPENDIX 2: CHAPTER INTERVIEWEES

Brian Abernathy	First Deputy Managing Director at City of Philadelphia. Formerly served as Executive Director of the Philadelphia Redevelopment Authority.
Martha Brown	Deputy Commissioner, Milwaukee Department of City Development.
Kathryn Dunn	Vice President, Community Investment at the Greater Milwaukee Foundation.
Jeff Hebert	Chief Resilience Officer and Executive Director of the New Orleans Redevelopment Authority.
Karla Henderson	Director of Strategic Planning and Facility Management at Wayne County Michigan and former Group Executive of Planning & Facilities for the City of Detroit.
Steve Janes	Assistant Commissioner of Research and Compliance for the City of Baltimore Housing Department.
Don Roe	Director of the Planning and Urban Design Agency, the City of St. Louis.
RJ Stidham	A community development consultant, who has worked with a number of cities on their development and implementation of the MVA, including Detroit and St. Louis.
Kyra Straussman	Director of Real Estate, The Urban Redevelopment Authority of Pittsburgh.

IV. IS THE URBAN MIDDLE NEIGHBORHOOD AN ENDANGERED SPECIES? MULTIPLE CHALLENGES AND DIFFICULT ANSWERS

By Alan Mallach, Center for Community Progress

This chapter looks directly at the challenges facing middle neighborhoods in legacy cities. As the title suggests—and as the entire thrust of this book suggests—those challenges are serious and complex. As I describe, the challenges are multidimensional, with demographic, physical, and economic factors interacting with and reinforcing one another. I am not suggesting that change and revitalization are impossible; rather, I am laying out the multifaceted and complex nature of the challenge in order to make clear that to be successful, strategies for change must in turn be multifaceted and sensitive to these complex realities.

I begin with a historical overview, reflecting my conviction that the seeds of many of today's challenges in middle market neighborhoods are rooted in their origins. Middle neighborhoods, as I define them here, are those residential areas within legacy cities that were historically occupied by those cities' large, stable working-class and middle class populations—and remained, at least through the beginning of the present century, viable if not always thriving neighborhoods.

The following sections address the different dimensions of the challenge, including demographic change; economic changes, including the impact of increasing inequality and the hollowing out of the middle class; challenges posed by the physical environment and housing stock; and the difficulty many cities are facing as they attempt to compete with their suburbs in increasingly competitive housing market environments. Although the erosion of homeownership is a significant factor in itself, I treat it only briefly here, given that I have devoted an entire chapter to that subject elsewhere in this book. Finally, a closing section addresses some of the opportunities and further challenges faced by those who are working to stabilize and rebuild middle market neighborhoods. As many other chapters in this book demonstrate, for all the manifold challenges, these neighborhoods offer opportunities as well—which have formed the basis for the successful revival of middle market neighborhoods across the United States.

THE CREATION OF A MONOCULTURE

The typical urban middle neighborhood, aside from a cluster of cities in the Northeast,[1] is a neighborhood of single-family homes. While each legacy city contains a central core—made up of the downtown along with the area in which major universities and medical centers are situated and a handful of immediately proximate residential areas—that central core typically covers 5 percent or less of its land area. The rest is made up of single-family residential neighborhoods, dotted with the factories, rail yards, and similar features that once sustained its industrial economy. Outside the central core, except for publicly subsidized lower-income rental housing projects, large multifamily apartment buildings are a rarity. The image of the early twentieth-century urban neighborhood as a tenement neighborhood is wildly misleading, and reflects the extent to which images of New York City—really only Manhattan—dominate our perceptions of that era. Even after decades of attrition and demolition, approximately 92 percent of all the residential structures in Baltimore today are single-family homes, as are 90 percent in Philadelphia, 81 percent in Cleveland, and 78 percent in St. Louis.[2]

In Philadelphia and Baltimore, these houses are usually brick row houses, while in the other cities they are more likely to be either brick or wood frame detached houses. Either way, these neighborhoods, which were created between the late nineteenth and the mid-twentieth centuries, were and remain fundamentally single-family house monocultures, interspersed with scattered convenience stores and crossed at regular intervals by wider streets along which more extensive commercial activities were concentrated.

The social function of these neighborhoods, whether made up of modest homes for industrial workers or more substantial dwellings for managers or merchants, was equally straightforward. It was to provide homes for couples, who would be spending much of their life cycle rearing children. The physical form of these neighborhoods—which offered each nuclear family the privacy of a separate house and a small back yard, yet with houses close enough to one another to foster walkability and neighborliness—was well suited to its purpose. The neighborhood commercial corridors, which were generally within walking distance of most residences, also ensured that families had adequate shopping opportunities in an era before widespread car ownership. In many cities, neighborhoods clustered around factories, which typically employed many, if not most, of the neighborhood's men, while in other cases places of employment were only a streetcar ride away.

Many of these neighborhoods are now facing a demographic trap: the demographic for which they were designed and which sustained them for most of the past century has declined

---

[1] For historic reasons, the principal house form in similar neighborhoods in a coastal belt including northern New Jersey and most of coastal New England was the two- and three-family house, in which the units were stacked on one another, known in Boston as "triple-deckers." Such houses, while not unheard of, make up only a small part of the residential stock in other American cities.

[2] U.S. Census Bureau, *American Community Survey* (Washington, DC: U.S. Department of Commerce, 2006–2011). I derived estimates of residential structures by using the data for units in structures from the 2006–2011 survey. Because the data are presented in ranges (3–4, 5–9, 10–19, etc.), I estimated the number of structures by taking the midpoint of each range. For buildings containing 50 or more units, I used 75 as the average for that category.

drastically as a share of the urban population and no new source of demand capable of sustaining these areas has emerged.

THE DEMOGRAPHIC CHALLENGE

In the middle of the twentieth century, before the effects of suburbanization were widely felt and when urban neighborhoods were arguably at their most stable[3] the great majority of all households in legacy cities were married couples, of which one-half or more were rearing children at any given point. In 1960, 68 percent of all households in Cincinnati were married-couple families; over half of these, or 39 percent of all households, were rearing children, close to the statewide percentage of 43 percent of all households. In both Dayton and Youngstown, the percentage of married couples raising children was even higher than the statewide level.

The share of married couples with children among all households has declined nationally, but the decline has been far more precipitous in older industrial cities. While married families' share of all households has declined in Ohio from 43 percent in 1960 to 20 percent today, it has dropped to 9 percent in Cincinnati, 8 percent in Dayton, and less than 8 percent in Youngstown. Of more than 100 census tracts in Cincinnati, only one has a share of child-rearing married couples equal to the statewide share. The effects of this demographic change reflect the classic problem of a monoculture, whether in nature or in the urban environment. They were designed for child-rearing households, and the partial substitution of single-mother families has not been adequate to sustain neighborhood stability.

In view of the sensitivity of these issues, it is important to be clear why this demographic change is of such significance for the future of urban neighborhoods. There is an extensive, albeit much contested, research on the difference between married-couple and single-mother households with respect to various social issues, most notably child outcomes. Whatever the merits of the arguments, these issues do not bear on my point here, which is more narrowly economic. There is a fundamental difference in the role each household type can play in sustaining the economic vitality or stability of their neighborhood, and that difference is driven by the extreme income gap between the two groups.[4]

The median income of single-mother households in most legacy cities is only 20 percent to 30 percent that of married-couple child-rearing households (Table 1). In most cases, between 5 percent and 25 percent of married-couple households with children at home fall below the poverty level compared with 45 percent to 60 percent or more of single-mother households. Although the latter is as likely to be working as female parents in married couples, most earn far less and are trapped in low-level, often transitory employment by low skills and limited educational levels.[5]

---

[3] R. Suarez, *The Old Neighborhood* (New York, NY: Free Press, 1999).

[4] Two other groups exist, including single-father households, whose economic condition falls in the middle between married parents and single mothers, and unmarried couples raising children. Their numbers, however, especially the latter category, are too small to affect the trajectory of urban neighborhoods to any meaningful degree.

[5] This in turn also reflects a separate issue; namely, the extent to which marriage in the United States has become in important ways a marker of social class; as Charles Murray writes, "marriage has become the fault line dividing American classes." C. Murray, *Coming Apart: The State of White America* (New York NY: Crown Forum, 2012), 153.

Table 1: Incomes and Poverty Rates for Married-Parent and Single-Mother Households

City	Median Household Income (households with children under 18)			Percentage of Households (with children under 18) below the Poverty Level	
	Married Couple	Female Head	Income Ratio*	Married Couple	Female Head
Baltimore	$90,604	$21,417	23.6%	10.1%	50.8%
Buffalo	$54,385	$15,964	29.4%	25.6%	57.6%
Cincinnati	$80,153	$14,524	18.1%	8.6%	57.7%
Cleveland	$48,358	$13,780	18.5%	22.6%	61.6%
Philadelphia	$67,458	$21,478	31.8%	15.5%	45.2%
Pittsburgh	$87,545	$22,685	25.9%	7.2%	47.0%
St. Louis	$62,790	$19,528	31.1%	18.5%	49.5%

*Median for female-headed households as percentage of median for married couples. Source: U.S. Census Bureau: One-Year American Community Survey (Washington, DC: U.S. Department of Commerce, 2013).

Taken as a whole, single-mother households lack the economic means to maintain economically vital neighborhoods. Their poverty or near-poverty means that most cannot realistically hope to become homeowners, or if homeowners, to sustain homeownership.[6] Many lack the financial resources to maintain single-family houses that are more than 50 years old and demand regular, expensive repairs and replacement. As tenants, they often cannot afford to pay enough to obtain decent-quality housing for themselves and their children, while, except for the fortunate few who win the housing voucher lottery and obtain a rent subsidy, chronic income insecurity makes them highly prone to residential instability. The exceptions, while real and important, are not numerous enough to change the generality of this picture.

Another group, the Millennials or people born in the 1980s and 1990s, is moving to these cities in large numbers. Although many can afford to maintain a house, few are likely to move to these neighborhoods, beyond the handful of areas that have particularly strong locational or other assets. The majority of urban neighborhoods outside the central core lack the distinctive features— high density, walkability, mixed residential and nonresidential land uses, high level of activity, and proximity to major locational assets such as downtown or major universities—that draw the

[6]   I am not familiar with any research that explicitly tracks homeownership survival or exit rates for single-mother families. There is, however, a substantial body of research that has found significantly greater exit rates, and lower spells of stable homeownership, for low-income and African American households. Given the extremely low incomes of the single-mother households in the urban neighborhoods discussed here, comparable exit rates can reasonably be inferred. C. Reid, "Achieving the American Dream: A Longitudinal Analysis of the Homeownership Experiences of Low Income Households," dissertation, (University of Washington, 2004); T. Turner, and M. Smith, "Exits from Homeownership: The Effects of Race, Ethnicity and Income," Journal of Regional Science 49, no.1 (2009): 1, 1–32; D. Haurin and S. Rosenthal. "The Sustainability of Homeownership: Factors Affecting the Duration of Homeownership and Rental Spells," (Washington, DC: U.S. Department of Housing and Urban Development, 2004).

Millennial generation to the same cities' central core areas. Although this could change if the Millennial generation chooses to remain in the city as they marry and raise children, it remains highly uncertain whether that will be the case.[7] In the meantime, as middle market neighborhoods lose the demographic element that was their economic underpinning, they are being further buffeted by powerful economic trends.

THE ECONOMIC CHALLENGE

The demographic changes taking place in legacy cities' middle market neighborhoods are paralleled by a series of economic changes, reflecting both national and local forces. These forces further weaken these neighborhoods' vitality and heighten their risk. Three different but related factors are at work. First is the impact of greater inequality and the thinning out of the middle class in the larger society. Second is the effect of increased residential segregation or "income sorting," which exacerbates the effect of inequality, while third is a steady erosion of both jobs and workers in those parts of legacy cities beyond their central core.

INEQUALITY

The pool of urban middle-income families has shrunk considerably during the past few decades, reflecting the shrinking middle of the national economic distribution as well as trends more specific to the cities themselves. As Table 2 shows, in 1970, well over 50,000 middle-income families (defined as having incomes between 80 percent and 120 percent of the city median) lived in Milwaukee, making up nearly one-third of all of the city's families. By 2013, the number had dropped to under 20,000, and this group's percentage of the total families in the city had dropped by more than one-half. By contrast, the number of low-income families (incomes less than 50 percent of the city median) remained roughly the same across the decades, while the number of upper-income families (incomes more than 150 percent of the city median) increased by more than 60 percent, despite the drop in the total number of families in the city. The pattern in St. Louis is similar but less pronounced. This is not, however, because growth in St. Louis has been more egalitarian, but rather because in 1970 St. Louis was already a more economically segregated city than Milwaukee. The effect of this increasing income disparity, and shrinking middle class, is exacerbated by the trend toward increasing economic segregation in these same cities.

---

[7] Although, as noted earlier, 25–34-year-old college graduates are significantly over-represented as a share of the city's population in cities such as Baltimore, Pittsburgh, or St. Louis, the opposite is true of college graduates ages 35 and older. Although 8.2 percent of Baltimore's population is made up of college-educated 25–34-year-olds compared with 7.5 percent of the statewide population, only 4.3 percent of Baltimore's population is made up of 35–44-year-old college graduates compared with 7.1 percent of the state's population.

Table 2: Distribution of Families by Ratio of Family Income to City Median Income, 1970 and 2013

St. Louis	0–50%	50–80%	80–120%	120–150%	150%+
Percentage of all families					
1970	20.5%	16.7%	25.0%	11.8%	25.9%
2013	25.4%	15.2%	16.9%	8.8%	33.8%
Number of families					
1970	30,765	25,057	37,413	17,680	38,829
2013	15,965	9,565	10,650	5,529	21,264
Percent change 1970–2013	-48.1%	-61.8%	-71.5%	-68.7%	-45.4%
Milwaukee					
Percentage of all families					
1970	18.1%	21.5%	31.9%	12.6%	15.9%
2013	24.5%	17.0%	15.4%	10.0%	33.2%
Number of families					
1970	30,208	35,785	53,153	21,007	26,446
2013	31,525	21,801	19,799	12,845	42,645
Percent change 1970–2013	+4.4%	-39.1%	-62.8%	-38.9%	+61.3%

Sources: U.S. Census Bureau: 1970 Census (Washington, DC: U.S. Department of Commerce); U.S. Census Bureau: One-Year American Community Survey (Washington, DC: U.S. Department of Commerce, 2013).

INCOME SORTING

The long-term trend toward increased family income segregation—the sorting of families by income into neighborhoods—has been extensively documented since 1970.[8] This phenomenon is distinct from the growing inequality in the distribution of incomes, although the two are related. Sorting is about the extent to which people of different income levels share the same areas, and for our purposes, the number of residential areas that can be characterized as middle neighborhoods; that is, neighborhoods where the median income of the families in the neighborhood is close to the middle of the citywide median. Such areas were widespread through the 1970s, but have diminished

[8]   J. Booza, J. Cutsinger, and G. Galster, "Where Did They Go? The Decline of Middle-Income neighborhoods in Metropolitan America," (Washington DC: Brookings Institution, 2006); S. Reardon and K. Bischoff, "Growth in the Residential Segregation of Families by Income," US 2010 Project (Providence: Brown University, 2011); and K. Bischoff and S. Reardon, "Residential Segregation by Income, 1970–2009," US 2010 Project (Providence: Brown University, 2013). Income segregation is "the uneven geographical distribution of families of different income levels within a metropolitan area." K. Bischoff and S. Reardon, "Residential Segregation by Income, 1970–2009," US 2010 Project (Providence: Brown University, 2013), 1.

markedly since then. Researchers Kendra Bischoff and Sean Reardon have found that the share of the national population living in neighborhoods where the median family income is between 80 and 125 percent of the regional median has dropped in the past 40 years from 65 percent to 42 percent of all U.S. families.

The same sorting patterns are visible in legacy cities. Indeed, the extent to which income segregation has increased even since 2000 is notable, as is the decline in the number of middle-income census tracts (defined as those in which the median family income is between 80 percent and 120 percent of the city median). Table 3 compares the change in St. Louis and Milwaukee from 2000 to 2013. As late as 2000, middle-income tracts—a reasonable surrogate for middle neighborhoods—made up more than one-third of all census tracts in both cities. In little more than a decade, their share of tracts dropped sharply, while the share of upper-income tracts (150 percent or more of city median) increased, particularly in Milwaukee, where the number of such tracts more than tripled.

Table 3: Distribution of Census Tracts by Ratio of Tract Median Family Income to City Median, 2000 and 2013

St. Louis	0–50%	50–80%	80–120%	120–150%	150%+
Percentage of all tracts					
2000	3.7%	26.2%	38.3%	16.8%	15.0%
2013	7.6%	37.1%	18.1%	16.2%	21.0%
Number of tracts					
2000	4	28	41	18	16
2013	8	39	19	17	22
Change 2000–2013	+4	+11	-22	-1	+6
Milwaukee					
Percentage of all tracts					
2000	8.9%	25.5%	33.9%	25.0%	6.8%
2013	5.2%	37.3%	21.2%	14.0%	22.3%
Number of tracts					
2000	17	49	65	48	13
2013	10	72	41	27	43
Change 2000–2013	-7	+23	-24	-21	+30

Source: U.S. Census Bureau, 2000 Census (Washington, DC: U.S. Department of Commerce); U.S. Census Bureau, 2009–2013 5-Year American Community Survey (Washington, DC: U.S. Department of Commerce).

The growth in upper-income tracts does not necessarily mean that these are areas of great wealth. What it shows is that in a city with anemic economic growth, those tracts that are above average to begin with—over 120 percent of the city median—tend to remain stable or grow wealthier relative to the rest of the city. Those below that level tend to move downward. Between 2000 and 2013, of the 41 middle-income tracts in St. Louis, 19 moved downward economically, five moderately upward, and two sharply upward, going from middle- to upper-income income status. Only 15 remained economically stable.

Sadly, there is nothing in either macroeconomic trends or forthcoming public policies to suggest that this trend is likely to change meaningfully in the foreseeable future. Although the downward progression from middle-income to moderate-income may not be the same as neighborhood decline, it sharply increases the risk of decline. The simultaneous decline in homeownership in these areas is arguably both a symptom of economic decline and a potential trigger for further decline.

EROSION OF JOBS AND WORKFORCE

At the same time as increased inequality and income sorting are leading to a decline in the economic base of middle market neighborhoods, trends in the distribution of both jobs and jobholders within legacy cities are further undermining them. As legacy cities undergo selective revitalization, they are seeing a twofold shift in their job patterns: Jobs are increasingly being concentrated in the cities' central core areas, particularly around major institutions such as universities and medical centers, and the people holding these jobs are increasingly likely to live in the suburbs and commute to the city, rather than live in the city. The number of city residents holding jobs in the city where they live, and the size of the city's employed workforce in general, are both rapidly declining.[9] Urban neighborhoods outside the central core have seen substantial losses in both jobs and job holders.

This point is most vividly apparent in St. Louis, an archetypal legacy city. The total number of job holders living in the city (whether working inside or outside the city) declined by 15 percent from 2002 to 2011. The decline in the city's southern ZIP codes, which contain the great majority of the city's remaining middle market neighborhoods, was also 15 percent, representing a total loss of more than 10,000 employed residents (Table 4). In the northern ZIP codes, the decline was 27 percent, or nearly 11,000 workers. Only in the central core area did the number of employed residents increase, by a modest 3 percent. In both the south and the north, the decline in the number of employed residents was roughly double the decline in total population.

9   A. Mallach, "The Uncoupling of the Economic City: Increasing Spatial and Economic Polarization in American Older Industrial Cities," *Urban Affairs Review*, June 25, 2014.

Table 4: Change in Distribution of Workers by Worker Residence in St. Louis, 2002–2011

	Workers 2002	Workers 2011	% 2002–2011	Population % 2000–2010	Share of Total City Workers	
					2002	2011
South	70,389	59,972	-14.8%	-8.0%	51.6%	51.7%
Central	25,985	26,755	+3.0	+2.6	19.0	23.1
North	40,059	29,234	-27.0	-15.0	29.4	25.2
City*	136,433	115,961	-15.0	-8.3	100%	100%

*Source: U.S. Census Bureau, On-The-Map (Washington, DC: U.S. Department of Commerce), available at http://onthemap.ces.census.gov; population data from http://www.city-data.com. *Citywide figures represent sum of figures for ZIP codes located entirely within city boundaries, and are approximately 2 percent smaller than actual city totals.*

The change in jobs followed a similar pattern, although the number of jobs in the city declined much less during that period, by only 3.5 percent. The number of jobs in the southern ZIP codes declined by more than 17 percent, while the total in the northern ZIP codes by a smaller amount, less than 6 percent (Table 5). The central area gained jobs, although modestly, increasing its share of citywide jobs from 68.5 percent to 71.4 percent.

Table 5: Change in Distribution of Jobs by Job Location in St. Louis, 2002–2011

	Jobs 2002	Jobs 2011	% 2002–2011	Share of Total City Jobs	
				2002	2011
South	38,253	31,680	-17.2%	18.1%	15.5%
Central	144,716	145,721	+0.7	68.5	71.4
North	28,152	26,572	-5.6	13.3	13.0
City*	211,391	203,973	-3.5	100%	100%

*Source: U.S. Census Bureau, On-The-Map (Washington, DC: U.S. Department of Commerce). *Citywide figures represent sum of figures for ZIP codes located entirely within city boundaries, and are approximately 2 percent smaller than actual city totals.*

Patterns are similar elsewhere. In Baltimore only the central core ZIP codes (21201, 21202, and 21239) gained employed residents, with an average 16 percent loss elsewhere in the city between 2002 and 2011. Eight of 18 ZIP codes outside the city's central core lost 20 percent or more of their jobholders, with five of these losing more than 25 percent.

The relationship between the loss of jobs and workers and the declining economic condition of middle market neighborhoods produced by increased inequality and income sorting is a difficult one to untangle. Whatever the causal links may be, it is clear that these forces reinforce one another, and collectively further destabilize large numbers of middle market neighborhoods in legacy cities.

THE PHYSICAL CHALLENGE

Within the parameters of a predominately single-family inventory, the housing stock in legacy city middle market neighborhoods is quite varied. Houses vary by size, architectural character, materials, and other features. That stock, however, shares one feature: It is old. Moreover, as a largely single-family stock, regardless of age, it may no longer be a good fit with today's housing market demands.

Legacy city neighborhoods were typically built between the late nineteenth century and the early 1960s. Since the 1960s, developers have built little new housing in these neighborhoods, with the exception of housing developments financed with public subsidies. For example, 80 to 90 percent of owner-occupied single-family homes in these cities predate 1960 as do approximately two-thirds of the renter-occupied single-family stock (Table 6).[10] Although a handful of older homes have been extensively rehabilitated, largely with public funds, their numbers are modest as a share of the total housing stock.

Table 6: Share of All Single-Family Structures Built Before 1960 by Age of Structure and Tenure

	Owner-Occupied	Renter-Occupied
Baltimore	85.3%	78.1%
Cincinnati	80.0%	65.9%
Dayton	81.0%	71.9%
St. Louis	85.8%	64.2%
Syracuse	86.8%	66.5%

Source: U.S. Census Bureau, 2009-2013 Five-Year American Community Survey (Washington, DC: U.S. Department of Commerce).

At the same time, to the extent that the demand for urban housing today is disproportionately from young, single individuals, couples, and people living in informal living arrangements, much of the housing in middle market neighborhoods may not draw their interest. Although those few neighborhoods with distinctive architectural or historical character, or those in close proximity to major employers or other centers, may draw greater demand, most middle market neighborhoods lack those special features.

In this context, the effects of an aging housing stock raise particular problems for middle market neighborhoods. Although there is little or no research on this point, anecdotal evidence from

---

[10] The larger share of newer single-family rentals, compared with owner-occupied units, can be attributed to the widespread preference, particularly since 2000, among many developers and community development corporations (CDCs) to use single-family housing types (particularly row houses) as the design scheme for subsidized rental housing developments.

many different cities suggests that the majority of older houses in these neighborhoods have not been upgraded or modernized to any significant degree, while many—particularly those owned by lower-income elderly people or absentee landlords—suffer from significant deferred maintenance and repair needs. Without an infusion of significant capital, either public or private, in the coming years, a large part of the housing in middle market neighborhoods could deteriorate further, perhaps to the point of no return. At that point, the question arises whether the capital is available and the market demand exists to replace these houses with new houses or apartments better reflecting market demand.

Assembling the capital to either to repair and upgrade, or to replace, existing housing in middle market neighborhoods may be extremely difficult. Public funds are likely to fall far short of what is needed, and in any event, are likely to be restricted in large part to means-tested households, typically with incomes of 80 percent or less of the HUD-defined area median income. Building new subsidized housing to replace older market housing is unlikely to stabilize middle market neighborhoods and may, under certain conditions, further destabilize them.[11] Thus, the fate of these neighborhoods is likely to depend ultimately on their ability to attract private capital—whether in the form of individuals buying and improving homes—or private market developers rehabilitating existing houses or building new homes or multifamily buildings.

Whether an influx of private capital takes place will depend on attracting not only enough private market demand, but enough demand at income levels capable of moving neighborhood market prices to the point where they support substantial investment in existing houses as well as construction of new housing without public capital subsidy.[12] Given not only the demographic and economic forces working against middle market neighborhoods described earlier—but also the generally low market values in legacy cities, continuing shortfalls in mortgage access in urban areas, and the ongoing competition from nearby inner-ring suburban markets—this is likely to be a daunting challenge for those neighborhoods that lack the special attributes likely to render them particularly desirable.

The magnitude of the challenge is reflected in trends in homeownership and rental tenure in legacy cities. These trends reveal a substantially greater loss of homeowners in legacy cities since the end of the housing bubble than in the United States as a whole. Although the number of homeowners declined by 2 percent between 2007 and 2013 nationally, the number of homeowners declined by 8 percent in Philadelphia, 13 percent in St. Louis, and 17 percent in Detroit. As Table 7 shows, these cities' homeownership rates declined at roughly twice the national rate of decline during the same period.

---

[11]   L. Deng, "Assessing Changes in Neighborhoods Hosting the Low-Income Housing Tax Credit Projects," Center for Local, State and Urban Policy working paper (Ann Arbor: University of Michigan, 2006).

[12]   Public funds for capital subsidy should be ruled out, both because of their scarcity and because they are likely to be means-tested. Abatements of local property taxes, however, should be considered as a means of filling a market gap, as they could be different forms of state tax credit, analogous to historic preservation tax credits.

Table 7: Change in Number of Homeowners and Homeownership Rate, United States and Select Legacy Cities, 2007–2013

	United States	Cleveland	Detroit	Philadelphia	St. Louis
Homeowners 2007	75,515,104	77,178	153,708	323,021	71,725
Homeowners 2013	73,843,861	69,845	127,502	297,098	61,551
Change in number of homeowners 2007–2013	-2.2%	-9.5%	-17.0%	-8.0%	-14.2%
Change in homeownership rate 2007–2013	-5.5%	-8.9%	-9.9%	-11.2%	-11.9%

Source: U.S. Census Bureau, 2007 and 2013 1-Year American Community Survey (Washington, DC: U.S. Department of Commerce).

Although data limitations make it difficult to pinpoint the same trends as shown in Table 7 for individual census tracts,[13] in view of the demographic and economic trends discussed earlier, it is likely that many, if not most, middle market neighborhoods in these cities show similar trends. A continued shift from owner occupancy to rental tenure in these neighborhoods is unlikely to lead to the level of capital investment necessary to provide for either long-term maintenance or replacement of their aging housing stocks.

THE COMPETITIVENESS CHALLENGE

The last area I would like to address is harder to quantify, and yet may ultimately be the most challenging for those seeking to bring about the long-term stabilization of urban middle market neighborhoods in legacy cities, specifically, the challenge of suburban competition. The core market for middle market neighborhoods, with relatively few exceptions, is not the highly educated Millennial single individual, but the remaining pool of working-class and middle class households, neither affluent nor poor, including large numbers of child-rearing families. The particular features that have drawn Millennials away from the suburbs and into urban central core areas are not necessarily important to this middle market, and moreover, even if they found them appealing, most urban middle-income families would be unable to afford the downtown lofts or upscale townhouses being created to cater to affluent newcomers. Competition for the city's middle-income families does not come from the central core or the city's few gentrified neighborhoods, but from its suburban neighbors.

In that respect, legacy city neighborhoods are at a particular disadvantage. In contrast to rapidly growing regions—where homes in even relatively modest suburbs tend to sell for prices out of reach of most working-class families, and many urban middle-income families may have no realistic

---

[13] The one-year ACS data that was used to create the table, and that enables one to track the entire period from the end of the housing bubble to near the present, is not available at the census tract level; the best available data at the census tract level comes from the five-year ACS. While that data would enable one to compare 2005–2009 with 2009–2013 data, the margin of error in the data is significant and problematic.

alternative but to remain in the city—inner-ring suburbs around legacy cities such as Detroit, Cleveland, or Cincinnati tend to be far more reasonably priced, and often accessible to families with incomes of $30,000 or less.

Moreover, these suburbs appear to offer clear advantages over neighborhoods in the central cities, particularly to families with children. With respect to both education and crime, relocation to the suburbs appears to confer significant benefits, at relatively modest incremental cost. Table 8 shows median house prices, violent crime rates, and school graduation rates (used as a proxy for quality of the school district) in Detroit and Dayton and in several of their inner-ring suburbs. Moreover, as a growing share of the urban workforce works in the suburbs, the appeal of living in the suburbs is likely to become that much greater.

Table 8: Median Home Prices, Graduation Rates, and Violent Crime, Detroit and Dayton

	Median Home Sales Price (2013)	Violent Crimes per 100,000 Population (2012)	Average Graduation Rate of Entering Freshmen (2008–2009)
Detroit (city)	$17,222	2,547.5	45.1%
Detroit Inner-Ring Suburbs			
Oak Park	49,750	548.6	86.0%
Southfield	70,000	487.1	75.7%
Ferndale	82,500	414.9	100.0%
St. Clair Shores	82,724	252.3	87.5%
Dayton (city)	$24,600	973.7	45.9%
Dayton Inner-Ring Suburbs			
Trotwood	26,325	385.6	61.7%
West Carrollton	55,000	189.4	73.1%
Kettering	92,000	88.6	84.7%
Clayton	103,000	67.2	80.9%

Source: Reinvestment Fund, PolicyMap (Philadelphia: author, 2016) (median sales price and freshman graduation rate); U.S. Department of Justice, FBI Uniform Crime Reports (Washington, DC: author).

With mortgage interest rates at approximately 4 percent, a moderate-income family earning $35,000 to $50,000 could easily afford to buy a home in any of the suburban communities shown in Table 8. Although some families may find it difficult to get a mortgage, or come up with a down payment, the increase in investor activity in many of these towns has also meant that an increased supply of single-family homes are available for rent, making that an affordable alternative.

Suburban flight from the cities is an old story. It has historically been associated, however, with "white flight" during the 1950s through the 1980s. What appears to be taking place now, and which appears to have markedly accelerated during the past decade or so, is the movement of middle class African American households from the cities to the suburbs. Although the dynamics of this trend have yet to receive systematic scholarly attention, they have been the subject of many journalistic accounts, including detailed reporting from Philadelphia[14,15] and Detroit[16], as well as more modest but credible accounts from many other cities including Birmingham, Dallas, Los Angeles, Memphis, and Oakland. All of these accounts add credence to the possibility that cities are losing a critical battle for the population that more than any other has sustained their middle market neighborhoods for many decades—the African American working- and middle class family.

Table 9 illustrates the change in the African American population by income (in constant 1999 dollars) in eight legacy cities and for the United States as a whole between 2000 and 2008–2012. Every one of these cities saw sharp declines in middle- and upper-income African American households and simultaneous increases in lower-income households. Although nationally, the number of African American households with incomes greater than $50,000 held steady during this period, and the number with incomes between $35,000 and $49,999 grew by 5 percent, both groups saw losses in all of these cities, in most cases by more than 20 percent.

Table 9: Change in Number of African American Households by Income, 1999 to 2008-2012 (in constant 1999 dollars)

	<$35,000	$35,000–$50,000	$50,000+	Total
Baltimore	-0.6%	-5.2%	-17.6%	-5.1%
Philadelphia	14.4%	-32.0%	-21.1%	2.7%
Pittsburgh	-1.9%	-9.9%	-25.5%	-7.7%
St. Louis	4.4%	-22.3%	-31.6%	-4.9%
Cincinnati	4.0%	-19.9%	-32.2%	-4.9%
Cleveland	10.3%	-32.0%	-47.3%	-4.7%
Detroit	2.9%	-35.4%	-57.7%	-20.1%
Milwaukee	28.4%	-6.1%	-23.6%	13.2%
United States	25.0%	4.7%	0.2%	15.1%

Source: U.S. Census Bureau: 2000 Census and 2008-2012 5-Year American Community Survey (Washington, DC: U.S. Department of Commerce).

[14] T. Ferrick, "Black Exodus: Part One," *Metropolis*, October 7, 2011. http://www.phlmetropolis.com/2011/10/black-exodus.php.
[15] M. Mallowe, "Black Exodus: Part Two," *Metropolis*, October 6, 2011. http://www.phlmetropolis.com/2011/10/black-exodus-part-two.php.
[16] A. Kellogg, "Black Flight Hits Detroit," *Wall Street Journal*, June 5, 2010. http://www.wsj.com/articles/SB100014240527 4870429200457523053224871585.

Whether cities will be able to withstand this challenge will depend in large part on their ability to provide public services of reasonable quality to middle market neighborhoods, not only decent schools and public safety, but also services such as street and sidewalk repair, street lighting, park maintenance, garbage pickup, and other services that translate directly into residents' quality of life. That in turn is closely related to the fiscal constraints under which most, if not all, legacy cities and their school districts operate. Although those constraints may become marginally less severe as the economy improves, they are unlikely to improve in the foreseeable future to the point where school quality, safety, and service delivery will be seen as comparable to the cities' suburban neighbors.

CLOSING NOTE: CONFRONTING THE CHALLENGES
The purpose of this chapter has been to describe the challenges facing middle market neighborhoods rather than the solutions, which are the subject of many of the other chapters in this volume. It would be inappropriate, however, to end without at least a brief discussion of the policy implications of the challenges sketched out above.

First, the challenge facing these neighborhoods is a multifaceted one. As such, the response cannot be a matter of identifying a single problem and zooming in on it with a laser-like focus. Rather, it will require recognizing the multidimensional nature of the problem and tackling it in systematic, comprehensive ways that reflect an understanding of its complexity and the interrelationship of its many parts.

Ultimately, the challenge facing legacy cities' middle market neighborhoods is one of demand. Although supply is an issue, as discussed above (the physical challenge), that problem would be far more easily manageable if it did not exist within a framework of limited and often diminishing demand. Rebuilding demand must be the driving force of any strategy to stabilize or revitalize middle market neighborhoods, whether in the form of getting more people to buy and improve homes in the neighborhood or making it easier—through greater access to mortgage and home improvement loans, incentives to restore vacant properties, or other means—for those who want to stay to do so.

The process of restoring demand is likely to take more than marketing and branding strategies, as described by David Boehlke and Marcia Nedland later in this volume. Important as they are, it is likely to require increased access to financing and incentives to overcome the market gap. In the long run, however, any effort to rebuild middle market neighborhoods must also address the economic issues and improve access for urban residents to job opportunities, and even more directly, must confront the competitive challenge these neighborhoods face. No amount of marketing or branding can overcome deficiencies in the underlying product. However attractive a neighborhood's housing stock may be, ultimately people need to feel that the neighborhood is a good place to live, and that its trajectory is upward, or at least stable, rather than downward. As the stories in this volume show, many neighborhoods have been able to make this happen, although it has often required years of dedicated effort.

As one looks at the success stories in the context of the larger trends discussed earlier, another question arises: Can every neighborhood be saved? The thinning of the middle class from growing income inequality coupled with the decline in child-rearing households generally, and married-couple child-rearing households in particular, means that the pool of potential demand for middle market neighborhoods in legacy cities has shrunk considerably during the past few decades. The hollowing out of the middle class and the decline in married-couple families with children is not limited to cities; it is taking place throughout these cities' regions, thus reducing the source from which the greater part of any future demand will be drawn.

Fifty years ago, roughly one-third of Milwaukee's residents were middle income, and—an educated guess—half of its neighborhoods could probably be considered middle market neighborhoods. Today, less than one-sixth of the city's residents are middle income and barely 20 percent of its neighborhoods are middle market. Many urban areas that are devastated and disinvested today were once middle market neighborhoods. The power of the larger economic and demographic trends affecting these areas is such that, despite our best efforts, the erosion is likely to continue. That does not mean that our efforts are in vain. It does mean, however, that we may have to be selective with those efforts and identify what can be saved.

Writer, scholar, practitioner and advocate, Alan Mallach has been engaged with the challenges of urban revitalization, neighborhood stabilization, and housing provision for 50 years. A senior fellow with the Center for Community Progress, he has held a number of public and private-sector positions, and currently also teaches in the graduate city planning program at Pratt Institute in New York City. His publications include many books, among them Bringing Buildings Back: From Vacant Properties to Community Assets *and* A Decent Home: Planning, Building and Preserving Affordable Housing, *as well as numerous articles, book chapters, and reports. He has a B.A. degree from Yale College, and lives in Roosevelt, New Jersey.*

V. HOMEOWNERSHIP AND THE STABILITY OF MIDDLE NEIGHBORHOODS

By Alan Mallach, Center for Community Progress

Homeownership, although far from universal, forms a central part of what might be called a national ethos, in which owning one's own home is associated with middle class status and the American dream achieved.[1] Yet, a recent article by Ryan Cooper bore the grandiose title, "It's Time to Kill the American Dream of Homeownership."[2] Whether homeownership is or is not a good investment for a middle class family is not the issue here, although there is a compelling case that it still is.[3] The question this chapter will attempt to answer is a different one; namely, what role does homeownership play in the vitality of middle neighborhoods in legacy cities?

This question is particularly timely for a number of reasons. First, as Cooper noted, many support the proposition that homeownership is overrated or irrelevant, or, in the recent words of a respected colleague, "it's time to get over homeownership." Second, the years since the bursting of the housing bubble in 2006 and 2007 have shown not only a widely reported decline in homeownership rates nationally, but a significantly greater decline in homeownership rates—and in the absolute number of homeowners—in legacy cities.

If a relatively high level of homeownership is indeed an important factor in fostering neighborhood stability, a different phenomenon—a growing number of single-family homes purchased by absentee investors—should be a source of considerable concern to those who care about the future of middle neighborhoods. My case for this proposition is circumstantial; homeownership is interwoven with many other factors affecting neighborhoods, and, as I will discuss, the pathways by which it affects neighborhood vitality are complex and multifaceted.[4] At the same time, I would argue that the case is strong, and that homeownership should be at the forefront of policies and strategies to stabilize or revive urban middle neighborhoods.

---

[1] It is worth noting, however, that although homeownership may play a more potent ideological role in the United States than elsewhere, when it comes to actual homeownership rates, the United States is roughly in the middle of the pack among developed nations. While the homeownership rate in the United States is higher than that of many European nations like Germany or France, it is much lower than in Italy or Spain, and slightly lower than in other predominately English-speaking countries like the United Kingdom or Canada. In many of these countries, such as Italy, Spain and Israel, homeownership in multifamily housing is much more the norm than in the United States.

[2] Ryan Cooper, "It's time to kill the American dream of homeownership," *This Week*, April 25, 2014.

[3] Alan Mallach, *Building Sustainable Ownership: Rethinking Public Policy Toward Lower-Income Homeownership* (Philadelphia: Federal Reserve Bank of Philadelphia, 2011).

[4] In addition, the problems obtaining reliable data at the neighborhood level are considerable.

At the same time, it is important to stress that arguing for the value of homeownership does not imply that rental housing is unnecessary or that renters are in some fashion second-class citizens and cannot contribute to their neighborhoods. Rental housing is a vital part of any community, particularly those with large numbers of lower-income families for whom homeownership may not be a realistic or desirable alternative. While maintaining a high homeownership rate may be a desirable public policy, policies that focus on homeowners and fail to address both the importance of a sound rental housing stock and engaging renters fully in their communities are as unbalanced as strategies that ignore homeownership entirely.

This chapter is in four sections. The first provides a brief historical introduction to homeownership in middle neighborhoods, while the second discusses the research evidence for the neighborhood effects of homeownership and explores some of the pathways by which those effects are experienced. The third describes the erosion of homeownership in legacy cities and their neighborhoods— including a case study of Trenton, New Jersey, where I have been able to use a unique neighborhood-level data set showing the trends in owner-occupant and investor home purchases from 2006 through 2013. The final sections explore the features of a model that links different homeownership effects to neighborhood change and suggest some policy implications for middle neighborhoods.

THE HISTORICAL BACKGROUND

The middle neighborhoods of legacy cities were developed beginning in the late nineteenth century through the early 1960s. They were historically, and remain today with few exceptions, neighborhoods of single-family homes.[5] In Camden, Baltimore, and many coastal cities, these homes were row houses—while in Toledo, Detroit, and most inland cities, they were detached houses on small, usually narrow, lots. Homeownership rates in legacy cities from 1920 on were often comparable to or higher than the national homeownership rate (Table 1). By 1930, one-half or more of the single-family houses in most of these cities were owner-occupied.

[5]   For obscure historic reasons, the dominant urban neighborhood house form in a coastal belt including northern New Jersey and most of coastal New England was the two- and three-family house, in which the units were stacked on one another. In Boston, they are known as "triple-deckers." Such houses, while also found elsewhere, make up only a small part of the residential stock in other American cities.

Table 1: Homeownership Rates in Select Legacy Cities, 1900–1960

City	Homeownership Rate			
	1900	1920	1930	1960
Flint, MI	51.8	NA	60.7	79.4%
Youngstown, OH	45.2	47.8	52.1	66.8
Grand Rapids, MI	41.4	50.1	60.1	64.4
Camden, NJ	24.9	40.5	49.8	64.1
Toledo, OH	42.9	49.4	50.6	63.9
US	46.5[6]	44.8	47.8	61.9
Trenton, NJ	26.2	35.3	54.3	58.4
Detroit, MI	39.1	38.3	42.0	58.2
Dayton, OH	38.0	41.9	48.1	55.1
Baltimore, MD	27.9	46.3	51.5	54.3

Cities with homeownership rates above the national average are shaded. Source: U.S. Bureau of the Census, 1900, 1920, 1930, and 1960 Census of Housing,(Washington, DC: U.S. Department of Commerce).

Homeownership rates in the cities in Table 1 grew at a far more rapid pace than the national average from 1900 to the Great Depression and World War II in the 1930s and 1940s. Homeownership also was common in urban areas well before the reforms of the New Deal. Between 1900 and 1930, the number of homeowners in Baltimore more than tripled, to 97,000, while the number of renters grew much more modestly, from 70,000 to 92,000. The number of Trenton homeowners also more than tripled, to nearly 15,000, while the number of renters increased by fewer than 2,000. In both cities, the character of the housing stock, mainly single-family row houses, did not change materially. In all likelihood, what was happening was that many rented houses became owner-occupied and that the majority of the new houses built were sold to homebuyers rather than absentee landlords.

Homeownership growth in many cities did not end with the Depression. A number of cities, including most notably Toledo and Detroit in (see Table 1), saw dramatic increases in homeownership following World War II. Between 1930 and 1960, the number of homeowners in Detroit doubled, to 299,000, while the number of renters barely grew, from 211,000 to 215,000. Clearly, and contrary to widespread belief, the increase in homeownership during the immediate postwar period was not a purely suburban phenomenon.

Although data do not exist to enable one to zoom in on particular neighborhoods in these cities, it is reasonable to assume that middle neighborhoods, being inhabited largely by middle-income

---

[6] This obscures a significant difference between rural and urban housing; in 1900, the non-farm homeownership rate was only 36.4 percent.

families and occupying the middle of the local housing market, had homeownership rates similar to or higher than those shown in Table 1—and that well before World War II, homeownership was already a central element in the character of the typical urban middle neighborhood. As I suggest, both here and in Chapter IV, the recent drastic drop in homeownership in many of these neighborhoods has been a significant factor in their decline.

NEIGHBORHOOD EFFECTS OF HOMEOWNERSHIP

With homeownership looming so large in the American ethos, it is not surprising that an extensive body of research exists on its effects, whether in terms of wealth-building, behavior and family outcomes, or neighborhood conditions and dynamics. In this section, I summarize the research findings in five separate areas: residential stability, property values, property condition, social/behavioral factors, and social capital and collective efficacy.

All of this research shares the problem of how to isolate homeownership from other social and economic factors. Although the research, particularly more recent work, typically tries to control for socioeconomic differences between owners and renters, such as income or race, it is more difficult to pin down the extent to which homeownership is affected by self-selection; in other words, whether people who choose to become homeowners have different attitudes or values than people of similar social and economic status who choose not to become homeowners. This may in turn affect their behavior and their effect on their surroundings.[7]

Although this does not affect the relationship between homeownership and whatever neighborhood feature one is trying to measure, such as stability or civic engagement, it means that one can never be completely certain that one is measuring the effect of homeownership or the effect of some other social factor that is, in turn, linked to homeownership. For that reason, the nature of the pathways through which homeownership exerts its influence, which I address later, becomes particularly important.

RESIDENTIAL STABILITY

Residential stability in legacy city middle neighborhoods is declining as homeownership declines. Residential stability or turnover appears to be an important element in neighborhood health, with high turnover or "churning" seen as a factor leading to decline.[8] Homeownership is statistically associated with greater length of tenure; the 2013 American Community Survey finds that the median length of residence for homeowners in their current home is 11 years. This compares with fewer than three years for tenants. The tenure gap is even greater in legacy cities, as shown in Table 2.

---

[7]   Not only is this inherently difficult to measure, but the difficulty is compounded by the effect of homeownership itself; in other words, the process of becoming a homeowner may change the individual's values and attitudes in significant ways. A fascinating study from Argentina offers strong evidence of those effects (Rafael Di Tella, Sebastian Galiani, and Ernesto Schargrodsky, "The Formation of Beliefs: Evidence from the Allocation of Land Titles to Squatters," *Quarterly Journal of Economics* 122, no. 1 (2007): 209–241).

[8]   Claudia Coulton, Brett Theodos, and Margery A. Turner, *Family Mobility and Neighborhood Change: New Evidence and Implications for Community Initiatives* (Washington DC: Urban Institute, 2009).

Table 2: Average Tenure for Owners and Renters in Select Legacy Cities

City	Median Tenure (years)*		Percent of Renters with Tenure Less than Two Years
	Owners	Renters	
Baltimore	15	2.1	48.3
Detroit	20	2.1	47.3
St. Louis	14	1.7	58.2
Buffalo	15	1.9	51.5
Cleveland	17	1.8	53.7

*Medians for renters calculated by author from grouped American Community Survey data. Source: U.S. Census Bureau: 1-year 2012 American Community Survey (Washington, DC: U.S. Department of Commerce).

Analysts have raised the question of how to separate the impact of homeownership as such from the impact of long-term tenure stability.[9] Some research has found that the effect of homeownership on child outcomes drops significantly when controlling for mobility.[10] Thus, in theory, one might be able to achieve outcomes similar to those associated with homeownership by stabilizing the tenure of renters or by fostering intermediate forms of tenure, such as rental with tenure rights or share appreciation, as exist in some European countries.

In practice, though, this may not be a realistic option. First, evidence is strong that homeownership improves residential stability independent of other socioeconomic factors.[11] This may be a function of the greater transaction costs for homeowners associated with moving or it may reflect some of the value or attitudinal changes associated with homeownership, as noted earlier. Second, the magnitude of the tenure gap between owners and renters is so great that it is hard, if not impossible, to conceive of a plausible strategy that would eliminate it. Although some advocates have suggested that a landlord-tenant regime that incorporates security of tenure and rent control would have such an effect, the experience in New Jersey, where security of tenure is enshrined in state law and

---

[9] National Association of Realtors, *Social Benefits of Homeownership and Stable Housing* (Washington, DC: NAR Research Division: 2006).
[10] David Barker and Eric A. Miller, "Homeownership and Child Welfare," *Real Estate Economics* 37, no. 2 (2009): 279–303
[11] William Rohe and Leslie S. Stewart, "Home Ownership and Neighborhood Stability," *Housing Policy Debate* 7, no. 1 (1996): 37–81.

rent control is legal and widely used, does not support that proposition.[12] Increasing tenants' tenure through legal and economic strategies is a desirable policy objective. It would almost certainly yield significant benefits for tenants and may also yield some potential community benefit. However, it is unlikely in the extreme to be able to substitute for homeownership as a means of fostering neighborhood stability.

It is not enough to encourage families to become homeowners. It is equally or more important to ensure that they become stable, long-term homeowners, and that they do not involuntarily lose their homes through foreclosure, tax delinquency, or other controllable factors.[13] There is abundant evidence that involuntary loss of homes is severely destructive to both the homeowners and their neighborhoods, potentially exceeding whatever benefits were gained by becoming homeowners in the first place.[14]

PROPERTY VALUES

The value or sales prices of homes in a neighborhood is arguably the single most direct measure of the economic vitality of a neighborhood. Rising property values are a direct indicator of positive economic change in a neighborhood, and declining values equally directly measure negative change. Because homeowners tend to have higher incomes than renters do, it stands to reason that property values would be higher in areas with high homeownership levels. There is considerable evidence, however, that, independently of income, homeownership and property values bear a strong relationship to each other.

A number of studies have found that newly constructed, subsidized housing for owner occupancy increases the value of nearby homes.[15] Although these effects may have as much to do with the replacement of vacant lots or derelict buildings, research has found significant price increases with increases in homeownership rates, even after systematically controlling for both neighborhood

---

[12]   New Jersey landlord-tenant law prohibits eviction except for cause. Tenants are deemed to have indefinite tenure, and unlike most parts of the United States, may not be evicted simply because their lease has expired. Other than for cause, such as non-payment of rent, the only grounds for eviction are that the owner needs the house or apartment for their personal use. Moreover, rent control is permitted at local option by state law, and is widely used. While the average length of tenure for tenants in New Jersey is slightly longer than in the United States as a whole (45 percent moved in the previous two years, compared to 56 percent), the difference is roughly proportionate to the difference for homeowners (11 years compared to 13 years), suggesting that the difference is associated with lower in- and out-migration levels for New Jersey, rather than any effect of greater security of tenure on rental stability. However, comparing New Jersey to states with similar migratory profiles, such as Connecticut and Ohio, we find a slight difference (45 percent in New Jersey compared to 49 percent in Ohio and 51 percent in Connecticut), suggesting that the different landlord-tenant regime in New Jersey may have some effect on tenure. If so, it is a very modest one, representing a difference of at most a few months.

[13]   Alan Mallach, *Building Sustainable Ownership*.

[14]   The recent foreclosure crisis has spawned a substantial body of research on the impacts of foreclosure on neighboring properties, which makes a compelling case for its destructive effects. A recent study is particularly worth noting, in that it found a causal relationship between foreclosure and subsequent decline. The authors note, "The completed foreclosure indicator was strongly predictive of three other indicators: property crimes, total home purchase loan amounts, and mean home purchase loan amounts." (Sonya Williams, George Galster, and Nandita Verma, "Home Foreclosures as an Early Warning Indicator of Neighborhood Decline," *Journal of the American Planning Association* 79, no. 3 (2013): 201–210). They characterize foreclosures as an "early warning indicator" of neighborhood change.

[15]   Ingrid Gould Ellen, Michael Schill, Scott Susin, and Amy Ellen Schwartz, "Building Homes, Reviving Neighborhoods: Spillovers from Subsidized Construction of Owner-Occupied Housing in New York City," *Journal of Housing Research* 12, no. 1 (2002): 447–77.

and individual characteristics.[16] Chengri Ding and Gerrit-Jan Knaap have looked at the converse, finding that the loss of homeowners from Cleveland neighborhoods reduced property values in those areas.[17] William Rohe and Leslie Stewart have found that the relationship works in reverse as well; healthy property value appreciation triggers greater homeownership.[18] This last point offers insight into an important aspect of the pathways that drive neighborhood effects, the process by which households decide where to buy homes.

PROPERTY MAINTENANCE AND CONDITION

The condition and maintenance of properties are important elements in a neighborhood's stability and health. Although research finds a strong relation between homeownership and property maintenance and condition, it also finds that the relationship is contingent, in the sense that homeowners' maintenance decisions are strongly influenced by other neighborhood features. Both George Galster[19] and Yannis Ioannides[20] found that the level of social interaction and social cohesion in a neighborhood significantly influences property upkeep. Put differently, a homeowner's maintenance and investment decisions are influenced by neighborhood expectations and by what he or she sees neighbors doing. Their findings suggest a possible link between homeownership, property upkeep, and collective efficacy. This would be a fruitful area for further research.

Who owns the home is also important. My research in Las Vegas found a significant difference in property conditions between owner-occupied and absentee-owned properties within the same block or neighborhood.[21] Figure 3 illustrates the difference in property conditions in Flint, Michigan, for owner-occupied and absentee-owned properties, as well as the effect of higher homeownership rates on the condition of rental properties.[22] The census tracts shown along the X-axis (horizontal) in Figure 3 are organized in order of homeownership rate from low to high. The Y-axis shows the average condition score for properties, using a 4-point scale in which properties in good to excellent condition were scored 1, and dilapidated properties scored 4.

[16]   N. Edward Coulson, Seek-Joon Hwang, and Susumu Imai, "The Value of Owner-Occupation in Neighborhoods," *Journal of Housing Research* 13, no. 2, (2002): 153; N. Edward Coulson, Seek-Joon Hwang, and Susumu Imai, "The Benefits of Owner-Occupation in Neighborhoods," *Journal of Housing Research* 14, no. 1, (2003): 21.
[17]   Chengri Ding and Gerrit-Jan Knaap, "Property Values in Inner City Neighborhoods: The Effects of Home Ownership, Housing Investment and Economic Development," *Housing Policy Debate* 13, no. 4 (2003): 701–727.
[18]   William Rohe and Leslie S. Stewart, "Home Ownership and Neighborhood Stability," *Housing Policy Debate* 7, no. 1 (1996): 37–81.
[19]   George Galster, *Homeowners and Neighborhood Reinvestment.*
[20]   Yannis M. Ioannides, "Residential neighborhood effects," *Regional Science and Urban Economics* 32, no. 2, (2002): 145–165.
[21]   Alan Mallach, "Lessons From Las Vegas: Housing Markets, Neighborhoods, and Distressed Single-Family Property Investors," *Housing Policy Debate* 24, no. 4 (2014): 769–801.
[22]   Alan Mallach, *Housing Market Conditions Assessment: City of Flint, Michigan.* (Flint: Center for Community Progress: 2014).

Figure 1: Tenure and Property Condition by Census Tract in Flint, Michigan

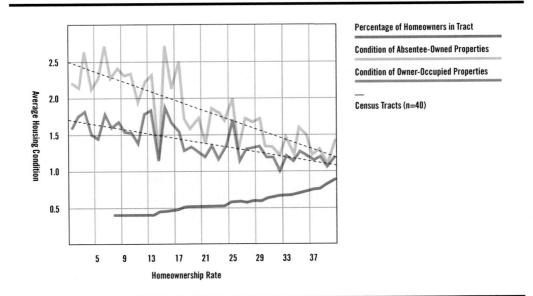

Source: Analysis by author of data from U.S. Census Bureau, 2010 Census (Washington, DC: U.S. Department of Commerce) (homeownership rates); 2012 Flint Parcel Survey (average housing condition) and Genesee County, Genesee County Property Records (Flint: author, 2014) (homeowner/absentee-owner distribution.)

Figure 1 supports the research findings that neighborhood peer behavior plays a major role in driving maintenance decisions. The higher the homeownership rate, the better properties are maintained and the better their condition. At every point on the continuum, moreover, owner-occupied properties are better maintained than absentee-owned properties, with the quality gap largest in areas where homeownership rates are lowest.

At the same time, one should not infer that the effects seen in Figure 1 are necessarily caused by higher homeownership rates. Higher homeownership rates are associated with higher incomes and higher property values, and it is likely that these effects are the result of the interplay between these (and perhaps other) factors.

MORTGAGE FORECLOSURE AND TAX DELINQUENCY

A number of studies have found that absentee owners are more likely than owner-occupants to allow their properties to go into mortgage foreclosure. Richard Todd, who studied Cuyahoga County, Ohio, early in the foreclosure crisis found that nearly three times as many non-occupant owners in Cuyahoga County had a foreclosure notice filed on their mortgage by April 30, 2008, than owner-occupants (28 percent vs. 9 percent).[23] Even when controlling for such factors as income, borrower's race, and neighborhood housing values, the foreclosure rate on mortgages to non-occupants was at

---

[23]   Richard M. Todd, *Foreclosures on Non-Owner-Occupied Properties in Ohio's Cuyahoga County: Evidence from Mortgages Originated in 2005–2006* (Minneapolis: Federal Reserve Bank of Minneapolis: 2010).

least double that of owner-occupied mortgages. Other research found that the disparity between foreclosure rates for owner-occupants and absentee owners was significantly greater in the midwestern states, where legacy cities are typically located than in Sunbelt states such as Nevada and Florida.[24]

Little or no published research exists on the relationship between homeownership and tax delinquency, although logic would suggest that the same disparities apply. My work in Trenton, New Jersey, supports that proposition. I was able to use parcel-level data to compare tax delinquency and redemption rates for owner-occupants and absentee owners of single-family homes (Table 3).

Table 3: Percentage of Absentee-Owner Properties with Tax Liens on File in 2014 in Trenton, New Jersey

Year	Absentee-Owner Percentage of Single-Family Tax Liens	Absentee-Owner Percentage of All Single-Family Properties (2014)
2014	53.4%	
2013	62.2%	} 49.7%
2012	63.8%	

Source: City of Trenton Tax Collector. Analysis by author.

Table 3 suggests that although the likelihood of early tax delinquency is only moderately greater for absentee owners (+15 percent), the likelihood of long-term delinquency—reflected in the failure to redeem 2012 and 2013 tax liens as of late 2014—is significantly greater (+65–75 percent) for absentee owners than for owner-occupants.

SOCIAL AND BEHAVIORAL CONDITIONS

Many studies find a strong connection between homeownership and different family social or behavioral conditions, and these conditions can affect neighborhood stability in important ways. Changes in child and youth outcomes may affect crime through lower dropout rates, leading in turn to lower juvenile delinquency; or through lower teen pregnancy rates, leading in turn to lower poverty rates in the next generation. These relationships reflect the well-established link between teen pregnancy, single-female parenthood, and poverty. Richard Green and Michelle White found a strong relationship between homeownership and greater educational attainment, lower dropout rates, and fewer teen pregnancies.[25] Other researchers have found that the children of homeowners are more likely to achieve higher levels of education and subsequent earnings, controlling for other relevant social and economic factors affecting educational outcomes and

---

[24] Breck L. Robinson and Richard M. Todd, *The Role of Non-Owner-Occupied Homes in the Current Housing and Foreclosure Cycle.* (Richmond: Federal Reserve Bank of Richmond: 2010); Breck L. Robinson, "The Performance of Non-Owner-Occupied Mortgages During the Housing Crisis," *Economic Quarterly* 98, no. 2 (2012): 111–138.

[25] Richard K. Green and Michelle J. White, "Measuring the Benefits of Homeowning: Effects on Children," *Journal of Urban Economics* 41, no. 3 (1997): 441–461.

earnings.[26] It is likely that a strong feedback chain exists between such behavioral changes at the family level and neighborhood conditions.

Research also has found that homeownership is associated with better physical and psychological health,[27] overall life satisfaction,[28] and owners' greater sense of control over their environments.[29] The extent, however, to which these factors affect neighborhood conditions remains uncertain.

It should be stressed that these positive effects are the product of successful homeownership, reinforcing the point made earlier that public policy should not aim simply to create homeowners but to foster sustainable homeownership. Homeowners who are delinquent on their mortgages or mired in foreclosure proceedings suffer from increased stress, depression, and mental illness.[30] The possibility should not be dismissed that these psychological effects contribute to the well-documented powerful negative effects of foreclosure on neighborhood vitality.

SOCIAL CAPITAL AND COLLECTIVE EFFICACY

Social capital can be seen as a combination of civic engagement and trust or the extent to which people feel mutual obligations to one another.[31] Kenneth Temkin and William Rohe studied change in Pittsburgh neighborhoods between 1980 and 1990 and found that "neighborhoods with relatively large amounts of social capital are less likely to decline when other factors remain constant."[32] A related concept linking social dynamics to neighborhood change is collective efficacy, or the "social cohesion combined with shared expectations for social control."[33] This concept echoes a much earlier formulation by Jane Jacobs, who wrote "a successful neighborhood is a place that keeps sufficiently abreast of its problems so it is not destroyed by them."[34]

[26] Thomas P. Boehm and Alan Schlottmann, "Does Home Ownership by Parents Have an Economic Impact on Their Children?" *Journal of Housing Economics* 8, no. 3 (1999): 217–232.

[27] Peter H. Rossi and Eleanor Weber, "The Social Benefits of Homeownership: Empirical Evidence from National Surveys," *Housing Policy Debate* 7, no. 1 (1996): 1–35; Luis Diaz-Serrano, "Disentangling the housing satisfaction puzzle: Does homeownership really matter?" *Journal of Economic Psychology* 30, no. 5 (2009): 745–755.

[28] William Rohe and Victoria Basolo, "Long-Term Effects of Homeownership on the Self-Perceptions and Social Interactions of Low Income Persons," *Environment and Behavior* 29, no. 6 (1997): 793–819.

[29] Kim Manturuk, "Urban Homeownership and Mental Health: Mediating Effect of Perceived Sense of Control," *City & Community* 11, no. 4 (2012): 409–430.

[30] Janice Bowdler, Roberto Quercia, and David A. Smith, The Foreclosure Generation: *The Long-Term Impact of The Housing Crisis on Latino Children and Families* (Washington, DC: National Council of La Raza, 2010); Craig Evan Pollock and Julia Lynch, "Health Status of People Undergoing Foreclosure in the Philadelphia Region," *American Journal of Public Health* 99, no. 10 (2009): 1833–1839.

[31] Robert D. Putnam, "The Prosperous Community: Social Capital and Public Life," *The American Prospect* (1993).

[32] Kenneth Temkin and William Rohe, "Social Capital and Neighborhood Stability: An Empirical Investigation," *Housing Policy Debate* 9, no. 1 (1998): 61–88. Social capital in their study combined institutional infrastructure and sociocultural milieu, which they define as "a construct that attempts to capture both observable behaviors of neighborhood residents and their unobservable affective sentiments toward the area" (p. 69).

[33] Robert J. Sampson, Great American City (Chicago: University of Chicago Press, 2012). They defined collective efficacy by (1) constructing an index of social control, in which they asked respondents how they would react (on a scale of 1 to 5) to various situations, such as if a fight broke out in front of their house, or they saw children spray-painting graffiti on a nearby building; and (2) constructing a similar index of social cohesion, asking respondents how they felt about statements such as "People in this neighborhood can be trusted" (p. 27). Finding that the two scales correlated very strongly with one another, they combined them to create their measure of collective efficacy.

[34] Jane Jacobs, *The Death and Life of Great American Cities*, 112.

Notably, however, "social control," Sampson, Raudenbush, and Earls write, "should not be equated with formal regulation or forced conformity by institutions such as the police and courts. Rather, social control refers generally to the capacity of a group to regulate its members according to desired principles—to realize collective, as opposed to forced, goals."[35] They found that collective efficacy is "a robust predictor of lower rates of violence," after controlling for neighborhood characteristics.[36] Later research has found that the absence of collective efficacy to be a strong predictor of homicide rates.[37]

Homeownership is positively associated with social capital. Homeowners are much more likely to participate in activities that increase neighborhood social capital, such as volunteering or participating in block group meetings.[38] Manturuk, Lindblad, and Quercia found similar patterns when looking specifically at the behavior of low- and moderate-income homeowners.[39]

Other research has found strong relationships between homeownership, collective efficacy, and neighborhood crime and disorder.[40] Lower homeownership, or lower collective efficacy, are both associated with higher levels of crime and disorder. This relationship is again subject to the homeowner having a sustainable mortgage. Two European studies also support the link between homeownership and collective efficacy. A Danish study found a strong association between greater homeownership and lower crime in a neighborhood, while controlling for multiple economic and demographic variables,[41] while a German study found that homeowners were less willing to accept deviant behavior and more ready to intervene when they observed such behavior.[42]

In conclusion, the relationship between homeownership and neighborhood change is complex and multidimensional, yet it appears clear that increasing stable, sustainable homeownership can significantly further positive neighborhood change through many different pathways, while a decline in homeownership is likely associated with neighborhood decline.

[35] Robert J. Sampson, Stephen W. Raudenbush, and Felton Earls, "Neighborhoods and Violent Crime: A Multilevel Study of Collective Efficacy," *Science* 277 (1997): 918–924, 918.

[36] Ibid, 923.

[37] Jeffrey D. Morenoff, Robert J. Sampson, and Stephen W. Raudenbush, "Neighborhood inequality, collective efficacy, and the spatial dynamics of urban violence," *Criminology* 39, no. 3 (2001); 517–558.

[38] Roland Cheo, Eric Fesselmeyer, and Kiat Ying Seah, "Revisiting the Effect of Homeownership on Social Capital," IRES *Working Captial Series*, 2013, at http://www.ires.nus.edu.sg/workingpapers/IRES2013-022.pdf

[39] Kim Manturuk, Mark Lindblad, and Robert Quercia, "Friends and Neighbors: Homeownership and Social Capital among Low- to Moderate-Income Families," *Journal of Urban Affairs* 32, no. 4 (2010): 471–488.

[40] Mark Lindblad, Kim Manturuk, and Roberto Quercia, "Sense of Community and Informal Social Control among Lower Income Households: The Role of Homeownership and Collective Efficacy in Reducing Subjective Neighborhood Crime and Disorder," *American Journal of Community Psychology* 51, no. 1 (2013): 123–139.

[41] Jorgen Lauridsen, Niels Nannerup, and Morten Skak, "Owner-Occupied Housing and Crime Rates in Denmark." Paper presented at the 2006 ENHR Conference, Ljubljana, Slovakia (2006).

[42] Jurgen Friedrichs and Jorg Blasius, "Attitudes of Owners and Renters in a Deprived Neighborhood." Paper presented at the ENHR Conference, Ljubljana, Slovakia (2006).

THE EROSION OF HOMEOWNERSHIP IN LEGACY CITIES

Although homeownership rates in legacy cities tended to parallel and even exceed national trends between 1900 and 1960, the trends have sharply diverged since then. In those cities, homeownership is declining and investor purchases are rising. Given the importance of homeownership to neighborhood health, as described above, this is a problematic trend.

All of the cities shown initially in Table 1 saw their homeownership rates drop after 1960—in some cases sharply, as in Flint or Camden, and in others more gradually, as in Toledo or Grand Rapids (Figure 2). Although homeownership rates have declined nationally in recent years, the long-term national trajectory over that period, as shown in Figure 2, was upward.

Figure 2: Homeownership Rates in Select Legacy Cities, 1900–2010

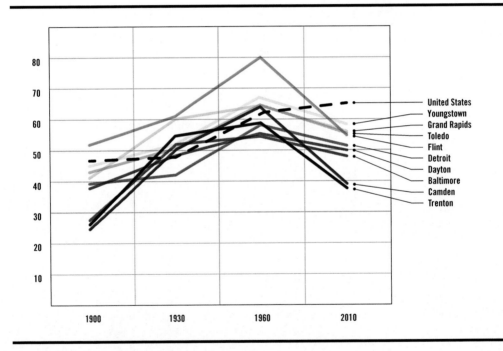

Source: U.S. Census, 1900, 1930 and 1960 Census of Housing; 2010 Census of Population (Washington, DC: U.S. Department of Commerce).

Figure 2 is somewhat misleading, however, given that it implies that homeownership has been declining since 1960 for all of these cities. Instead, many legacy cities saw continued growth or only modest declines in homeownership rates until the collapse of the housing bubble in 2007, at which point the rate plummeted. Table 4 shows the trends for a cluster of large legacy cities.

Table 4: Change in Homeownership Rates, Select Cities, 1960–2007 and 2007–2013

City	1960 (home-ownership)	2007 (home-ownership)	Average Annual Change 1960–2007	2013 (home-ownership)	Average Annual Change 2007–2013
Baltimore	54.3%	51.4%	-0.1%	46.2%	-1.5%
Detroit	58.2%	55.4%	-0.1%	49.9%	-1.7%
St. Louis	38.2%	50.7%	+0.6%	43.8%	-2.5%
Cincinnati	40.4%	43.0%	+0.1%	38.0%	-2.0%
Cleveland	44.9%	46.7%	+ <0.1%	42.5%	-1.5%
Philadelphia	61.9%	57.4%	-0.2%	51.0%	-2.0%
Pittsburgh	48.8%	53.8%	+0.2%	49.8%	-1.3%

Source: U.S. Census Bureau, 1960 Census of Housing, 2007 and 2013 1-year American Community Survey (Washington, DC: U.S. Department of Commerce). The cities included had one-year ACS data available for both 1960–2007 and 2007–2013.

Four of the seven cities in Table 4 saw homeownership growth between 1960 and 2007, modest in most cases, but substantial in St. Louis. Since 2007, all seven have seen sharp declines in both homeownership rates and in the number of owner-occupant households (Table 5). As a whole, these seven cities lost 11 percent of their homeowners, or more than 94,000 homeowner households.

An initial inference might be that the changes in legacy cities are no more than a reflection of the erosion of homeownership nationally during this period. This is incorrect, as not only is the rate of decline in these cities more substantial than the national rate of decline, but the numerical decline is far more substantial, as a percentage of the homeowner base, than nationally. The number of homeowners in these cities is declining at a rate of 1 percent to nearly 3 percent per year in the case of Detroit.

Table 5: Change in Number of Homeowners, Select Cities, 2007–2013

City	Homeowners 2007	Homeowners 2013	Change	Percentage Change
Baltimore	119,820	112,858	-6,962	-5.8
Detroit	153,708	127,502	-26,206	-17.0
St. Louis	71,725	61,551	-10,174	-14.2
Cincinnati	55,087	50,701	-4,386	-8.0
Cleveland	77,178	69,845	-7,333	-9.5
Philadelphia	323,021	297,098	-25929	-8.0
Pittsburgh	70,262	64,906	-5,358	-7.6

Source: U.S. Census Bureau, 2007 and 2013 1-year American Community Survey (Washington, DC: U.S. Department of Commerce).

During this same six-year period, the number of renters increased in each of these cities, in some cases substantially. Even in Detroit, where the total population continued to decline precipitously, the number of renters increased by more than 3,000 households.

Several factors have driven this erosion of homeownership, but one factor is clearly the increasingly dominant role of investor-buyers in legacy city housing markets. It is hard to measure this trend with precision, although a comparison of total sales volumes with the number of purchase mortgages in the same community during the same period can provide a rough sense of the trajectory of change.[43] Table 6 compares sales volumes with purchase mortgage volumes for three cities between 2006 and 2012. Mortgages declined from 42 percent of sales in Cleveland in 2006 to 20 percent by 2012, and in Pittsburgh from 46 percent to 22 percent. In Detroit, where the market collapse was pronounced, mortgages in 2012 represented fewer than 2 percent of total sales.

Table 6: Ratio of Purchase Mortgages to Total Sales, Select Cities, 2006–2012

City	Category	2006	2008	2010	2012
Cleveland	Sales	8,235	6,816	4,258	4,114
	Mortgages	3,490	1,597	993	824
	Mortgages of sales	42.3%	29.6%	23.3%	20.1%
Pittsburgh	Sales	6,487	8,787	8,281	7,381
	Mortgages	2,958	1,988	1,671	1,662
	Mortgages of sales	45.6%	22.6%	20.2%	22.5%
Detroit	Sales	29,230	21,006	13,814	12,579
	Mortgages	8,396	1,442	357	204
	Mortgages of sales	28.7%	6.9%	2.6%	1.6%

Source: Home Mortgage Disclosure Act, 12 U.S.C. § 301 (1975); Reinvestment Fund, PolicyMap (Boxwood Means data).

At the same time, Table 6 makes clear that total sales volumes also dropped significantly; although Pittsburgh, which may have the strongest housing market among major legacy cities, was an

---

[43]   This is based on the proposition that investor-buyers are significantly less likely to obtain mortgages from HMDA-reporting sources than are homebuyers, particularly first-time homebuyers. This proposition is strongly supported by a 2011 analysis from Campbell/Inside Mortgage Finance, which found that 77 percent of investor-buyers bought with cash, compared to 26 percent of "move-up" homebuyers and 10 percent of first-time homebuyers. See Tracking Real Estate Market Conditions using the Housing Pulse Survey, available at http://campbellsurveys.com/housingpulse/HousingPulse_white_paper.pdf

exception because the sales volume dropped to a lesser extent. This drop in sales volume reflects the severe difficulty that would-be homebuyers have in obtaining mortgages in the post-bubble era; a recent Urban Institute report concluded that "tight credit standards prevented 5.2 million mortgages between 2009 and 2014."[44] Although investors have filled part of the gap in effective market demand, much remains unfilled, leading to greater property abandonment in weaker neighborhoods. Moreover, as I have discussed in detail elsewhere, depending on the underlying market conditions of the neighborhood, investor behavior may have significant destabilizing effects.[45]

My recent study in Trenton, New Jersey, offers a more detailed picture of increased investor activity.[46] I analyzed individual sales transactions between 2006 and 2013 to identify investor and homebuyer activity citywide and by neighborhood for each year.[47] The trend shows a pattern consistent with that shown by the comparison of sales and mortgage data. The number of sales plummeted, with the number of owner-occupant homebuyers declining from more than 1,000 in 2006 to an average of less than 200 for the past three years (Figure 3). The number of investors has remained relatively stable since 2007 but at a level considerably lower than in 2006, the last year of the housing bubble. In 2013, investors represented nearly 80 percent of all sales in Trenton, compared with 50 percent in 2006.

---

[44]   Bing Bai, Laurie Goodman, Jun Zhu, "Tight credit standards prevented 5.2 million mortgages between 2009 and 2014," *Urban Wire*, January 28, 2016, available at http://www.urban.org/urban-wire/tight-credit-standards-prevented-52-million-mortgages-between-2009-and-2014.

[45]   Alan Mallach, "Lessons From Las Vegas: Housing Markets, Neighborhoods, and Distressed Single-Family Property Investors."

[46]   Alan Mallach, *Laying the Foundation for Strong Neighborhoods in Trenton, New Jersey* (New Brunswick: New Jersey Community Capital and Washington DC: Center for Community Progress: 2015).

[47]   We used online databases maintained by the state of New Jersey for all real property records and for real property transactions, singling out what are termed Class 2 (one to four family residential) properties. Purchases by investors were defined as those where (1) the address of the property and the address of the buyer were different; or (2) for transactions where the addresses were the same, where the name of the buyer was clearly not an individual or couple (e.g., "233 Chestnut LLC" or "Flip-That-House, Inc.").

Figure 3: Sales Transactions by Type of Buyer in Trenton, New Jersey, 2006–2013

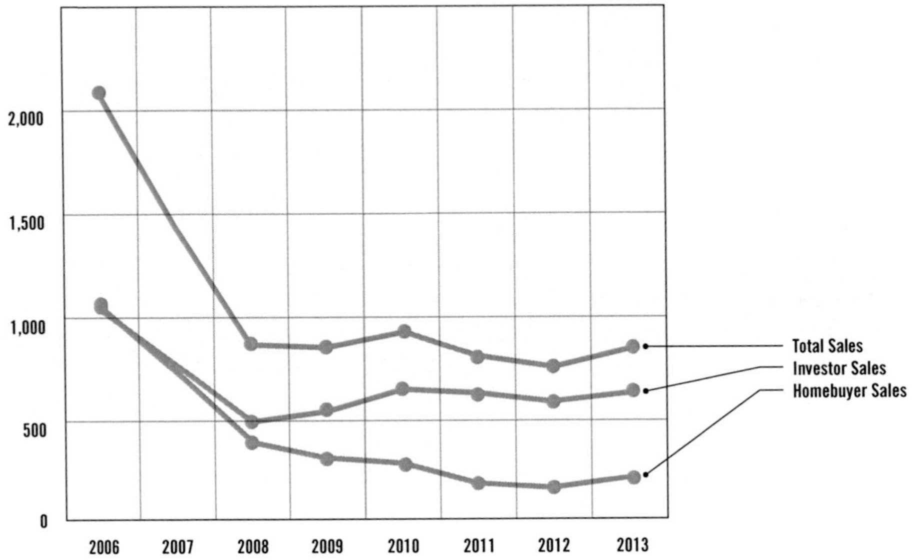

Source: New Jersey sales transaction database. Analysis by author.

Although in 2006, the percentage of investor-buyers was roughly proportional to their share of the city's housing stock, by 2013, the investor share was far higher, as illustrated in Figure 4 for two of the city's middle neighborhoods. Both of these neighborhoods still have relatively high homeownership rates (59 percent in Franklin Park and 64 percent in Parkside). Although investors own only 36 percent of the inventory in Parkside, they have accounted for 68 percent of the purchases there since 2006 and 86 percent since 2011. In Franklin Park, investors own 41 percent of the inventory, but they have accounted for 54 percent of the purchases since 2006 and 74 percent since 2011. The rate of erosion in homeownership in these neighborhoods is likely to be significant.[48]

---

[48]   It should be possible to calculate the rate of erosion using these databases by identifying investor vs. owner-occupant sellers and buyers. While such an analysis was beyond the scope of the Trenton study or this paper, it would be valuable, and I hope to be able to carry it out in the near future.

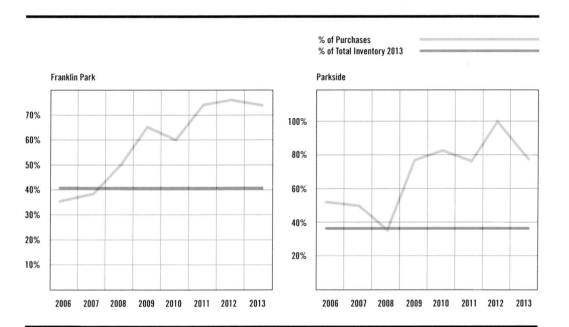

Figure 4: Investor Share of Inventory and Purchases, 2006–2013, in Two Trenton Neighborhoods

Source: New Jersey real property database and sales transaction database. Analysis by author.

MODELING THE RELATIONSHIP BETWEEN HOMEOWNERSHIP EROSION AND THE MIDDLE NEIGHBORHOOD

What, then, is the relationship between homeownership erosion and the decline of so many middle neighborhoods in legacy cities? In Chapter IV, I presented data showing the extent of that decline, while in this chapter I have tried to make two points: first, there is a compelling link between homeownership and a host of factors associated with stable, healthy neighborhoods; and second, decline in both the share and the number of homeowners in legacy cities and their neighborhoods has accelerated.[49]

Although the Trenton study finds a very strong relationship between the investor share of purchases (a reasonable proxy for homeownership erosion)—and factors such as median house price, violent crime rate, or tax foreclosure, all of which are associated with neighborhood strength and weakness[50]—one cannot necessarily conclude that the decline in homeownership causes neighborhood decline. Nonetheless, there appear to be clear associations between loss of homeownership and decline, and the findings on neighborhood effects suggest a number of the

---

[49] Regrettably, the ACS data that I used to present citywide data on homeownership erosion in Tables 4A and 4B do not exist in reliable form at the neighborhood (census tract) level. The only data available are from the five-year rather than one-year ACS, thus covering a narrower and more uncertain time period—and with a very large margin of error, which is particularly problematic when trying to compare relatively fine-grained changes.

[50] The investor share of single-family purchases by neighborhood showed very strong correlations (significance level of .99 or greater) with homeownership rate, tax delinquency, violent crime, vacancy, and median sales price.

pathways for such a relationship. The balance of this section explores these pathways and suggests a possible model of the relationship between homeownership and neighborhood change.

In doing so, it is essential to distinguish between those effects that appear to be properties of homeownership as such, which may be considered primary effects, and those that are the product of those factors, or secondary (or tertiary) effects. For example, even though there appears to be an association between collective efficacy and homeownership, that association may not be inherent to homeownership in itself, but could be seen as a secondary effect driven by primary features of homeownership—namely, the higher level of investment as well as the longer duration of tenure associated with homeownership.

Indeed, stripping it to its essence and disregarding the potential of homeownership as a means of building wealth reveals arguably only two salient features that intrinsically distinguish homeownership from rental tenure: the significantly longer duration of the tenure and the fact that homeownership represents a significant financial, and psychological, investment in a place. The two are closely interwoven. Although the financial investment may be independent of the duration of tenure, the psychological investment, to the extent it exists, is likely to be linked to duration of tenure. Duration of tenure, however, may also be linked to financial investment, if only because of the resulting greater "stickiness" of homeownership[51] and the higher transaction costs associated with selling a home than renting.[52]

Figure 5 is a conceptual model of the relationship between homeownership and neighborhood change. The extent to which the specific pathways in the model are supported by the body of research discussed earlier varies widely. The relationships between collective efficacy and crime incidence, or between crime and property values, for example, are strongly supported. The relationship, on the other hand, between length of tenure and collective efficacy is my hypothesis, drawn by inference from the research, rather than a relationship that has been explicitly established by research. Relationships that are more strongly established are shown with bold lines. Although the relationship between homeownership and foreclosure incidence is reasonably well established, the relationship between the financial investment in homeownership and foreclosure is inferred from the prior relationship, rather than being established in itself.

The model suggests a number of different pathways by which a relatively high and stable homeownership rate is likely to have a positive effect on the vitality of middle neighborhoods, and by extension, how the erosion of homeownership is likely to sap that vitality. As tenure shifts from ownership to rental, under the social and economic conditions affecting those neighborhoods, the neighborhoods are likely to see declines in property improvement and increased mortgage foreclosure and tax delinquency as direct results of the tenure shift. Indirectly, the increased residential instability and reduced investment associated with the erosion of homeownership may in

---

[51]   Lee Anne Fennell, *The Unbounded Home: Property Values Beyond Property Lines* (New Haven: Yale University Press: 2009).
[52]   Donald R. Haurin and H. Leroy Gill, "The Impact of Transaction Costs and the Expected Length of Stay on Homeownership," *Journal of Urban Economics* 51, no. 3 (2002): 563–584.

turn lead to reductions in collective efficacy and child outcomes, which in turn may trigger negative changes in crime incidence and property values, both of which are significant destabilizing factors.

I am not suggesting that these changes will necessarily take place. There are far more variables at play than can be suggested by the model, while there is no magic to any particular homeownership rate. However, it is important to stress that the erosion of homeownership in legacy city neighborhoods, particularly since the end of the housing bubble, is not taking place in a social or economic vacuum—It is taking place in the context of a series of powerful demographic and economic trends, all of which are having the effect of placing these neighborhoods increasingly at risk of destabilization. In that context, the erosion of homeownership in legacy cities should be a matter of substantial concern.

CONCLUSION

As with any complex policy issue, concern does not necessarily offer guidance on how the issue should be addressed. When it comes to the erosion of homeownership, and its effect on middle neighborhoods in legacy cities, this is particularly the case—since any policies to address this particular issue need to be carried out within the context of the highly problematic widespread decline of middle neighborhoods, which imposes significant constraints on what may be feasible.

Figure 5: Conceptual Model of Homeownership and Neighborhood Change

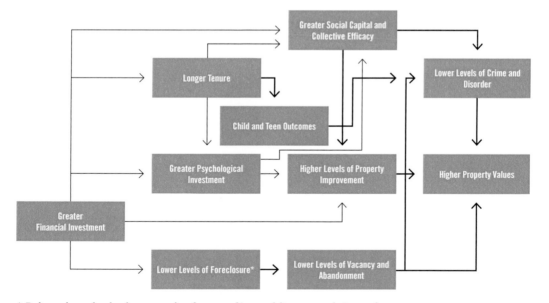

* Refers to lower levels of mortgage foreclosure and/or tax delinquency relative to absentee owners.

This is particularly true with respect to what might be seen as the obvious policy solution; namely, to encourage more people to become homeowners in middle neighborhoods. There appear to be severe limitations to what may be possible in this respect. The decline in the number of middle-income households in general—and the number of married-couple child-rearing households not only within the cities but also throughout metropolitan regions—means that the pool from which homebuyers come is a shrinking one. The weak competitive position of many legacy cities in their regions makes them a hard sell for many prospective home-buying households. Although some neighborhoods, with distinct locational, physical, or other assets, may—and should—become competitive for homebuyers, it is not likely to be an option available for all struggling middle neighborhoods.

A second approach—which is less often discussed but may have a wider potential reach—is how better to retain and engage the neighborhood's present homeowners, many of whom are not only disengaged, but actively fleeing the city for suburban areas.

Slowing their flight and engaging their energies in their neighborhoods are arguably the two most important steps to stabilize these neighborhoods. However, doing so will require some combination of both community-building strategies in the neighborhood—which most probably will depend on the existence of a strong Community Development Corporation (CDC) or other similar entity—and a responsive municipal government capable of improving public services and willing to give its residents a strong role in shaping the destiny of their neighborhoods.

Finally, although this chapter has focused on homeowners, it is important to pay greater attention to the renter population in middle neighborhoods as well as their landlords. Both groups have not received the attention their significant neighborhood role deserves—the former largely ignored and the later often demonized. Both, however, will have a significant impact on their neighborhoods' future. Creative organizing strategies to engage both tenants and landlords—and policy changes that encourage greater stability of tenure for tenants—could be important steps toward greater neighborhood stability, although perhaps not a substitute for homeownership. Moreover, because many tenants eventually do become homeowners, such policies would in all likelihood increase the probability that they buy in the neighborhood, rather than join the flight to the suburbs.

Writer, scholar, practitioner, and advocate, Alan Mallach has been engaged with the challenges of urban revitalization, neighborhood stabilization, and housing provision for 50 years. A senior fellow with the Center for Community Progress, he has held a number of public and private-sector positions, and currently also teaches in the graduate city planning program at Pratt Institute in New York City. His publications include many books, among them Bringing Buildings Back: From Vacant Properties to Community Assets *and* A Decent Home: Planning, Building and Preserving Affordable Housing, *as well as numerous articles, book chapters, and reports. He has a B.A. degree from Yale College, and lives in Roosevelt, New Jersey.*

VI. STRATEGIES TO IMPROVE MIDDLE NEIGHBORHOODS

By David Boehlke, czb planning & The Healthy Neighborhoods Group

ANOTHER MEETING; SAME OLD AGENDA

Those of us in the community development field spend many evenings at neighborhood meetings. At a typical meeting in any rec center, you might find a city planner, a community organizer, a police officer, perhaps a late-arriving city council member and, of course, the dozen residents who constitute the neighborhood association. Likely agenda items include complaints about landlords, crime, noisy teens, speeding traffic, and any other everyday problem that many older neighborhoods face. Consider just a few usual comments.

"We need to repair those abandoned houses and sell them to new homeowners."
"Everyone and that includes investors should be held responsible to meet all property codes."
"The crime and drug problems must be brought to the attention of the police, the politicians, and the media."
"The high rents landlords charge should shame them into better upkeep of their properties."

And, of course:

"It is just common sense. If we can get rid of problems, our neighbors and others will reinvest in the houses and the community."

Common sense—meaning a traditional attack on perceived problems—is repeatedly cited as the best way to improve a neighborhood. But after reviewing multiple attempts to address problems in middle neighborhoods, I would argue that common sense approaches are not working. What is needed is the substitution of "uncommon" sense strategies—innovative ways of moving middle neighborhoods to a better, more livable condition.

This chapter offers alternate approaches that are being used by residents and city officials around the country to reinvigorate middle neighborhoods.

UNIQUE REALITIES FOR THE MIDDLE

City officials, policy makers, and even residents typically undervalue middle neighborhoods. These neighborhoods are not thriving enough to attract sustained private investment, yet are not troubled enough to warrant concentrated public attention. Middle neighborhoods might have good houses on desirable blocks, many of which have a majority of homeowners and the remnants of a good reputation. But these places all face an unstated dilemma: a profound lack of confidence in the neighborhood, resulting in an inability to compete for the solid buyers and renters that every neighborhood must have to succeed.

To compete, middle neighborhood residents and their allies must understand the realities of their real estate market: high numbers of houses for sale, low prices, a lack of buyers, the community's negative image, and other market dysfunctions that undermine confidence in the future of the neighborhood.

What is needed to gain this understanding is a thorough assessment of the neighborhood as well as its assets, liabilities, and position in the market place. Any work plan must address actual dysfunctions. Rather than discussing code compliance or crime watches, attention should focus on critical conditions—such as the sales and rental markets, the competitive advantages of other neighborhoods, the declining disposable income of the residents, and the lack of a shared vision for the future. Unless a viable strategy reckons with the market realities of the neighborhood, no sustained change will happen.

This market placement dictum does not mean that crime reduction or the appearance of the neighborhood is unimportant. Such problems are always an issue, but there is a much larger dynamic also happening. Understanding how current residents, businesses, and institutions perceive the neighborhood is essential in formulating approaches that can make the neighborhood more competitive.

In this chapter, I discuss four core themes:
- The first asks, What is needed to shape approaches for stabilizing and strengthening middle neighborhoods? What do we need to know?
- The second focuses on how the real estate market can become more competitive. What are communities doing to be more competitive?
- The third theme examines how to stimulate investment in these communities. How can lending resources be expanded to reinforce the market?
- The fourth area addresses policies that are obstacles to middle neighborhood success. How are policies undermining the recovery of middle neighborhoods?

Each of these themes will be discussed and examples provided when possible.

STRATEGIZING FOR NEIGHBORHOOD IMPROVEMENT

Today, most neighborhood reinvestment efforts involve two quite different strategies—eliminating problems and creating new options, particularly for low-income households. Federal programs—such as Community Development Block Grants (CDBG), tax credits, and Department of Justice grants, among others—drive this approach, but they carry restrictions that can be harmful to middle neighborhoods. In particular, federal guidelines predetermine which problems to address and federal income regulations delineate who can be served and which assets can be added.

It is no surprise that rebuilding neighborhood confidence is not a typical federal program goal. Although building affordable housing or renovating foreclosed housing can be cast as improving the neighborhood, the reality is that further concentrating poor households and renovating hard-to-sell houses are ineffective strategies to help neighborhoods strengthen their positions in the marketplace. Neighborhoods won't thrive again through income-targeted efforts or public projects. They thrive when they offer the residents and newcomers what they want.

What then should be the primary goal of renewal strategies in middle neighborhoods? The answer is straightforward: Build confidence in the future of the neighborhood. Greater confidence is achieved when residents again feel pride in their homes and neighborhood, when real estate again sells and rents successfully, and when investments in houses again make economic sense. Such bold outcomes are not easily achieved and the work is complicated given that the approaches requires uncommon sense—taking actions that flow against the tide of governmental interventions that can weaken confidence.

Of course, building confidence is an unworkable strategy in severely troubled neighborhoods; one cannot build confidence in the face of overwhelming dysfunction. On the other hand, for stable and recovering neighborhoods, confidence is already achieved and the challenge in those places is how to shape the transformations to serve the full range of residents. However, in middle neighborhoods, confidence building is the critical element that will strengthen the community over the long haul. The central question is how can a middle neighborhood craft a workable strategy. Below, I offer basic steps that support strategy development.

USE REAL-TIME DATA
Challenge: Many neighborhoods still create and carry out programs on the basis of old census data, stale sales information, and out-of-date ownership records. For causing the recovery of a neighborhood real estate market, this data is obsolete. Old data often address concerns that no longer exist and overlook opportunities that can make the necessary difference.

One common lesson learned in middle neighborhoods is the need for good data and thoughtful analysis. For example, one middle neighborhood was viewed as stable because very few homes were for sale. However, closer examination showed that the aging homeowners were unable to sell their homes for what they thought they were worth, so they decided to stay put even though the houses were too large and much too expensive to maintain. Because there was no effort to attract younger buyers, many homeowners sold to investors when they could no longer stay in their homes due to financial or health reasons. If neighborhood leaders had analyzed who owned, who was selling, and who was buying, they could have identified the underlying problems and created promotions and homebuyer incentives to attract younger families to the neighborhood.

In contrast, the civic leaders of Jamestown in western New York decided to gather data on sales prices, ownership patterns, and market trends, and then hired a college student to visit each of the approximately 9,000 residences to rate the quality of upkeep and repairs as well as the extent of exterior reinvestment. This information was coupled with up-to-date data and gave civic leaders and city officials a comprehensive picture of neighborhood market conditions and behaviors. The leaders learned that although population loss was slowing, the process wasn't uniform and affected each neighborhood differently. They concluded that the middle neighborhoods most needed loans and self-help projects to build confidence. Information and analysis drove the program outcomes instead of government grants or "common sense" problem-solving strategies.

Takeaway: Knowing what is actually happening in the neighborhood marketplace is the best way to select and support strategies to effectively improve neighborhoods. With good data and clear benchmarks, residents and their allies can map their community's recovery and know if they are succeeding in improving the market position of the neighborhood.

IDENTIFY MARKET REALITIES

Challenge: Many middle neighborhoods were originally built to serve modest-income households. They offer traditional working-class housing that no longer attracts young families who often desire more than one bath and two bedrooms. Other middle neighborhoods were built with big houses for large families and today are seen as too expensive to own and maintain. Still other neighborhoods are considered too drab and it is hard to be confident about a place that is described as forgettable.

Although middle neighborhoods often have construction or design challenges, they also have a remarkable range of positive features. Promoting these qualities is key. Maybe the communities were constructed in the era of wide sidewalks or trees, or have many parks, or historic community facilities. Today these places might still have a solid social fabric and a reputation for imaginative holiday lights or lush gardens or active houses of worship. All of these features can support desirability so long as they are identified and promoted.

However, the positive features are not always self-evident. One Denver suburb was originally built with smaller 1950s tract houses so most buyers passed it by even though more recently built houses had three or four bedrooms. By helping buyers understand that a full range of houses was available, the diversity of housing in this middle community became a selling point. Buyers of varied needs could find the home they wanted.

Many cities are focused on demolition to change neighborhood investment psychology. Fortunately, removing buildings from dense older neighborhoods often gives the needed openness that cannot be found in other older areas. The critical question is how those open spaces are used. Cleveland is famous for innovations that have "re-imagined" hundreds of vacant lots. Neighborhood Progress Inc. of Cleveland even offers residents an impressive guidebook for addressing vacant space.

In another Ohio city, a neighborhood nonprofit partnered with a community arts group to improve lots that were not adopted by adjacent homeowners. A dozen orphan lots could have become eyesores but instead they are now known for their art and their uniqueness. When residents are being pro-active about their community, there is a noticeable increase in pride and confidence.

Takeaway: National experience is consistent: Selecting the best-suited strategies is critical. Even a disinvested tract house neighborhood or a community facing abandonment can be successfully marketed through a concentrated effort to find what makes the place special and what can be promoted, and to whom—that is, what market segment might be attracted to the neighborhood. When those elements are identified and leveraged, a market can be strengthened.

ASSESS STRENGTHS

Challenge: It is easy to enumerate problems to be solved, but that information does not promote investment. A thriving neighborhood must pay attention to its advantages and promote what makes it a good place for current residents to stay and for new residents to choose.

Neighborhood advantages are more varied than most people realize. Location is important, as is the quality of construction and the architectural appeal, but a neighborhood is much more. Some places are known for the friendly ways in which neighbors interact. Other communities are attractive because of their institutional anchors or a special cluster of unique houses or a remarkable history. Chicago bungalows and Baltimore row houses might be drab clichés to some people, but others see continuity and predictability as a virtue. Identifying defining features and using these as strengths is critical to any effort to reposition a middle neighborhood.

In the process, residents should be reminded of what is so good about the place that they have called home for years. Often they have become complacent about the neighborhood's positive features. One densely populated middle neighborhood on the East Coast acted as if the large stream valley park on its northern boundary was in someone else's neighborhood and the existence of a large city-owned golf course on its western edge was only a place to drive past and not something to be valued. Partnering with groups (environmentalists, golfers, etc.) who sought these amenities allowed the community to define itself as a much more desirable place to buy a home. This, in turn, encouraged public agencies and local nonprofits to make those purchases and rehabs easier. Coordinated open houses, direct marketing of the neighborhood, home tours, discounts for police officers to buy, small loans and grants, and dozens of other tactics were used to market the community as highly desirable.

Takeaway: If a middle neighborhood is to thrive again, the major focus cannot be on removing problems without an equal or greater focus on promoting the advantages of the place—which requires knowing the positive features of the place. People do not choose a neighborhood or choose to reinvest in their homes because the community no longer has certain problems; they choose a place because it offers them something they want.

THINK SMALL FIRST

Challenge: Middle neighborhoods lack high status; they are often labeled as average. Have you ever seen a bumper sticker announcing the proud parent of an average student? In middle neighborhoods, housing is solid but too much is a bit shabby. Public facilities are adequate but worn. Commercial areas are dated and do not attract many new customers. Often small steps are needed to reverse the negatives.

When residents feel unnoticed and uncared for, it is tempting to conclude that nothing will change unless there is a major breakthrough, such as a new housing project, a renovated community center, or an upgraded commercial strip—all actions that take considerable planning and public resource allocation. For example, one older middle neighborhood in the mid-South decided that new houses would be the answer. The resulting project followed the principles of New Urbanism: The lots were small and the porches nearly touched the sidewalks. However, the government subsidy needed to make the housing feasible restricted the incomes of potential buyers, many of whom barely qualified for financing and lacked the wherewithal to install landscaping, buy proper porch furniture, or manage even minor upkeep. Over time, this major project had the unintended consequence of weakening confidence in the future of the neighborhood.

For more than 20 years, one Great Lakes city sought to reposition troubled but viable neighborhoods with numerous large housing projects. But there was little positive carry-over to adjacent blocks. The projects were successful at many levels, but it took decades for nearby areas to reflect the change. Getting the large developments built required long lead times and substantial resources—and created long-term expectations that could not be met.

A better approach starts small. For example, for decades Rochester, New York, lost businesses and population mostly due to new technologies that were displacing jobs. As a response, city government developed a variety of large-scale projects, but the leaders of one area decided to also partner with a nonprofit to create small programs to rebuild confidence and to stimulate investment behaviors. The selected site surrounded a city-sponsored eight-house in-fill development. The neighborhood strategy focused on modest projects to improve the curb appeal of existing homes and to enhance landscaping. These efforts were conducted in partnership with the local real estate board. Reinforced by sophisticated market savvy from real estate agents, the small improvements reinforced standards of good maintenance and supported an active real estate market like other successful communities.

Takeaway: Large projects sound great and architectural renderings can be seducing. But middle neighborhoods usually are too vulnerable to wait for such projects. Smaller community-based initiatives are typically more effective at dealing with the core issues. However, if large projects should happen, there must be a companion plan to leverage positive impacts on the whole neighborhood.

FORGE RELATIONSHIPS AMONG NEIGHBORS

Challenge: Strategies do not work unless residents are integral to the work. Too many middle neighborhoods have lost the ties that once linked their residents together. Fewer households have children; there are new racial and ethnic groups; and many people are working two jobs. It is hard to have confidence in your neighbors if you do not know them.

If asked about what made their neighborhood attractive when they first moved in, many longtime residents speak about how neighborly the place was. They knew everyone on the block and people paid attention to one another. The sidewalk of the shut-in was shoveled. The missing dog was quickly found. The locked-out child was given a place to stay until his parents came home. People saw themselves as buying both a house and a neighborhood. Even though these memories are sometimes seen through rose-colored glasses, it is true that most middle neighborhoods were originally desired because of their stability and neighborliness.

Thriving neighborhoods are filled with people who know and trust their neighbors, so scores of middle neighborhoods employ block projects as powerful tools for improving ties. The stated goal is usually a cleanup or beautification, but the more important outcome is that neighbors are given a chance to interact. Instead of passively attending meetings, residents are bridging barriers of age, race, language, and income by working together to improve their neighborhood. Residents undertaking shared activities and socializing reignite the neighborliness that once made the place so attractive.

Engaging neighbors is a powerful strategy for improving middle neighborhoods and can be implemented for a variety of goals. In the Belair-Edison neighborhood in Baltimore, Maryland, the initial organizing was aimed at installing front porch lights to create a sense of oversight and to offer a welcoming feeling. After years of completing similar projects, teams of neighbors now host marketing parties in renovated houses for sale. They invite their co-workers, friends, and relatives as potential buyers. The intent is not only to sell the homes but also to create a sense of resident control over what was happening in the market.

Takeaway: Accomplishing physical change in the neighborhood is great, but building solid neighborly relationships has an even higher rate of return when it comes to successful middle neighborhoods. Particular programs such as home sales efforts and block projects empower the residents to shape their community in a positive way.

Clearly, there are many more elements in crafting strategies for middle neighborhoods, but the above examples demonstrate some of what needs to be done. Data must be up-to-date and useful. There must be an honest appraisal of the neighborhood's conditions and realities. Strategizing should move from cataloging problems to identifying marketable strengths. The first strategic steps in neighborhood change should be manageable and timely. Neighbors working together are critical to any strategic approach to change in middle neighborhoods. All of these actions should be seen as a form of uncommon sense.

REBUILD MARKET CONFIDENCE

Once workable realistic strategies for improving a neighborhood have been created, new action plans must focus on the market goals and should avoid whatever has not worked in the past.

To rebuild market confidence in middle neighborhoods, plans must make sense in the market context. Too often, the goal is building new housing or better parks or reopening the closed elementary school. But these actions seldom address what is hindering the neighborhood from competing well in the neighborhood marketplace. Moreover, investment does not follow from the removal of obstacles; investment follows when and where opportunities are increasing. As Marcia Nedland demonstrates elsewhere in this volume, successful creative efforts to strengthen markets in middle neighborhoods are already happening. What follows are examples of what to do to re-build market confidence and how different places are doing just that.

IMPLEMENT MARKETING CAMPAIGNS

Challenge: Neighborhoods cannot sustain confidence without a viable real estate market. Both neighbors and newcomers need to believe that buying a home or improving one will add to its value. Confidence building without positive change in the sales values and rents will ultimately fail, because people want to invest their time, effort, and money sensibly. Reaching the right market segments is a key to building market strength and increasing values.

Successful middle neighborhoods evaluate the competition and compete where there is a real chance for success. If there are only one or two niche markets, these must be the focus. Targeting market segments that are not likely to be attracted to the neighborhood is likely to be ineffective. Is the focus on current owners, new buyers, more desirable investors, or stronger tenants? The answer is important, because missteps are easy to make. Rehabbed houses that have no market or are in poorly chosen locations profoundly undermine stability. New houses that do not sell are disastrous to the market. Upgraded rentals that are empty reinforce a negative image.

The principle is to pick the most likely buyers and renters and then seek them out. Recognizing this, many middle neighborhoods target households with children because of the exceptional quality of the local elementary schools, while other neighborhoods target singles and childless couples where the schools are weak. One Michigan neighborhood targeted gay households to buy and restore very large 100-year-old homes. Other places market to young firefighters and police officers, many of whom qualify for special loans if they buy in their cities. Still other neighborhoods aggressively seek out quality investors to improve the rental market and many communities have developed incentive grants for real estate agents in order to stimulate sales. The common goal is getting more home buyers and solid landlords.

To make the most of these efforts, middle neighborhoods also must have the capacity for ongoing campaigns to inform the public about the real estate market. More than relaying numbers, marketing initiatives should describe the new buyers and the improvements they are making. Likewise, it is important to publicly congratulate long-term current owners who decide to reinvest—even with a 10 percent annual turnover of houses, home improvements by the remaining 90 percent of owners are pivotal.

These promotional campaigns should be brought directly to people in ways that readily engage the target audience. Muskegon, Michigan, county government hosted a holiday party at one of its renovated houses and provided access to other nearby restored houses. Even though there was bitter cold and snow, curiosity proved to be a powerful force in stimulating interest in the houses and in the neighborhood. In Cicero, Illinois, newly built properties were marketed by holding barbecues at the homes of recent buyers. Their invited friends were told of other homes for sale and were encouraged to join the newcomers in moving into the neighborhood. Another city created an involved agent list, which included those real estate agents active in the community who had completed additional training on special financing for middle markets. By having a targeted list of active agents, it was possible to fully educate them on what was happening and to arm them with the information needed to complete sales. The issue is not which specific programs are chosen; the key issue is using techniques that achieve sustainable market change.

Takeaway: Confidence does not grow without good communication and marketing does not mean much unless people act on the information. Better upkeep, more upgrades, and active sales all show a recovering middle market, which, in turn, feeds more confidence. With good data and clear benchmarks, residents and their allies can map their community recovery and determine if they are improving the market position of the neighborhood.

MANAGE THE NEIGHBORHOOD STORY

Challenge: Middle neighborhoods are not sexy; they do not command feature articles in the local newspaper, unless there is a problem. After a drive-by shooting, the local television news will describe where the event happened in detail and will surely interview a distressed resident. Something positive like a farmers' market or a park restoration might receive general mention, but the neighborhood might never be cited.

Residents of middle neighborhoods consistently complain that any news reported about their neighborhood is bad news. Middle neighborhoods are not good copy. There are few ribbon-cutting ceremonies on new housing projects and there are no gushing reviews about the latest new coffee house or trendy restaurant. Regrettably, instead of directly confronting this problem, too many neighbors concede to being labeled. But to rebuild a market, there must be a communications plan to create and promote the stories that convey the value of the neighborhood to existing residents and prospective newcomers. If not, information about most middle neighborhoods will continue to be controlled by others.

Fortunately, many middle neighborhood leaders are building market confidence by proactively crafting what they want to say. Neighborhoods, Inc. of Hammond, Indiana, works with a half-dozen older small cities east and south of Chicago. One successful project involves having homeowners agree to the installation of a park bench on their yards next to the sidewalk. This "public" bench gives an opportunity for people to stop, sit, and talk. The group also sponsors unique, upbeat events like community-wide dog walks and marching groups of neighbors all playing kazoos. These fun, tongue-in-cheek events are the centerpiece of the neighborhood newsletter, which conscientiously omits any police call reports and instead enthusiastically includes before and after photos of the property changes taking place. The message is consistently upbeat.

Youngstown, Ohio, has lost two-thirds of its population. As such, confidence should be at a low point—but to counteract this, each and every neighborhood improvement is given coverage in local media and especially in the neighborhood newsletters. Citywide newsletters convey images of a city filled with murals, renovated houses, new homebuyers, reclaimed vacant lots, resident-sponsored gardens, and restored park sites. These articles honor what the neighbors are doing, but just as importantly, they create a more positive story of where the community and middle neighborhoods are heading.

Takeaway: The challenge sounds simple: Create and promote a positive message to strengthen the neighborhood and the value of its real estate. However, the task is not easy. Neighborhood and city leaders need to commit to a new way of talking about communities so that positives are moved up-front and negatives are addressed in the background. The concept is not complicated, but the execution is very hard and requires conscious change from years of complaining.

CREATE POSITIVE IDENTITIES

Challenge: As any real estate agent will tell you, it is very hard to build market confidence in a place that does not have a name. Remarkably, many middle neighborhoods are distinct places but are lumped with other communities under names like the Westside or the Fifth Ward. However, such large areas usually have a great deal of variety, so if only a general name is used, the neighborhood takes on all of the baggage—good and bad—that applies to the whole area.

Geneva, New York—an attractive small city on a Finger Lake—recognized there were ongoing problems undermining neighborhoods in the city. Some parts of the city had poor-quality housing; other parts had large homes that were under-maintained. Some areas consisted of small houses built after World War II that were being converted to rental housing. To many residents, the city was just a list of problems, but the reality was much different. There were areas of older homes in beautiful condition; many of the largest houses had been fully restored. Some neighborhoods had incredible parks or attractive median strips leading to community facilities. But the positives could never be fully promoted because there were no distinct neighborhood identities.

Of course, residents were neighborly, but usually with other residents on the same block. The need was to define a larger area with enough similarities so residents could work for common outcomes. Yet these areas had to be small enough to be manageable. After months of analysis, a dozen neighborhoods were identified and were given distinct standing by city government and in the marketing of the city. Today many residents describe themselves as living in these newly named neighborhoods. The simple act of creating neighborhood identities empowered residents to act together for community change. Recently, this paid off when the city was nominated as one of 15 national finalists for the All-America City Award.

In a Michigan community, a large swath of the city was called the North Side, even though much of the area was actually northeast of the downtown. People avoided confusion by simply using street names as their identity, which in turn produced scores of identities. To untangle all of the confusions, local leaders decided to call the overall area The Historic Northside, but then identified each of a half-dozen distinct areas with specific neighborhood names based on history or prominent features. This created a sense of place and specialness.

Takeaway: A rose by any other name is still a rose, but what if it has no name, no identity, and no distinctness? In recovering middle neighborhoods creating identity is critical to sustaining the cohesiveness necessary for a more confident community and a thriving real estate market.

ACCENTUATE POSITIVES
Challenge: Neighbors often believe resources come to places with needs and not to places that are succeeding. But this view is often mistaken, especially when applied to middle neighborhoods. Public and private resources also come to places that offer potential and have a plan to initiate positive change.

The old common sense: To get attention and funding, one large urban East Coast neighborhood promoted its rat extermination campaign over many years and the area became well known for its infestation. Hardly a market builder. A community in the South faced a significant drug problem centered on one house and the neighbors used the media to effectively communicate that fact to the rest of the city, even though this just reinforced notions that the area had serious problems. And across the country, neighbors often appear before city councils to decry how troubled their neighborhoods are and, of course, these stories are repeated endlessly on city cable channels.

Such efforts to publicly address problems almost always create negative perceptions.

The uncommon sense: One older southern mill town offers cutting days, when long-term residents with established gardens provide plant cuttings to new neighbors. Another neighborhood does cleanups that include a public event for awarding prizes for the most improved alleys. And one small Indiana city makes a tradition of using public meetings to highlight the best blocks and the best rehabs. The ostensible reason for such efforts is to promote positive change, but the added outcome is to publicly and enthusiastically encourage both the residents and others to see the community in a more positive way, which is necessary for market recovery.

Takeaway: Touting neighborhood problems publicly typically has the unintended consequence of tagging the neighborhood as problem ridden. Meeting quietly, but effectively, with city officials to deal with problems can produce results without hurting a neighborhood's reputation. Positive strengths needed to be shouted.

CELEBRATE THE NEIGHBORHOOD

Challenge: As stated differently earlier, middle neighborhoods "don't get no respect." They cannot demonstrate significant distress; they are not able to be the squeaky wheel, and when they focus on problems, they often lower confidence. So middle neighborhoods need to create their own message and use every possible tool listed to make people feel confidence about these places.

One of the most underrated marketing tools is celebration. Neighborhoods that celebrate themselves are neighborhoods that build standing in the larger city. And, they build status with their own residents who take pride in their community. The Highlandtown neighborhood in Baltimore had long been a place of choice for various working-class ethnic groups. The level of pride was evident to the most casual observer. But change was happening and it was not clear where the neighborhood would end up. Would it be the next location for ethnic and racial transition? Would it transition from an elderly homeowner community to a place of choice for emerging young households of means? Would it be seen as a sustainable middle neighborhood?

In this case, the answer is all of the above. The neighborhood leadership group employs dozens of techniques to sustain a remarkable market mix. The leaders ensure that market concerns are addressed with first-rate counseling and with lending products for homebuyers supplemented with caring professional foreclosure assistance. Simultaneously, the historic park was rediscovered as a neighborhood and city resource. This Victorian greensward is now the "in" place for open-air plays and water ballets. At the same time, corner taverns that survived from the 1930s were promoted as places where "everybody knows your name." There are wine festivals that honor the homemade wines still being made by older ethnic families. The neighborhood cleanups have become excuses for block parties. The Main Street programs heavily tilt toward celebration, including parades of homemade lanterns around Halloween, widely promoted farmer markets, and cross-cultural events. The neighborhood also parlayed an arts district designation to engage residents from all backgrounds and ages in shared activities.

The results are outstanding, but perhaps the most important outcome is that the neighborhood has weathered both economic and ethnic transition and the recent downturn in prices better than many similar neighborhoods. The neighborhood thrives because it is known for its diversity, its respect for history, its stability, its sense of whimsy, and its healthy market.

Takeaway: As the saying goes, it is hard not to smile while eating ice cream. The leaders of middle neighborhoods must recognize that simply enjoying the people and values of the neighborhood can be a powerful tool for neighborhood market recovery.

Elsewhere in this book, there are more examples of marketing techniques to craft strategies for middle neighborhoods. The examples here are provided to show how strategies can be implemented with a bias toward neighborhood marketing. There should be an aggressive marketing campaign. Middle neighborhoods too often are treated as second choices in real estate marketing. To address this, the neighborhood needs to manage its own story and not expect others to promote it. Further, middle neighborhoods must create clear positive identities and must market their strengths. Finally, middle neighborhoods need to celebrate themselves as the special places they are.

INVESTING IN MIDDLE NEIGHBORHOODS

What we have seen in the above examples are ways that communities are strengthening their middle neighborhoods by creating effective, achievable strategies and by acting to reignite market confidence. To reinforce these actions, additional investment dollars are critically important—both from private sources and from public funds.

In terms of household or lender investment in middle neighborhoods, the proof of success is in changing behaviors. Moreover, some leaders in the lending community are making important headway in increasing lending in middle neighborhoods. Sometimes that means using or modifying a Community Reinvestment Act product and other times it means making loans to be kept in portfolio until seasoned. In many cases, the focus has been on purchase loans, but easier access to home improvement loans can be just as important. In some cases, leaders in the lending community have stepped up to do quite imaginative projects.

Some examples are at a significant scale, particularly the case of Baltimore, Maryland, where a the Healthy Neighborhoods program (described at length in Chapter VIII) has galvanized neighborhood groups, public programs, and lender commitments to set a high standard for investment in the target neighborhoods. But there are also many smaller examples that speak to similar lender involvement in neighborhood confidence building.

Canton, Ohio, uses various small strategies to impact specific areas, many of which are middle neighborhoods. The Community Building Partnership (CPB) is a nonprofit primarily focused on those neighborhoods, and part of their work involves partnering with lenders. In one case, Huntington Bank is aggressively making loans available through CPB. The underwriting is very flexible (580 credit score, $500 buyer cash, 3 percent required through the buyer or a grant, and no private mortgage insurance.) In the past year, 103 portfolio mortgages have been made, totaling a $13.2 million investment. Huntington Bank supported the work of CPB by paying $250 for each closed loan. Further, Fifth/Third Bank has granted $15,000 to CPB to provide incentive down payment assistance of up to $2,000 for each loan. And a large local credit union, CSE Federal, uses CPB to market home improvement loans. Each of these lenders recognizes that lending is a critical part of stabilizing a soft real estate market.

Oswego, New York, is a small city with houses ranging from grand to very modest in neighborhoods with a wide range of conditions. Neighborhood leaders decided to select specific middle market areas to promote homeownership and to encourage more improvement lending. One lender—Pathfinder Bank—committed to being a significant player. It makes an annual $25,000 contribution to the local revitalization organization and it is providing creative construction financing for an LLC controlled by 22 neighbors who are have bought and are restoring a vacant sorority house. The president of that bank is a hands-on participant in the work of the revitalization organization and has joined with a local foundation to support the activities of the group.

The results on the street testify that the dollars and leadership time have been effectively invested. But to further encourage home improvements, the nonprofit follows a program developed in Jamestown, New York, where small matching grants are given to homeowners in middle neighborhoods. In Oswego, 100 grants averaging $1,000 have resulted in over $200,000 of small-scale upgrades to houses on targeted blocks. The plan for next year is to include a lender home improvement loan option with this program.

Of course, expanding lending is not enough unless there is a commitment of the larger community to confidence-building initiatives. Although faced with significant funding obstacles, many cities recognize that investing in middle neighborhoods makes good economic sense. City investment preserves solid housing stock and infrastructure as well as builds the tax base cities need to provide services to all neighborhoods. It is much less expensive to reinvigorate middle neighborhoods than to recover failed neighborhoods.

For many cities, investing in middle neighborhoods is also a way to serve lower-income households. Some of these households live in these middle neighborhoods already and successful interventions can protect their equity and their quality of life. For low-income households elsewhere in the city, making sure that middle neighborhoods do not decline improves the standards of housing for neighborhoods they might someday call home.

Other communities are investing in middle neighborhoods because these neighborhoods provide a ladder of housing opportunities as households improve their economic situations. More neighborhood stability means additional opportunities for good rentals and affordable home buying in desirable areas. Solid renters and first-time buyers can locate in a thriving middle neighborhood and expect it to remain stable or even to improve.

Almost without exception, cities invest in middle neighborhoods as a low-cost strategy. The costs of buying and repairing sound older houses are far less than the costs of restoring failed housing. The program costs can be remarkably low in comparison to the positive impact on the city tax base.

Investing in middle neighborhoods is a tested strategy. Lenders know that involvement in these neighborhoods creates new market opportunities. Innovative cities have developed formats for tailored, low-cost interventions that increase housing values by addressing the need for more investment—often despite policy obstacles to neighborhood recovery.

ADDRESSING POLICY OBSTACLES

A focus on middle neighborhoods raises core public policy issues. Is "community development" actually just a term denoting work in low-income neighborhoods on issues such as affordable housing and community facilities or does it include efforts to recover at-risk communities that need to rebuild market confidence? Can the field change from a one-size-fits-all approach to one that recognizes the range of housing markets and neighborhood dynamics across the country and even across many cities?

The recent emphasis on foreclosure intervention through the Department of Housing and Urban Development's Neighborhood Strategy Program (NSP) illustrates the dilemma. In strong market cities, foreclosure assistance was helpful in nearly all qualified neighborhoods. But in weak market cities, the NSP's focus on more troubled areas meant that resources were not targeted to middle neighborhoods, but instead were spent on high-cost renovations on troubled blocks. Detroit, Flint, and Saginaw in Michigan are classic examples of this distorted investment scheme. Further, in many cases the appraised values of the renovated houses in the distressed neighborhoods were so low that lenders weren't willing to make such small home mortgage loans. Severely distressed markets like Gary, Indiana, faced no sales demand in the selected distressed neighborhoods. Gary saw costs of $80,000 to renovate a house appraised at $17,000 and no lenders wanted a 30-year loan or even a 15-year loan of less than $20,000. The realities of the real estate market just did not fit the NSP guidelines.

The decades of CDBG investments illustrate many of the same points. For example, funds can easily be spent on replacing existing sidewalks in low-income communities, but the rules often do not allow modest funds to be spent to repair walkways in many middle neighborhoods. With a few exceptions, CDBG rules essentially dictate that only low-income households can be assisted directly and only if the properties are brought fully to code—no matter if the economics make little sense in that market.

Policy obstacles do not stop at government. Foundations and corporate giving programs are often unwilling to assist middle neighborhoods. Their argument is that these places are not in the most need. Funders do not want to be seen as helping a place that is generally viewed as adequate. Of course, there are exceptions to these rules and some cities like Cleveland, Rochester, and Baltimore are home to funders that look beyond need to see potential.

Further, the pervasive national fixation on gentrification is often an impediment to government or philanthropic funding for middle neighborhoods. While middle neighborhood residents seldom worry about new neighbors who might be better off financially, these residents are warned that gentrification is a risk and cities like San Francisco and Washington, D.C., are used as illustrations. In reality, data from cities nationally shows that the bigger worry in middle neighborhoods is insufficient active investment. For most legacy cities, the central challenges are to maintain their tax bases, for households to conserve their equity, and for residents to live in neighborhoods of choice.

NEXT STEPS

Cities across the country are recognizing that middle neighborhoods are valuable assets that have been overlooked and allowed to slowly decline. Today these cities are being strategic about how they address their middle neighborhoods and how they develop work plans for positive change. They do this because it makes uncommon sense.

But too many middle neighborhoods continue to be forgotten—and public policies, especially federal community development programs, reinforce this problem by funding programs that undermine market recovery. If there is to be a future for middle neighborhoods beyond individual efforts like those listed here and elsewhere in this volume, the next steps will have to focus on a national policy that engages government, funders, and nonprofits with residents to achieve the confidence building that will strengthen these neighborhoods.

David Boehlke has 40 years' experience working in neighborhoods and assisting community-based nonprofits in more than 100 cities, especially places with declining populations. He uses "Healthy Neighborhoods" as an organizing concept to understand and direct community stabilization. The concept looks at what is working successfully and what is undermining stability. It identifies community assets and proactive ways to re-build the "demand" side of neighborhood investing while greatly strengthening resident involvement. As a consultant he works through czb planning in Alexandria, Virginia, and through The Healthy Neighborhoods Group in Ithaca, New York.

VII. USING PLACE-BRANDING STRATEGY TO CREATE HOMEBUYER DEMAND FOR LEGACY CITY NEIGHBORHOODS

By Marcia Nedland, Fall Creek Consultants

The fundamental law of supply and demand applies to neighborhoods as much as any other product or service. Leaders in legacy city neighborhoods know that when the supply of homes for owner occupancy seriously exceeds demand, it will also be immediately apparent whether their neighborhood is a place where people with choices will choose to live.

While developing quality homes for purchase through the Neighborhood Stabilization Program (NSP), those working on neighborhood improvement learned that a neighborhood's image is just as important to its success in reaching prospective buyers as the quality and price of an individual home. Image exerts an enormous influence over the behavior and choices of homebuyers, particularly in a weak market with many choices of homes and neighborhoods at affordable prices.

Neighborhoods are dynamic places. People move in and out, and homes turn over regularly. All neighborhoods need replacement households to thrive—but not just any replacement household. They need households who are able and willing to maintain neighborhood standards of property maintenance and community life in order to retain existing neighbors and attract new ones. Replacement households that do not contribute to these goals, such as investors who are incompetent or only interested in cash flow, undermine confidence and hasten the depopulation spiral.

When neighborhoods fail to attract appropriate residents, neighborhood leaders often think they need a promotion strategy to improve the neighborhood's reputation. But a promotion strategy will not work if the product—the neighborhood—is not competitive. The special challenge that legacy city neighborhoods face is that being just an adequate place to live is not enough to compete for a shrinking pool of homebuyers.

LEGACY CITY NEIGHBORHOODS NEED A SPECIAL STRATEGY FOR REVITALIZATION

In my experience working in legacy city neighborhoods throughout the Midwest, Southeast, and Northeast, I've seen many local governments and other community developers struggle to redirect declining neighborhoods. Besides the obvious market challenges, I believe there are two main reasons for this struggle.

The first is that community developers are working with tools that are designed to create housing supply instead of increasing demand in neighborhoods where there is already too much supply.

Federal housing policy has largely devolved into addressing only what policymakers living in major, high-demand cities see as the problem: scarcity of housing and high housing prices. The key tools and funding available to cities and nonprofits are the Community Development Block Grant (CDBG), the HOME Housing Investment Partnerships Program (HOME), and the Low Income Housing Tax Credit (LIHTC), all of which are income-restricted supply programs. These income constraints and the increase in supply makes sense in markets where, absent these programs, the neighborhoods would be flooded with high-income households, and where the absence of affordable housing would drive more moderate-income people out. This, however, is most certainly not the case in legacy cities. All of these federal programs are also focused on unit production, assuming that every place needs additional supply. In fact, new units in low-demand communities can draw the strongest households away from other housing, creating lower values and more vacancy.[1]

The second reason for the struggle in finding the right approach to neighborhood improvement is that planners, city officials, and neighborhood leaders tend not to see neighborhoods as competing with each other. They have been conditioned to seek only the perspectives of current residents and businesses in defining goals and strategies for improvement. This commitment to citizen participation in planning processes, while appropriate, has omitted a critical participant: the desires of new households. Without input from potential newcomers, planners and leaders may design approaches that reduce the number of deficits in the neighborhood, without creating and communicating net value that is meaningful to prospective homebuyers, who have many affordable choices of homes and neighborhoods.

A discipline called place or destination branding could transform work in legacy cities.

PLACE BRANDING: HISTORY AND DEFINITIONS

Branding is what creates the difference in our minds between a cup of coffee and Starbucks, between a room at a Holiday Inn and a room at a Hampton Inn, between a Budweiser and a Stella Artois. Product branding, therefore, differentiates a product from its competitors.

Place branding evolved as a fully integrated discipline distinct from product branding in the late 1990s. One of the earliest examples is the Australian "shrimp-on-the-Barbie" campaign for Australian tourism. Today, it is common for nations, states, and cities to adopt a brand strategy to take control of, or at least shape, their reputation with important target markets.

Place branding is not the same as marketing a home for sale or even designing a logo for a neighborhood. Place branding is an integrated approach to repositioning a place to attract demand, whether it be visitors, home buyers, business interests, or development. Place branding views the place as a product competing with others for target customers. A brand is how others see the place, rather than how those in the place see themselves. It is the place's reputation, created by the experience others have when they come into contact with the neighborhood, either by visiting and experiencing it for themselves or hearing about it from others.

---

[1]   This could be a fine strategy if the only goal is to replace substandard housing, but to avoid further weakening the market, one would have to remove the substandard housing altogether.

Place branding helps leadership develop a guiding vision for a place with the target markets necessary to its survival, and then aligns all actions and communication to support and reinforce the brand. In place branding, this vision takes the form of a brand statement or brand promise. A brand statement is king. It is arrived at through a well-researched process in which leadership prioritizes goals for demand, identifies target markets that can deliver that demand, understands what these market segments want, and compares those customer wants with what the place has to offer.

Brand statements (which are akin to a vision statement in terms of prominence in the planning hierarchy) are built around a small number of attributes of the place that meet three criteria:

- **They are important to target markets:** Low-demand neighborhoods must prioritize the assets and amenities they want to invest in. One way is to focus on what matters to the prospective households. For example, a social service agency may be seen as an asset to current residents, but if it is not a compelling attribute to potential homebuyer target markets, it will not be useful as a core brand attribute.

- **The place can deliver the attributes reliably and well:** It is not useful to build a neighborhood's reputation on an attribute that the neighborhood does not excel in. For example, good schools are often highly important to homebuyers. But improving under performing schools is a long process. In the near term, it may be better to market the neighborhood to the many childless households that might be attracted to the neighborhood for its other assets, such as an urban feel with closeness to downtown.

- **The place delivers the attributes better than competing places:** A neighborhood should build its brand around attributes that are special enough to give a target homebuyer a reason to choose that neighborhood over other similarly priced neighborhoods. In a legacy city, there may be many low-cost neighborhoods that have old houses with character, but only one that also has recreational trails or an international restaurant scene or an annual jazz festival or is next door to a university.

The attributes that meet all of these criteria become the core brand attributes around which the brand statement is created. For example, a group of five neighborhoods in Pocatello, Idaho, decided to co-brand under the name "The Neighborhoods of Historic Old Town." After many focus groups, interviews, and other market research, the Old Town neighborhoods decided their core brand attributes would be:

1. Healthy, Active Lifestyle: These neighborhoods are home to trailheads of a wonderful new Portneuf Greenway, many parks, easy access to the foothills, and are very walkable with a dense grid layout.
2. Exciting Downtown Location: One of the five neighborhoods in Old Town includes the historic downtown business district, which has many events, eclectic dining, and specialty shopping.

3. Friendly Neighbors: The local NeighborWorks network affiliate, NeighborWorks Pocatello, is organizing neighbors in each of the five neighborhoods through social and beautification activities to leverage the existing sense of community spirit.

Based on these core brand attributes, leaders crafted the following brand statement:

"For people who want a healthy, active lifestyle in a downtown location, the Neighborhoods of Historic Old Town are the gateway to a unique mix of urban vibe, outdoor recreation, and eclectic dining and shopping—all in a walkable community with friendly neighbors."[2]

Once a community has identified its core brand attributes and its brand statement, partners are trained on the brand, and all of the actions taken in the neighborhood and messages communicated about it are shaped to ensure that the neighborhood delivers on its promise.

ADAPTING PLACE BRANDING TO LEGACY CITY NEIGHBORHOODS

Place branding adds a useful and novel perspective to the typical program planning process for neighborhood improvement. First, it does not limit target markets to current residents. If goals for neighborhood health include typical market indicators such as more owner-occupant homebuyers, stronger home values, and less vacancy, target markets will include prospective homebuyers and real estate agents as well as existing residents. The place branding process will compel leaders to learn a lot about what these target markets want and who their competition is.

Second, in the course of thinking beyond the needs and interests of existing neighborhood residents, neighborhood leaders typically see their community with fresh eyes. The definition of success becomes making the place good enough to attract newcomers as well as retaining existing residents. In legacy cities, any standard less than this will fail to restore neighborhoods to a healthy market condition.

Successful place branding requires leaders to identify and strengthen those attributes of a place that meet all of the three criteria noted above. Once identified, these core attributes are worked into a brand statement that expresses who might be attracted to the neighborhood and why. Once that brand statement is created, the goal is to organize resources (programs, communications, events, incentives, projects) to build on and reinforce the promise the brand statement makes. A basic principle of place branding is that every act of promotion, communication, policy, or program must be seen not as an end in itself but as an opportunity to build the place's image and reputation.

One of the challenges in rebranding a neighborhood and identifying prospective buyers is to match the assets of the neighborhood to the many niches in the housing market that might be attracted to a neighborhood. Existing residents and planners often have a narrow view of the kinds of movers who might be interested in the neighborhood. They often think in general terms, when far more calibrated analysis is needed. For example, discussions about attracting newcomers often get bogged down in quality of schools. Yet, two-thirds of households in the United States do not have school-

---

[2]   NeighborWorks Pocatello worked with Fall Creek Consultants (with which the author of this chapter is affiliated), a neighborhood branding and market-rebuilding company based in Ithaca, New York.

aged children. More households have dogs than children in the United States. Millennials, for example, may be attracted to a particular neighborhood because of its location, housing style, or access to parks and other outdoor recreation. Empty nesters seeking urban living may want smaller homes and yards, walkable access to downtown retail and cultural events, and a neighborhood with the character and charm that was lacking in the suburbs in which they raised their children. These Millenials and empty nesters are two categories of households without children, and there are many subcategories. One leading housing market analyst lists 15 subcategories for each of these two groups.[3]

PLACE BRANDING AT WORK IN WEAK MARKET NEIGHBORHOODS

A small but growing number of legacy city neighborhoods are using a place-branding approach to neighborhood revitalization. I outline a few below.

NOBO, COLUMBUS, OHIO

One of the most common ways for community developers to use place branding is through clustered real estate development, like that in the North of Broad neighborhood in Columbus, Ohio. Homeport is the non-profit developer that managed the project and worked with existing neighborhood leaders to create the NoBo brand strategy.

NoBo, or "North of Broad," refers to an area along North 21st Street that is north of Broad Street. This area—which includes approximately 200 households along Long Street, North 20th, North 21st, and North 22nd streets—has a rich history of African American culture and music. During the 1930s through the 1950s, the neighborhood was a hub of the African American community, with many jazz clubs and African American–run businesses. The neighborhood began to decline in the 1960s with the construction of Interstate 71, which cut through the city and isolated many parts of the neighborhood. Vacant properties soon became common and many homes were converted into poor-quality rental properties. Some buildings were torn down, and fires destroyed others.

Homeport planned carefully to make sure all of the ingredients of a successful revitalization project were present, or achievable before they decided on a target area. One of the primary considerations was scale. The neighborhood that was later defined as "NoBo" is positioned in a much larger neighborhood—called "King Lincoln"—that suffered from all of the same negative impacts of disinvestment. By focusing first on a smaller area, Homeport felt it could better control and manage the redevelopment—and maintain a vibrant perception of the many exciting changes about to take place, including removal of blighted and abandoned houses as well as construction of new homes.

---

[3]   Laurie Volk and Todd Zimmerman, "American Households on (and off) the Urban-to-Rural Transect," *Journal of Urban Design* 7, no. 3 (2002): 341–352. Available at http://www.zva.cc/zva_transect.pdf

The neighborhood had declined to a point where new construction was seen as the right strategy to invigorate reinvestment. The first buyers of new homes were "urban pioneers" (people who had a high tolerance for risk and valued an urban environment) and people that were already affiliated somehow with the neighborhood. They were already interested in moving into the neighborhood, and Homeport helped them do that by building a housing product they liked, with financing they could access.[4]

The next wave of buyers were people priced out of adjacent neighborhoods, who could see high-quality development happening and felt confidence in the future of the neighborhood. As more construction could be seen on North 21st Street, Homeport received more contracts for new homes. This all happened during a very weak national market, 2009–2012.

Leadership knew that the homes would not sell unless Homeport also "sold" the neighborhood. To do that required dispelling misperceptions and focusing on the area's many attractive features. North of Broad needed to be rebranded.

The NoBo brand focuses on 1) high-quality new homes with attributes that are competitive with suburban options; 2) youthful, urban, trendy location; and 3) jazz music history in the neighborhood.

Homeport created marketing messages that played up the 1930s and 1940s jazz theme, using taglines such as "Cool digs, right downtown" and "Jazzed up homes in a grand old neighborhood." A new logo played off that same jazzy theme: a penguin in a tuxedo. This identifiable character drew attention to the neighborhood and helped give it a new persona. All marketing materials include a tagline and the logo and bright, modern colors to give a positive and exciting impression.

The brand guides the overall neighborhood revitalization strategy. In addition to housing strategies, for example, Homeport teamed up with a historic theater in the neighborhood that had a vacant storefront. Homeport established an art gallery there and now pays the utilities for the space. The gallery features local artists on a six-week rotation, and presents information on Homeport programs and homes for sale. Volunteers operate the art gallery, and local businesses and nonprofits host occasional happy hours and other events in the space.

The agency integrated its marketing and homeownership strategies through monthly strategy meetings. Homeport also worked closely with a real estate agent who held all of the North of Broad listings.

While many other city neighborhoods in Columbus saw decreases in home values, appraisals in the North of Broad neighborhood grew. In a deliberate market-building strategy, Homeport sold the first

---

[4]   The City of Columbus assisted by providing subsidy raised through a bond issue that helped bridge the difference between development cost and appraised values—with no income restrictions. A special first mortgage product was created by Huntington Bank especially for buyers of the new NoBo homes. This portfolio product allowed for a low downpayment and modified underwriting during the worst of the national credit crunch. Later, NSP funds were also used as subsidy.

homes in the $125,000 range. Gradually, sales prices moved up to the $140,000 price range. Attracting mixed-income buyers supports Homeport's desire to create long-term, sustainable neighborhoods that are not solely dependent on subsidies to grow and thrive.

Homeport has begun the same process on adjacent blocks, incorporating a rehab component into the development strategy in an effort to save the large, stately brick duplexes on North 20th and surrounding blocks.

MIDDLE MAIN, POUGHKEEPSIE, NEW YORK

In the 1800s, Poughkeepsie was known as the "Queen City of the Hudson" for its thriving shipping trade, paper mills, and breweries. Like other manufacturing cities, Poughkeepsie suffered economic decline in the late twentieth century, followed by residential disinvestment and blight. Many of the old mill buildings were demolished to make way for new development, but the area continued to struggle.

Hudson River Housing was formed in 1982 to provide shelter and services to a growing population of homeless people in Poughkeepsie. During the last decades, Hudson River Housing expanded its work to develop permanent affordable housing for people of a variety of incomes, focusing much of its efforts in the northern part of Poughkeepsie, home to many of the city's low-income and minority residents.

Hudson River Housing focused its redevelopment efforts on the Middle Main neighborhood, which includes a five-block stretch of mixed-use Main Street and surrounding residential blocks. As part of a NeighborWorks America program, the agency received a grant and technical assistance to develop a brand strategy and marketing campaign for the neighborhood. A national place-branding consultant worked with staff and the neighborhood on a brand and campaign.

Goals for the neighborhood's revitalization include cultivating a thriving retail district on Main Street, redeveloping a vacant mill building as mixed-income housing, and attracting and retaining a diverse group of neighbors committed to improving the quality of life in the neighborhood. The neighborhood's brand was built around its eclectic and quirky mix of neighbors and businesses, openness to new ideas and possibilities, and up-and-coming position as a place of opportunity.

Middle Main's brand statement is expressed in a "brand platform" format that addresses the target audience, a geographic frame of reference, the "point of difference" or competitive edge the neighborhood has, and the benefit the neighborhood offers its target audience.[5]

MIDDLE MAIN NEIGHBORHOOD BRAND PLATFORM

Target Audience: for people energized by differences and interested in making one.
Frame of Reference: Middle Main, along Poughkeepsie's historic Main Street.
Point of difference: is a close knit neighborhood celebrating diverse cultures and flavors.
Benefit: where collaboration and creativity are at your front door.

---

[5]   Hudson River Housing worked with the place-branding company Northstar, headquartered in Nashville, Tennessee.

The neighborhood also created a logo, including the tagline "just a little off center" to recognize both its geographic location (a block off the main downtown business district) and its quirky eclecticism.

Strategies to promote the brand included a mix of promotional, community building, economic development, and physical improvement strategies, as one might expect with any revitalization plan. However, Middle Main's strategies are all inspired by and operate within the framework of the brand statement. This coordination works to leverage the power of each strategy, but the most important difference is that all strategies are oriented to rebuilding the market and cultivating demand.

Staff maintains an active Facebook page for the neighborhood and fills it with posts that reinforce the brand elements. A "Made in Middle Main" campaign signs up neighborhood businesses to be active partners in promoting the brand. In turn, the businesses are heavily marketed on Facebook and through other channels. Hudson River Housing supports and promotes neighborhood events celebrating cultural history (such as a Dia de la Muerta cookie-decorating event at a local bakery) in partnership with local businesses, and businesses have access to business and leadership education.

EARLY RESULTS INCLUDE:

- Hudson River Housing trained 15 community leaders through its first Leadership Training Program, taught entirely in Spanish. Several leaders subsequently launched new initiatives in the neighborhood, including a 24/7 Spanish-language radio station with nine live programs; a bi-weekly "Intercambio" language exchange; and a Multicultural Council hosting monthly movie nights, special events, and planning for a Multicultural Festival this summer.
- The Dia de la Muerta 2014 festival brought 400 people to the neighborhood (up from 40 in its first year, 2011), some coming from more than 20 miles away.
- Seventeen businesses participate in the Made in Middle Main campaign. A series of workshops (pizza making, flan making) is being launched to highlight them.
- A 2014 inventory of businesses showed that vacant storefronts decreased by 26 percent in the previous year.
- A resident survey showed 74 percent of residents are satisfied with the community, and 68 percent would recommend it to others.
- There has been an uptick in inquiries regarding properties for redevelopment, with six private investors/developers reaching out for information or partnership possibilities in a recent six-month period.

The mill building is in the process of being developed; Hudson River Housing hopes the place branding and business development work will be a major factor in building greater residential demand (from a variety of income groups) for both existing homes and those in the mill building. Meanwhile, the organization is turning current residents into enthusiastic brand ambassadors.

LAYTON BOULEVARD WEST, MILWAUKEE, WISCONSIN

The Layton Boulevard West neighborhoods—Silver City, Burnham Park, and Layton Park—are clustered on the southern border of the Menomonee Valley, a 300-acre brownfield redevelopment area that runs through the center of Milwaukee, Wisconsin.

In the late 1800s, the Valley employed thousands of workers in industrial jobs, and they established the first residential neighborhoods west of downtown. But by the late 1900s, as manufacturing practices changed, the Valley became a blighted area with abandoned, contaminated land and vacant industrial buildings. Bridges into the Valley were demolished, and businesses left. The neighborhoods adjacent to the Valley declined along with it, losing jobs and population.

In 1998, city leaders joined forces to create a redevelopment plan for the Valley, and in the past 10 years, 39 companies have moved in and 5,200 jobs have been created. The contamination of the site has been mitigated and the Valley now enjoys 45 acres of native plants, seven miles of trails, and a nationally recognized storm water treatment system. The Valley is the location of the Milwaukee Brewers' stadium, and 10 million people visit the Valley for recreation and entertainment each year.

Meanwhile, the nonprofit Layton Boulevard West Neighbors (LBWN) has been working on revitalizing the three neighborhoods it serves through a market-building strategy that seeks to rebrand the area, build confidence in the future among internal and external stakeholders, update housing stock and attract owner-occupant homebuyers.

In the mid-2000s, LBWN developed a neighborhood marketing plan[6] that focused on the goal of reversing the trend of home sales to absentee investors. The plan identified target markets for new homebuyers by examining recent buyers, who represented young, multicultural households seeking high-quality homes in a friendly, urban location. One of the first strategies was to produce a video with testimonials by these recent buyers talking about why they chose the neighborhood. Talking points included high-quality homes with character; friendly, diverse neighbors; access to recreational opportunities in the Valley; and the international flavor of retail businesses.

LBWN promotes these key assets through an array of events such as tours of homes for sale, historic home tours, and the Silver City International Food and Art Walk; a website; a newsletter; partnerships with Realtors; and more videos and related marketing materials.

The rebranding of the Layton Boulevard West neighborhoods has had a great impact on the area's image and on home sales.

---

[6]   With Fall Creek Consultants in Ithaca, New York.

- Since 1995, LBWN has connected neighbors with resources to renovate over 1,000 homes, resulting in $7.2 million in neighborhood investment.
- Since 2006, LBWN has facilitated 71 home sales, resulting in $6.2 million in neighborhood investment.
- Since 2012, LBWN has conducted two Tour of Homes events each year to attract new homebuyers to the neighborhood. As part of the tours, LBWN administers pre- and post-event surveys to gauge perceptions of the neighborhood. In aggregate, responses show a pre-tour "positive perception" of 78 percent and post-tour positive perception of 87 percent.
- While this 9 percent increase is significant, even more significant is that prior to the summer 2013 tour, the normal starting point on the pre-tour survey would range from 50–60 percent. Because of the other branding work LBWN did leading up to summer 2013, the organization believes that more recent home tour attendees start with a much higher positive perception of the neighborhood, which increases even more with the tour.

GENEVA, NEW YORK

The small city of Geneva (population 13,199) is located in western New York state's Finger Lakes region. Despite its location at the top of the beautiful 38-mile Seneca Lake, and its status as the home to William Smith and Hobart Colleges, the city in 2008 was declining by a number of measures. Population was declining, poverty was concentrating, owner-occupancy and property values were down, and city leadership felt it was not getting the kind of results it sought for investment of money and staff resources.

As the largest town in a rural area, Geneva attracted a disproportionate share of social services and very low-income households. Its reputation in the region was increasingly associated with urban problems that drive buyers with choices away. Residents of all incomes felt overwhelmed and unable to control their environments.

The City engaged a planning firm that specializes in residential market-building strategies,[7] which advised them to organize the residential blocks into neighborhoods, name them in dialogue with residents, and begin investing in a number of strategies to build social connections and leadership within the newly defined neighborhoods. This leadership was incentivized with small grants and staff support to raise standards of curb appeal and improve quality of life in other ways that were meaningful to them.

BRAND ESSENCE (DNA, HEART AND SOUL)

Beautiful: Perhaps the most inarguable part of the brand, the beauty of the area speaks for itself. It applies to the natural beauty as well as the aesthetic appeal of the built environment.

Historical: Geneva's architecture has remained intact amid the urban renewal era, adding greatly to the beauty of Geneva. This architectural wonder is situated in a part of the country rich with unique stories to be told.

---

[7]   czb LLC, headquartered in Alexandria, Virginia.

Uniquely urban: A cross between a small town and a big city, Geneva's downtown has a palpable vibrancy, where there is always something to do. This element also speaks to the diversity—of the population, backgrounds, perspectives—all of these bring something different and unique to Geneva. Residents and visitors find a wide—and growing—selection of restaurants and a vibrant college community.

Meanwhile, the City examined and reorganized all City services to build confidence in the future of the city and its neighborhoods; both with existing residents and businesses, and with potential ones. Services were analyzed to focus on how traditional service delivery platforms aligned with neighbor expectations, and amended where appropriate. The City reorganized its community development programming and rebranded the vehicle for delivery as the Office of Neighborhood Initiatives. Its chief product, the Geneva Neighborhood Resource Center, was relocated to a downtown storefront, and serves today as a hub for neighborhood support activities.

The City very consciously decided not to add any new supply of housing units because of the weak demand for its existing supply. Instead, it opted to encourage reinvestment by existing residents, hoping to update the existing stock and set it on a path to growing value and greater appeal to replacement buyers as it turned over. Among other strategies, GNRC offers free architectural design services to any resident of the city, regardless of income. Staff works to source good contractors and good materials for those contractors. The city is too small to receive very much HUD funding. It uses the CDBG and HOME grants it has, combined with general revenue and foundation grants, to focus heavily on building curb appeal and social connections.

During the implementation of the neighborhoods strategy, the City contracted with the Ad Council of Rochester, New York, to create a brand strategy, which dovetails nicely with the market-driven neighborhood strategy. The core elements of the brand are "beautiful, historical and uniquely urban," described above as the "brand essence."

The city created a new logo, and each neighborhood has been developing its own logo, with matching entryway signage and street sign toppers.

The city heavily integrated brand elements and neighborhood strategic planning efforts into the annual budget and operational planning exercises. At the onset of each investment strategy round, City departments and any other organization seeking City funds are provided with copies of the brand elements, and charged with tying any request for discretionary spending to an element of the brand. Investment proposals for programs, services, or facilities are ranked according to their alignment with branding and neighborhood strategy.

This intense focus on brand and market-based strategy is beginning to pay off. The City recently conducted an update to its block-level analysis of housing conditions. In areas where neighbors engaged in strategic planning and branding efforts, housing conditions are showing marked improvement. Nine of the City's 11 originally identified neighborhoods have active neighborhood associations, all of which have engaged in strategic planning and place-based branding and marketing.

In 2014, the City began an aggressive program of marketing the neighborhoods—contracting with nearby Neighborworks Rochester to engage a communications staffer in promoting the assets of each neighborhood through traditional and social media. The City also engaged directly with area Realtors, providing neighborhood "personality profiles" and recruitment toolkits in order to present prospective residents with an array of positive choices and neighborhood-crafted messaging designed to highlight the most marketable aspects of each place.

IMPLICATIONS FOR PRACTITIONERS AND POLICYMAKERS

A place-branding approach to rebuilding demand in weak neighborhood housing markets has important implications for practitioners and policymakers.

For many practitioners, the special challenges of place branding will require new ways of thinking and acting. These include:

1. Understanding that the proper goal in many legacy city neighborhoods is rebuilding neighborhood real estate markets to a sustainable point of demand and supply. Without this goal, actions often do not help the neighborhood compete for a dwindling supply of homebuyers, good landlords, and renters.
2. Understanding that practitioners must view the neighborhood brand as a strategic framework for all other actions, rather than as incidental or secondary to core business.
3. Understanding that neighborhood revitalization is different from providing affordable housing, and that neighborhood branding strategies should focus on reaching new market segments, without regard to income limits.
4. Understanding that practitioners must help current residents, staff, board members, and funders transform fears of gentrification (which are largely irrational in weak markets) into an informed, thoughtful course of action that translates goals for the neighborhood into concrete target markets and strategies to recruit homebuyers, landlords, and renters.
5. Ensuring that neighborhood leaders, real estate agents, and others concerned with neighborhood recovery understand the local market and its competitors, and remain objective about the extent to which the neighborhood is succeeding or failing to attract target markets.
6. Understanding that neighborhood revitalization strategies must balance the interests of current residents with the preferences of those being wooed to the neighborhood. Planners are very good at the former, but need more skills in reading the interests of the potential newcomers.

7. Understanding that someone is needed to train, influence, and coordinate a large number of stakeholders who influence the neighborhood's brand, but who are independent of the lead organization.

8. Creating organizational and neighborhood leadership that works to maintain a culture in which everyone is responsible for applying the brand in communications, program design, activities, events, policy and behavior, not just the "brand manager."

Although these may seem like big changes, the place-branding industry[8] has strategies and best practices developed to work with municipal and national clients that can help.

Policymakers have their own set of perspectives and practices that could be better aligned to produce market change through place branding:

1. For funders, gentrification in middle neighborhoods in legacy cities should not be the primary concern: continued decline is the bigger worry.

2. Funding should be available for demand strategies, not just for building supply. Nowhere is this more critical than at HUD because HOME, CDBG, and LIHTC (and previously NSP) are the sources of funding on which so many practitioners rely. HUD needs an ability to distinguish weak and hot markets, and adjust expectations and funding accordingly.

3. Because they are so much more attuned to regional and local markets, states should invest in place-branding strategies, particularly in ways that align with economic development strategies.

4. Where lack of demand by homebuyers is a critical factor in decline and vacancy, funding should allow for housing products and incentives without regard to income limits (that is, not just for those earning below 80 percent of area median income).

5. New partnerships should be forged between community developers (especially those focused on housing) and organizations that are historically more market savvy and demand-oriented—such as local tourism bureaus, some real estate boards, chambers of commerce, and the more entrepreneurial economic development departments. The natural instincts of these types of organizations could lend perspective and capacity to nonprofits and housing departments trying to adapt.

6. Training for practitioners should more effectively build capacity to implement demand strategies, including place branding. This includes helping practitioners cultivate and maintain detailed, timely knowledge of local housing markets that will help them adjust strategies to compete effectively.[9]

---

[8] Entities in the industry of place or destination branding include for-profit brand development agencies; convention and visitor bureaus, which are sometimes generically called "destination management organizations" or DMOs; and two national trade associations, one for the for-profits—the Association of Destination Management Executives or ADME—and one for the nonprofits—Destination Marketing Association International or DMAI. The industry seems to be more weighted to tourism than other goals.

[9] For example, with my colleague Karen Beck Pooley of czb LLC, I have been examining shares of sales to owner-occupants and to investors against price range and number of bedrooms and baths. I am finding that homes priced below $50,000 and homes with only one bathroom are very difficult to sell to an owner-occupant buyer. Neighborhoods with a big share of these homes must develop strategies to update them physically and build values to get mortgage-qualified owner-occupants to even look at them. But most community development organizations lack this kind of market data.

NEIGHBORWORKS AMERICA'S NEIGHBORHOOD MARKETING PROGRAM

Both Homeport and Hudson River Housing are graduates of NeighborWorks America's Neighborhood Marketing Program, the only national example of an effort to build the capacity of community development organizations to promote place branding in neighborhoods. NeighborWorks America launched its Neighborhood Marketing Program in 2012 to partner with communities to create strong neighborhood brands and rebuild market demand. Through the first two rounds of the program, NeighborWorks supported 33 of its network member organizations across the country in developing neighborhood brands and implementing a range of creative strategies aimed at bolstering neighborhood strengths, increasing pride and confidence, and attracting and retaining residents, businesses, and investment.

Through a competitive proposal process, grant winners receive the services of a branding and marketing consultant[10] to help articulate goals, research the market, and develop a brand statement and strategies for cultivating the brand. Where needed, NeighborWorks provides the services of a graphic designer to create a logo for the neighborhood. A small cash grant is awarded to seed implementation of the strategies, and grantees share challenges and successes through peer exchanges and other training. Funding for the program has come from Wells Fargo Housing Foundation, Citi, and Capital One.

The program is administered by NeighborWorks America's Community Stabilization Initiative, a department initially created in response to the foreclosure crisis to assist member organizations that were working to stabilize neighborhoods hit hard by foreclosure. Most often, the organizations were redeveloping foreclosed property as subgrantees to participating jurisdictions in the federal NSP program. Like many NSP grantees, these organizations often faced challenges selling redeveloped homes because of a weak market and a scarcity of qualified buyers. The other clear impediment was the image of the neighborhoods in which homes were located, and their inability to compete against places with better-known amenities and positive reputations.

From this experience, NeighborWorks developed the Neighborhood Marketing Program as a hybrid marketing/revitalization strategy framework that helps nonprofits reposition neighborhoods and rebuild healthy real estate markets that can attract the replacement households they need to grow and prosper. Key elements from this approach include:

- **An Assessment of Neighborhood "Readiness:"** Neighborhoods have varying levels of "readiness" to undertake a neighborhood marketing campaign—especially a campaign focused on attracting new homebuyers. In selecting participants for the program, NeighborWorks America seeks to identify neighborhoods where community stabilization efforts have resulted in tangible strengths. That's not to say that everything needs to be perfect. But there should be signs of growing optimism and confidence in the future of the

---

[10] NeighborWorks America contracts with a number of consultants who have experience with branding or with weak market neighborhood revitalization, or both. One of the growing accomplishments of the program is the development of a pool of contractors that understands both disciplines and can combine them in hybrid branding/revitalization plans.

neighborhood (e.g., residents speak favorably of the neighborhood, the housing market has stabilized, and efforts to address blight or crime are gaining ground).

- **Resident and Stakeholder Engagement:** Place brands need to be owned at the grassroots level. No single organization or entity can (or should) control the brand. In order to be sustainable, residents and other stakeholders need to embrace the brand and adopt it as their own. The Neighborhood Marketing Program includes steps to engage residents, business owners, nonprofits, real estate agents, media, anchor institutions, and other community stakeholders in the process of defining the new brand and implementing the resulting marketing campaign.

- **Internal vs. External Marketing Strategies:** Related to the points above, the Neighborhood Marketing Program encourages participants to undertake marketing strategies directed at both internal and external audiences. Internal marketing is aimed at creating pride among existing residents and inviting their participation in community-building activities. This serves to create confidence, build excitement and reinforce the strengths that underlie the new brand. As a result, internal marketing creates the preconditions necessary to begin to market the neighborhood to external audiences (e.g. new homeowners).

- **Building on Strengths:** Place branding is inherently asset based; the goal is to identify, enhance and promote the special qualities that make these neighborhoods unique. This is different from many revitalization planning efforts that begin with a problem statement and offer strategies to address deficiencies. The asset-based orientation that is at the core of the Neighborhood Marketing Program approach serves to energize residents and stakeholders who might not get involved in traditional "crime and grime" efforts. Instead of responding to problems, residents and stakeholders are encouraged to participate in fun activities that create a sense of pride and buzz for the neighborhood.

- **Taking Risks:** The work of place branding is substantially different from many of the Neighborhood Marketing Program participants' core business of real estate development. Place branding requires a holistic view of the neighborhood's place in the regional marketplace, brand attributes, and target markets. Marketing campaigns aimed at attracting homeowners, businesses, and investment requires testing new ideas and exploring creative ways to make the neighborhood stand out amid the competition. Taking a risk on an edgy marketing tactic (e.g., the North of Broad penguin or the Middle Main "little off center" tagline) can pay dividends. The Neighborhood Marketing Program participants are also equipped with an evaluation framework to assess what works (and what does not) so they can continue to innovate and adapt to ensure that the marketing messages are having the desired effect.

NeighborWorks organizations that are participating in the Neighborhood Marketing Program have reported gains in two main areas. First, the program has fundamentally reshaped the way many of the participants approach their community stabilization efforts. Realizing that the new brands need to be reinforced by positive conditions on the ground, the participants are undertaking creative strategies to bolster neighborhood strengths. This asset-based approach has led to renewed enthusiasm and engagement among residents and has leveraged additional partners and funding to support the neighborhood marketing and community stabilization efforts.

Second, the participants have made tangible gains in fostering neighborhood pride and attracting attention from their key target markets, including external audiences. This has been accomplished through a wide range of marketing tools and strategies, including neighborhood websites, newsletters, videos, events, and more. Although the campaigns are still in the initial stages, several organizations have also credited the program with enhancing their ability to sell homes in their target neighborhoods.

CONCLUSION

For a low-demand neighborhood to stand any chance in catching the eye of real estate agents and homebuyers in a highly competitive marketplace, it is essential that everyone is playing from the same sheet of music. Everything the neighborhood does and says, how others talk about it and make policy about it, and how it looks and feels to current and prospective residents, must reinforce the same compelling story, the same values, and the same personality. This story must be one that conveys the neighborhood's unique and positive attributes to households who have choices among many neighborhoods, and the revitalization strategy must prioritize the cultivation of those attributes. Place branding offers a method and perspective that can help community developers and neighborhood residents determine what that story is and to organize a broad range of stakeholders and interventions to deliver it.

Marcia Nedland is the principal of Fall Creek Consultants, a national firm delivering training and technical assistance to nonprofits, government, national intermediaries, funders, and other policymakers on neighborhood revitalization and stabilization in weak markets. Nedland specializes in marketing neighborhoods and building demand from strong homebuyers and renters for homes in those neighborhoods. Nedland is an award-winning trainer at the national NeighborWorks Training Institute on topics related to neighborhood stabilization, marketing, and sales.

VIII. THE HEALTHY NEIGHBORHOODS PROGRAM: A MIDDLE NEIGHBORHOODS IMPROVEMENT STRATEGY

By Mark Sissman, Healthy Neighborhoods, Inc.
and Darlene Russell, Greater Milwaukee Foundation

As this volume has shown, relatively few well-organized programs are aimed at strengthening middle neighborhoods. Two exceptions are the Healthy Neighborhoods programs in Baltimore and Milwaukee,[1] which are both are asset-based and market-driven programs. They are asset-based because their basic premise is that the neighborhoods they target have many assets and reasons to live there, which residents, real estate agents, and potential newcomers often overlook. The programs generally choose neighborhoods that have few vacant properties and a strong community organization, yet a housing market that is persistently stagnant. The program is market-driven because it understands that its target neighborhoods exist in a market (neighborhoods compete with one another for residents and investment), and the goal of the program is to strengthen their competitive position in the city or regional market.

In many respects, Healthy Neighborhoods is a twenty-first century version of the Neighborhood Housing Services (NHS) organization begun in Pittsburgh in 1968, and promulgated by NeighborWorks America. Like NHS, Healthy Neighborhoods targets middle neighborhoods and combines efforts of neighborhood residents, lenders, city government, and the nonprofit sector to prevent abandonment, increase investment (particularly in homeownership) and stabilize or increase property values. All this is done in an effort to protect and expand homeownership equity. However, unlike the NeighborWorks model, there are not income restrictions on who can participate in the program.

THE KEY ELEMENTS OF THE HEALTHY NEIGHBORHOODS MODEL

The programs in Baltimore and Milwaukee seek to increase homeownership in their target neighborhoods by marketing (with incentives) the neighborhoods to existing residents and prospective buyers. The goal is to improve these neighborhoods and to make it more likely that homeowners will be able to build equity through increased home values.

---

[1]   The name "healthy neighborhoods" does not describe a health initiative in the neighborhoods, but rather an approach to keep the middle neighborhoods strong and vibrant, hence, "healthy."

Operationally, the programs follow similar principles. These are:

1. **Improve the neighborhood by working from the strongest areas outward.** This approach targets neighborhood improvement by building on assets rather than fixing the biggest problems. This principle may appear to be counterintuitive, but building from the strongest areas spreads market strength and avoids the common problem of having investments made in weak areas chewed up by decline, and uses scarce financial resources wisely. This strategy gains momentum from success that can be reinvested, improvement-by-improvement, until it affects the entire neighborhood. For example, if a quality school is an asset for a particular neighborhood, then efforts should focus on building additional support in the community for that school. This could mean working with the school principal and staff to offer additional recognition and access to school facilities or afterschool activities. Helping current and prospective parents connect with the school as a resource is one approach to neighborhood improvement. It can also mean connecting with real estate agents so they know that the schools will be an important asset in marketing homes in the neighborhood.

2. **Support residents in working together to establish and enhance individual neighborhood identities by marketing strengths.** This is often accomplished by direct neighbor-to-neighbor contact, in which residents focus on what they like about their neighborhood, and not on its liabilities. As a starting point, everyone should know the name of their neighborhood and be able to articulate the key reasons for living there. There should be general agreement about what is important and why most people choose to live there. Knowing neighborhood history helps to build this solidarity, as do programs such as walking tours, community newsletters published by residents, and other similar efforts. This positive approach can be challenging because neighborhood residents are typically organized to confront problems and their sources. Helping resident associations adopt positive messaging while still confronting the sources of neighborhood problems requires ongoing coaching and technical help. Residents must find the right balance between promoting the neighborhood as a good place to live, while demanding solutions to problems from city government when warranted.

3. **Help residents become spokespeople and "sales agents" for the area.** Healthy Neighborhoods programs help organize active residents to speak articulately about their neighborhoods and actively promote its virtues to friends, relatives, and coworkers. Baltimore uses the terms "neighborhood ambassadors" or "'I Love City Life' ambassadors" for its program of city residents who are actively involved in the community and volunteer at neighborhood events and other opportunities. The positive messages about the neighborhoods are also conveyed through active, well-maintained websites, given that large numbers of homebuyers use the web to scout out homes and neighborhoods. Of course, neighborhood "sales agents" must work with the real estate agents who sell homes in the neighborhoods to ensure they have up-to-date information on the assets in the neighborhoods and the positive activities underway.

4. **Help people of all income levels invest in their properties by offering economic incentives to get financing for home improvements.** To encourage people to invest in their properties, Baltimore's Healthy Neighborhoods program has organized with a group of lenders in a loan program to provide home improvement loans and home mortgages at slightly below-market prices, which residents can access in an expedited manner. All the loans require some home renovation, particularly on home exteriors. Healthy Neighborhoods encourages homeowners to make external, visible improvements because these changes can become contagious in a positive way, with homeowners following suit once they see their neighbors making improvements. Loans can exceed the after-rehabbed value of the home.

5. **Market the neighborhood and its assets to people who may want to move in—and knowing the market segments that are likely to move into the neighborhood.** A key starting point is simply to market the neighborhoods to people with similar income levels and to be strategic in reaching out to those who would find the neighborhoods attractive as a place to live and invest. The Internet is the most important means of communication.

6. **Tackle crime aggressively.** People do not choose to live in unsafe neighborhoods.

7. **Clean up physical problems in the neighborhood. Vacant homes, uncut lawns, abandoned cars, and vacant and littered lots must be tackled to improve the look of the neighborhood.** Philadelphia offers as a model the vacant land treatment program created by New Kensington CDC, along with the Pennsylvania Horticultural Society, which is a bottoms-up approach to controlling abandoned land.

8. **Help residents be directly involved in and take personal responsibility for improving their blocks through small, inexpensive improvement projects.** Not only do greening, improved lighting, and other efforts help to beautify a neighborhood and improve home values, but the process of making the improvements also helps to create a community fabric. Contrary to conventional beliefs about neighborhood revitalization, an effective strategy is to go to the strongest block in an area and support a park or school, rather than just focusing on a group of kids causing trouble on a corner. Rather than merely focusing on solving the toughest, most expensive physical problems, the efforts should build on the existing strengths of these areas—leveraging them to make them even stronger and more self-sustaining. In addition to supporting residents' investments in their own properties and acting as agents for their neighborhood, the Healthy Neighborhoods goal is to help residents to take action that helps them to have a sense of ownership of and connection to where they live.

9. **Build community spirit through picnics, block parties, and other festive events.** These activities make it fun to live in the neighborhood and build stronger bridges among different groups (young and old, schools and community, etc.). Living in a good neighborhood is about people enjoying living together, not about spending time

complaining about problems. Events that celebrate the quality of life that people have chosen helps to build community spirit. Neighborhood greening and "farming" activities are also important marketing activities.

10. **Tailor approaches to suit particular neighborhood conditions and see to it that the different assets of the neighborhood fit together and reinforce one another.** This may lead to different strategies for different places—a focus on "aging in place" for neighborhoods with large numbers of seniors, a school-focused strategy to increase resident involvement in school improvement efforts, and similar targeted approaches.

11. **Measure results as a means to provide feedback to resident leaders and their partners on progress or lack of it.** Although stories about actions that improve neighborhoods are of value, hard data matter more. The Healthy Neighborhoods programs track changes in property values through sales price changes, days on market, the number of rehabilitation permits issued, changes in the number of vacant properties—all data that is locally available and relatively easy to collect and report on.

Several critical elements underlie each of these principles:

- Residents, merchants, property owners, and neighborhood institutions must take responsibility for improving their neighborhood.
- Concessionary rate and non-income-restricted mortgages are a critical incentive for improvement and investment, given that neighborhoods compete for homebuyers.
- Government is supportive of, but does not lead, the process. Government identification with neighborhood improvement efforts can have the unintended consequence of damaging neighborhood confidence by sending the message that the neighborhood is bad enough to need government support. Government's role is to make the streets safe, invest in infrastructure as needed, pick up trash and keep the neighborhood clean, and improve schools. In addition to providing these city services, Baltimore City government provides local funds without income restrictions on the users to stimulate homeownership and investment in the neighborhoods. Using income-restricted funds complicates the simple message that these are neighborhoods where anyone can and will buy a home. It instead suggests that the only buyers are low- and moderate-income households who are moving in because they are receiving federal support.
- Execution of the plan in each neighborhood will, and should, vary. The approaches are by no means "neighborhood improvement by formula," but rather, approaches that seek to unleash invention and creativity in neighborhoods. Successful execution requires significant volunteer time and energy and neighborhood leadership.
- Many forces will work against the improvement of these areas. Although these neighborhoods may seem "good enough" to some, hard work is needed to ensure they are on a path to becoming improved places to live and invest.
- The neighborhoods must be carefully selected. They must be large enough that their improvement can spread to bordering areas, yet the strategies targeted enough that

change is visible in a year or two. Residents and outsiders alike must develop a growing confidence that the neighborhood is on the road to improvement.

- A nonprofit organization should serve as an intermediary between neighborhood leadership, city government, the school board, lenders, and other partners. In Baltimore, this nonprofit is Healthy Neighborhoods, Inc., which was incubated by the Baltimore Community Foundation and then spun off. In Milwaukee, the nonprofit is the Greater Milwaukee Foundation.

THE EXPERIENCE IN BALTIMORE

The Healthy Neighborhoods program was begun in 2004 as a pilot program of the Baltimore Community Foundation (BCF) with the single goal of strengthening middle neighborhoods in a city that had been losing population since the end of World War II. BCF raised the initial funds for the program and recruited a strong board, which consisted of executive leadership from three banks, foundations, and other civic leaders. The board hired a seasoned president with substantial knowledge of Baltimore neighborhoods and housing finance, and a deputy who had been leading a middle neighborhood program in Baltimore.

During the program's 10-year history, it has worked with 14 neighborhood groups to improve 41 neighborhoods, with private and public capital exceeding $150 million in investments in these neighborhoods. Healthy Neighborhoods chose neighborhoods through a "request for proposal" competitive process. Neighborhoods must have met the definition of a middle neighborhood, and neighborhood groups were selected on the basis of neighborhood capacity and willingness to participate in an approach that builds on assets and property. Each neighborhood receives $40,000 annually for program staffing, and each neighborhood is also eligible to receive funds to take on community improvement projects.

The neighborhoods targeted their efforts to the strongest blocks in the neighborhood, following the "build from strength" principle. The program leaders also understood that private financing could provide attractive terms and incentives without income or price restraints. Healthy Neighborhoods organized a pool of loans from 10 lenders totaling $40 million. These loans were special in two ways. First, the loans could be up to 120 percent of post-rehab appraised value. Three local foundations and the Maryland Housing Fund made these loans possible by guaranteeing the top 10 percent of losses to the lenders. Second, loans were made to qualified buyers at a percentage point below-market rates as an incentive to draw buyers into the neighborhoods. No mortgage insurance premium was charged to the borrowers. A second $30.5 million loan pool was organized when all the funds from the first were committed. In all, these loan pools have originated 352 loans totaling $53.6 million. Defaults have cost the program 2.5 percent of capital. In addition to mortgage loans, the program provides matching grants of up to $10,000 to homeowners who are willing to improve their homes. This program component has led to 179 rehabbed homes, with $1.6 million allocated in matching grants.

Baltimore City has been supportive of the HNI program, providing city funds for operations and matching grants. These funds are local funds, not federal funds—because federal funds, such as

Community Development Block Grants or HOME funds—carry restrictions on the borrowers' incomes. The programs provide ongoing training and mentoring for nonprofit staff and the board on the specifics of the Healthy Neighborhoods model. This training includes content on marketing and organizing, loan products, advice on development projects, public policy, and block projects to help neighbors feel more positive about their neighborhoods. Forty-one neighborhoods have participated in the program, supported by 12 neighborhood (sometimes CDC) organizations. The program is modest to operate compared with most community development programs. The annual program costs in 2015 were $1.3 million.

The Baltimore program was also a successful applicant for Neighborhood Stabilization Funds from the federal government. The city used these funds to work with developers to successfully renovate and sell 205 formerly vacant or foreclosed housing units in the targeted neighborhoods. Although the NSP component is not a fundamental part of the Healthy Neighborhoods model, its use in Baltimore's targeted neighborhoods has had a significant impact on home values and neighborhood conditions.

The program monitors its own progress quarterly, measuring its success through changes in sales prices of homes, rehab permits issued, and days on market of homes (to measure market strength) as well as other real estate measures. Through 2008, results were positive, with neighborhood values keeping up with or exceeding the city's trend lines. The recession did harm the city and those neighborhoods particularly where development drove up values artificially or there was predatory lending. However, home values are again increasing in these neighborhoods.

The program is successfully improving these neighborhoods and their competitiveness, without gentrification. The median income in the middle neighborhoods in Baltimore has risen, on average, slightly above that of the city overall. The three neighborhoods that experienced a sharp rise in median income are near Johns Hopkins University and adjacent to neighborhoods with very strong markets. Even in these neighborhoods, what is occurring is not gentrification, but a slow replacement of owners who have aged in place with newcomers who have higher incomes. However, the essential character of the neighborhoods has not been disrupted.

Table 1. Median Household Income in Select Neighborhoods

Neighborhood	Median Household Income		
	2000	2006–2010	% Change
Highlandtown	$28,180	$59,210	110.1%
Lauraville	$44,870	$56,061	24.9%
Medfield/Hampden/Woodberry/Remington	$ 22,426	$49,204	119.4%
Patterson Park Northeast	$27,663	$48,889	76.7%
Belair-Edison	$36,512	$42,921	17.6%
Edmondson Village	$33,032	$40,122	21.5%
Orangeville/East Highlandtown	$ 28,003	$38,988	39.2%
Howard Park/West Arlington	$37,099	$38,218	3.0%
Greater Mondawmin	$27,105	$37,034	36.6%
Forest Park/Walbrook	$28,766	$36,859	28.1%
Glen-Falstaff	$32,508	$35,785	10.1%
Midtown	$22,426	$35,394	57.8%
The Waverlies	$32,492	$34,787	7.1%
Downtown/Seton Hill	$21,723	$33,874	55.9%
Brooklyn/Curtis Bay/Hawkins Point	$26,358	$32,888	24.8%
Midway/Coldstream	$27,712	$32,544	17.4%
Greater Charles Village/Barclay	$21,068	$31,659	50.3%
Pimlico/Arlington/Hilltop	$26,012	$28,815	10.8%
Greater Rosemont	$24,682	$28,810	16.7%
Penn North/Reservoir Hill	$22,287	$27,874	25.1%
Upton/Druid Heights	$14,487	$13,811	-4.7%
Average of Healthy Neighborhoods	$27,877	$37,321	33.9%
Baltimore City	$30,078	$39,386	30.9%

REVITALIZING MILWAUKEE'S MIDDLE NEIGHBORHOODS

Milwaukee has been working to improve middle neighborhoods for over a decade. In 2006, the Greater Milwaukee Foundation launched the Healthy Neighborhoods Initiative, a public-private partnership with the city of Milwaukee. The program has operated in 18 neighborhoods in Milwaukee and two neighborhoods in Waukesha, a nearby suburb. The program targets neighborhoods in the middle—those generally stable, affordable places that are neither high-demand neighborhoods promoted by real estate agents nor the distressed neighborhoods receiving public policy attention. They are, nonetheless, neighborhoods important to the future well-being of the city.

HEALTHY NEIGHBORHOODS' APPROACH

Milwaukee Healthy Neighborhoods program has three main goals:

- Restore market confidence in selected neighborhoods through investment, reinvestment, and strategic physical improvements.
- Help neighborhood residents build wealth, primarily by restoring homeowner equity and market appreciation.
- Strengthen and enhance the social fabric of neighborhoods by supporting neighborhood organizations and community-building activities.

The foundation identifies and works with designated neighborhood lead organizations that engage residents and manage the program on the ground. They helped residents improve more than 1,300 properties, representing more than $23 million in neighborhood reinvestment. The foundation also collaborates with a broad array of public and nonprofit organizations that agree to work together to make the program successful. Neighborhood lead organizations must be committed to Healthy Neighborhoods values, have dedicated staff, systems for finance and administration, and sources of funding other than the foundation.

Resident engagement is a key driver of success for the program. Since its inception, more than 900 block activities and community events have engaged more than 70,000 residents. More residents are choosing to invest in their homes because the program is increasing their confidence that their neighborhood is improving. This was evident in 2015 when 59 homeowners in the Silver City, Burnham Park, and Layton Park neighborhoods participated in the Most Improved Home Contest. The residents invested more than $232,800 in curb appeal enhancements that boost neighborhood appearance, pride, and confidence.

THE FOUNDATION'S ROLE IN HEALTHY NEIGHBORHOODS

The Healthy Neighborhoods program developed in a fairly organic way in Milwaukee. Initially, neighborhood lead organization conducted only a cursory assessment to identify suitable neighborhoods. Over time, the foundation brought more discipline and analysis to select the target neighborhoods. In 2012, the foundation and other stakeholders engaged The Reinvestment Fund to conduct a market value analysis for Milwaukee, a tool described in the third essay in this volume. As the foundation prepared to redesign the program in 2014, it used this tool to confirm its designated neighborhoods and identify new middle market neighborhoods. During this process, the foundation learned the neighborhoods it designated as "Healthy Neighborhoods" were indeed middle neighborhoods with the exception of two, which were healthy enough that they graduated from the program.

The foundation's commitment to middle neighborhoods is evident in the human and financial capital it has contributed to the program. A program officer provides key leadership, identifying training needs and appropriate training resources for the lead agencies. Some of this training has touched on topics such as understanding the Healthy Neighborhoods approach, branding and marketing, the importance of working with real estate agents and using LinkedIn, just to name a few.

Since the program's inception, the foundation has coordinated monthly meetings among the neighborhood lead agencies. These meetings create synergy, build trust and understanding, and create a learning community. Neighborhood coordinators come prepared to share resources and information about upcoming projects, and to collaborate on projects across neighborhoods. In addition, the program officer identifies and acquires financial resources, whether from the foundation's unrestricted funds or by partnering with other philanthropic entities. An example of unrestricted funds is the foundation's Model Block Project. The project provides grants to make the neighborhood more physically attractive to newcomers and to strengthen social connections among neighbors. Block projects make an immediate physical improvement or tie closely to a target block strategy. Block projects involve residents in planning, implementation, and ongoing maintenance.

In commemoration of the foundation's centennial, the Healthy Neighborhoods Art Initiative—in partnership with the Greater Milwaukee Foundation Mary L. Nohl Fund—helped create art in public spaces. The Mary L. Nohl Fund is among the foundation's largest funds dedicated to investing in local arts education programs and projects. Five neighborhoods received more than $80,000. The project was also supported by the Neighborhood Improvement Development Corporation, which provided matching grants of up to $20,000.

THE VITAL ROLE OF PARTNERSHIPS IN HEALTHY NEIGHBORHOODS

None of the work is done in isolation. A critical feature of the program's success in strengthening neighborhoods is the large number of partnerships and collaborations. The foundation has developed relationships with city government, philanthropic partners, and banks to bring needed capital to the program. One of the foundation's central partners is the city of Milwaukee's Neighborhood Improvement Development Corporation, which provides eligible homeowners with a forgivable, low-interest loan of up to $15,000 through its Target Investment Neighborhood strategy. In addition, each designated Healthy Neighborhoods lead agency qualifies for up to $10,000 in matching grants through its Community Improvement Projects program.

The foundation is one of the founding partners of the Community Development Alliance (CDA), a consortium of philanthropic and corporate funders that have been working to align place-based activities and investments in Milwaukee's neighborhoods since 2010. The alliance combines resources to make contributions to neighborhood improvement.

The CDA is guided by the belief that successful neighborhood leadership is the key to neighborhood stabilization and growth. The foundation, along with its community development philanthropic partners, created two comprehensive leadership programs: The Neighborhood Leadership Institute (NLI), and the Community Connections Small Grants program. The NLI develops the skills of neighborhood leaders through a free 10-month program for neighborhood residents. The program pairs two people who live, work, or volunteer in the neighborhood. By the end of 2016, more than 60 leaders will have completed the training.

The small-grants program also provides support by building social connections. It provides up to $750 to a group of residents to implement projects that benefit their neighborhood. The review committee is made up of residents, many of whom have participated in the NLI. Examples of projects include backyard composting, family unity craft projects, healthy cooking classes, block parties, positive body image workshops for young girls, and alley clean ups. This is an example of how partnerships help enhance the social fabric in neighborhoods.

In 2015, the foundation and Wells Fargo partnered to establish a $1 million pool of funds to strengthen Milwaukee neighborhoods. A portion of the funds focuses on a targeted housing preservation strategy that supports homeownership by building equity. The Healthy Neighborhoods Minor Home Improvement Pilot Program is part of that strategy. It works to stabilize three designated Healthy Neighborhoods. The program provides matching grants to homeowners to complete minor exterior home improvement projects.

In summary, both the Baltimore and Milwaukee Healthy Neighborhoods programs have their roots in the foundation, nonprofit, and neighborhood sectors—and both are showing genuine progress in strengthening middle neighborhoods. Relative to many other neighborhood programs, the administrative costs are very small, demonstrating that middle neighborhoods programs can be very cost-effective.

Mark Sissman served the Enterprise Foundation for 14 years as president of the Enterprise Social Investment Corporation ("ESIC"). Under his leadership, ESIC was the nation's foremost syndicator of low-income housing tax credits. In January 1999, he joined Bank of America as senior vice president. Mr. Sissman was the Deputy Housing Commissioner for Baltimore City. For 11 years, he has served as president of Healthy Neighborhoods, a Baltimore community development intermediary and CDFI organized by financial institutions, foundations and neighborhood organizations to improve neighborhoods by increasing home values, rehabilitating homes, and marketing neighborhood assets. Sissman was president and chief executive officer of the Hippodrome Foundation, the local partner for the redevelopment of the abandoned Hippodrome Theater, a $70 million, 2,250-seat world-class performing arts center.

Darlene C. Russell brings more than 15 years of nonprofit experience to her role as a foundation program officer. In addition to participating in the discretionary grant review process, she manages the Greater Milwaukee Foundation's Healthy Neighborhoods Initiative and serves on several nonprofit advisory committees. Prior to joining the foundation in January 2011, Russell worked with a number of organizations to help increase college access to students in the greater Milwaukee area. In her role as senior outreach consultant at Great Lakes Higher Education Guaranty Corporation, she worked to help low-income, first-generation college students access post-secondary education by partnering with nonprofits that helped students and families prepare and pay for college. She graduated with a B.A. in community leadership and development from Alverno College and earned an M.S.M. in management from Cardinal Stritch University.

IX. UNDERSTANDING MIDDLE NEIGHBORHOODS AS VITAL PARTS OF REGIONAL ECONOMIES

By Robert Weissbourd, RW Ventures, LLC

Over the past decade, it has become increasingly clear that geography plays a key role in economic prosperity. Industrial, human capital, and innovation assets concentrating in metropolitan areas are the drivers of economic growth in the twenty-first century economy.[1] Metropolitan leaders are developing comprehensive economic growth plans tailored to enhancing the productivity of these assets in their regions. (See Metropolitan Business Planning sidebar.) Most of these assets are located in neighborhoods. As a result, both the regional growth and neighborhood development fields are focusing on how the component parts of the regional economic geography—particularly its neighborhoods—define, participate in, and contribute to regional economic performance, and vice versa. In the long run, neighborhoods and their regions thrive or fail together.

This essay describes the connection between neighborhood and regional economic growth, and proposes, "neighborhood business plans" as a method of undertaking neighborhood development aligned with and contributing to regional growth in today's economy. The market-based development principles that underlie this connection highlight the importance of building from and fully deploying neighborhood assets as vehicles for economic growth, individual wealth creation, poverty alleviation, and improved amenities. This approach offers particular opportunity for middle market neighborhoods.

---

[1] This section draws heavily on Robert Weissbourd and Mark Muro, *Metropolitan Business Plans: A New Approach to Economic Growth* (Washington, DC: Brookings Institution Metropolitan Policy Program, 2011); Gretchen Kosarko and Robert Weissbourd, *Economic Impacts of GO TO 2040* (Chicago: Community Trust, 2011); Gretchen Kosarko et al., *Implementing Regionalism: Connecting Emerging Theory and Practice to Inform Economic Development* (New York: Surdna Foundation, available at http://rw-ventures.com/publications/downloads/Surdna%20Final%20Paper%20-%20Combined%20112111.pdf; Robert Weissbourd, Riccardo Bodini, and Michael He, *Dynamic Neighborhoods: New Tools for Community and Economic Development*, (New York: Living Cities, 2009), see esp. chapter 8; *Economic Place-Making: How to Develop a 'Neighborhood Business Plan'* (Chicago: RW Ventures, 2014), available at http://www.rw-ventures.com publications/downloads/Choice_NBP_Training_May.pptx); and The Greater Chatham Initiative, http://www.greaterchathaminitiative.org.

GROWTH IN THE TWENTY-FIRST CENTURY ECONOMY

The global economy is experiencing a fundamental transformation, characterized by:

Knowledge intensity: Knowledge, embedded in people and technology, is the most critical factor driving productivity and growth. The nature of knowledge assets, and their increasing returns, means that innovation and growth increasingly flow from continuous cross-fertilization and synergies among economic activities. This makes it important to reduce "transaction costs"—the costs associated with economic actors finding, evaluating, and engaging with each other. As a result, collaboration and connectedness—through rich, flexible, tangible (e.g., infrastructure) and intangible networks—are critical to efficiently deploying and redeploying assets, whether in labor markets, business networks, or cross-sector partnerships.

Dynamism: We are going through a period of "creative destruction" in which knowledge intensity makes the economy more dynamic as products, firms, industries, and markets emerge, develop, and transform at an increasingly rapid pace. This also rewards close, nimble economic networks and the ability to continually adapt and redeploy human capital and other assets.

Regional synergies: In short, physical proximity matters. In particular, people and other assets are increasingly concentrating in metropolitan areas—exactly because they are disproportionately productive when concentrated. A person or firm with the same characteristics, if located in a metropolitan area with others like them, is likely to be more productive and profitable. Metropolitan areas have thus become the global economy's primary unit of geography, where market systems operate and interact with characteristics of place to create unique economies.

Analysis of these new dynamics within regions reveals five market levers that enable these synergies and so drive the efficiency and productivity of a place, determining its economic prosperity: industry clusters, deployment of human capital, innovation, spatial efficiency, and governance. These are detailed below in Drivers of Neighborhood Growth.

In today's economy, sustainable growth also mandates inclusion, because the places with the least inequity perform best.[2] This is, in part, simply a matter of economic efficiency: Excluding particular populations or locations in a region is a waste of economic assets because human capital, businesses, land, and other fundamental contributors to economic growth remain latent or underdeployed. In

---

[2]   Robert Weissbourd and Christopher Berry, *The Changing Dynamics of Urban America* (Cleveland: CEOs for Cities, 2004), available at http://rw-ventures.com/publications/downloads/Changing%20Dynamics%20report.pdf; Jonathan D. Ostry, Andrew Berg, and Charalambos G. Tsangarides, "Redistribution, Inequality, and Growth," IMF Staff Discussion Note (April 2014), a http://www.imf.org/external/pubs/ft/sdn/2014/sdn1402.pdf; OECD Directorate for Employment, Labour, and Social Affairs, "Does Inequality Hurt Economic Growth?" *Focus on Inequality and Growth* 9 (December 2014).

addition, economic exclusion of people and places incurs the high economic and social costs of poverty.[3]

The great paradox—and challenge—of to-day's economy is that the drivers of growth often exacerbate inequality (primarily by increasing returns to capital over labor), but successful regional economies require inclusion for sustainable growth. The twenty-first century economy is propelling shifts to new industries, demanding new labor force skills, and reshaping urban form as new density and mixed uses develop. As a result, people and places in legacy or disconnected businesses, jobs, and neighborhoods are frequently left behind. At the same time, all of these changes create new value and new opportunities for inclusion to drive and capture value—for aligning poverty alleviation with economic growth. Indeed, inclusive economic growth has become an economic imperative for achieving both poverty alleviation and prosperity.

A necessary element of inclusive regional growth is to connect neighborhood growth

---

Metropolitan Business Planning

Metropolitan Business Planning (MBP) is a relatively new approach that applies the practice of private-sector business planning to regional economic growth planning and implementation.[3a] To date, MBP has been piloted in a dozen regions across the country. MBP principles are equally applicable to smaller geographies and to neighborhood business plans. These principles include the following:

- Apply a market-driven and disciplined approach, building from areas of strength and seeking to create and capture value;
- Identify key, mutually reinforcing strategic initiatives, tailored and targeted to build from the particular assets and dynamics of place;
- Implement new products and enterprises to drive growth—the plan is only the first step, its end goal must be action;
- Expect the plan to evolve over time as conditions change, as progress and impact are measured and as course corrections are made; and
- Ensure that inclusivity, collaboration, and transparency inform the process of creating and implementing the plan.

---

planning with regional economic planning. Because regional economies rely on neighborhoods for critical human, physical, financial, and institutional capital, this new generation of growth planning must tailor market analysis, strategy development, and initiative design and implementation to the challenges and opportunities of particular geographies. It must deliberately and strategically link communities' assets (e.g., workers, businesses, land) to opportunities throughout the region (e.g., cluster supply chains, high-growth occupations, resources for innovation and entrepreneurs, etc.) to drive the entire region along a prosperous trajectory.

---

[3]   See Weissbourd, *Into the Economic Mainstream: Bipartisan Policies for Inclusive Economic Growth* (Philadelphia: Opportunity Finance Network; Washington, DC: CFED, 2006), available at http://www.rw-ventures.com/publications/downloads/Distribution%20Draft%20IEM%20Paper%208-6-06%20rw.pdf.

[3a] For details, see Robert Weissbourd and Mark Muro, *Metropolitan Business Plans: A New Approach to Economic Growth* (Washington, DC: Brookings Institution, 2011) at http://www.brookings.edu/research/papers/2011/04/12-metro-business-muro.

THE FUNCTIONS OF NEIGHBORHOODS IN REGIONS

Just as regions depend on their neighborhoods, neighborhoods are best understood in the context of their regions. In fact, neighborhoods do not have economies: their dynamics and trajectories are determined by their economic and other connections to the regional economy, whether through labor markets, business supply chains, or real estate markets, all of which are larger than the neighborhood.

Neighborhoods arise and change as their assets and built environment interact with economic, social, and political systems that are usually larger than the neighborhood itself. A neighborhood's character and development are driven primarily by the movement of people: who chooses to move in, stay, or move out over time. In an iterative cycle, new residents are followed by new businesses and amenities to serve them, which then attract more people and businesses of the same kind and so on (see Figure 1).

Figure 1. The Economic Life Cycle of a Neighborhood

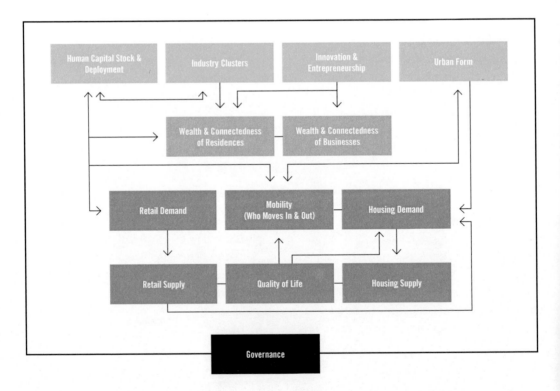

The connections to regional and business markets influence how residents and businesses thrive, and how the cycle turns as a result. Different types of neighborhoods follow different trajectories as the cycle produces specializations to serve particular groups, such as young professionals, families, immigrants, or others.

This dynamic process means that two primary sets of factors determine a neighborhood's vitality: internal characteristics of place, and connections between community assets and the broader regional economy. Characteristics of place are mainly oriented to serving residents and directly define a particular neighborhood's personality and quality of life. They include housing; commercial amenities such as retail, services, restaurants, and entertainment; public goods and services such as safety, schools, and parks; support services for youth, the elderly, and others; and institutional and cultural qualities.

TYPES OF NEIGHBORHOODS

There are many types of neighborhoods, differentiated by factors that include location; characteristics of the built environment (for example, density, age of the building stock, and so forth); household demographics; the nature of the local business environment; and many others. Particular combinations of these attributes appeal to different segments of the regional population. Young professionals, for example, will tend to be attracted to a different kind of neighborhood than growing families, new immigrants, retirees, or other types of households.

Having many diverse neighborhood types is important to regional growth because it helps the region attract and retain the many and varied types of workers that are necessary to drive growth in the twenty-first century economy. It also provides residents with many potential communities of choice, ensuring that there are places in the region that fit their current and changing needs.

The Dynamic Neighborhood Taxonomy (below)[4] provides a useful typology for analyzing and understanding the many different types of neighborhoods and their trajectories.

Dynamic Neighborhood Taxonomy

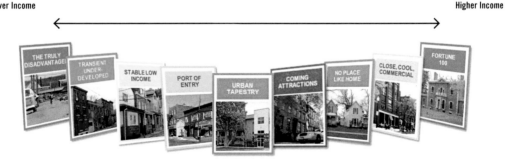

A neighborhood's connections to the regional economy affect the flow of income, wealth, and investment into the community, which indirectly influences local buying power and support for

---

[4]   The neighborhood typology was developed as part of a multi-year study that examined hundreds of indicators of neighborhood change in four cities (Chicago, Cleveland, Dallas, and Seattle) from 1986 to 2006. See Weissbourd, Bodini, and He, *Dynamic Neighborhoods*.

local amenities. These connections are primarily about the extent to which a neighborhood's assets are effectively deployed into regional markets: its residents into the labor force, its businesses into high-growth supply chains, and its land and structural assets into regional real estate markets.

These two sets of factors—local amenities and regional economic connectedness—interact with one another in a cycle that can either be virtuous or vicious. A neighborhood's degree of connectivity to regional economic opportunities is a primary driver in the cycle. A neighborhood attracts people and businesses when it offers good job access, strong connections to suppliers and customers, and other factors that enable the creation of income and wealth. The resulting income, and wealth trigger public and market-based investments in local amenities, goods, and services to meet new demand (e.g., particular types of housing and retail, parks and libraries, and so forth).

Where people choose to live is also a function of which local amenities are in a given neighborhood. Young professionals, for example, might choose a neighborhood not only because of its proximity to downtown jobs, but also because it already has some of the amenities they most value, such as reasonably priced apartments, a fitness center, coffee shops, and casual restaurants or trendy clothing stores. The same holds true for businesses, which choose to locate in neighborhoods that provide access to their customers and suppliers, but also to other factors that contribute to their success, such as transit access for workers, high-speed broadband service, and other specialized infrastructure.

At particular points in a neighborhood's life cycle, local amenities can have a particularly high impact on which residents and businesses stay, move in, or move out.[5] The goal of neighborhood growth planning is to propagate a cycle of positive change through the interaction and iteration of characteristics of place and connectedness to the broader regional economy.

COMMUNITIES OF OPPORTUNITY AND CHOICE

Exploring these dynamics of neighborhood change reveals two key economic functions of neighborhoods. Neighborhoods serve as communities of opportunity by developing and deploying their economic assets—workers, businesses, real estate and so on—into regional economic opportunities. Communities of opportunity foster businesses and enable their participation in the supply chains of regional industry clusters. They support residents in developing their skills and connecting to opportunities in the occupations demanded by regional employers. They also cultivate connections between entrepreneurs and small businesses and the regional resources and networks that can enable and catalyze their growth.

Neighborhoods also serve as communities of choice, attracting and serving particular segments of the regional population. Communities of choice offer unique combinations of goods, services and other amenities that attract and retain the individuals and households that most value that

---

[5] Overall, economic connectivity remains paramount in determining neighborhood health, as amenities are generally derived from or follow the demand generated by the enhanced economic prosperity flowing from connectedness. A well-connected neighborhood, producing income and wealth, will attract amenities. An amenity-rich neighborhood that is disconnected will have a harder time becoming connected just by virtue of its amenities.

particular bundle of characteristics. The status of neighborhoods as communities of choice for particular populations is also affected by their connectivity (both physically and through market activity) to economic opportunities. These roles necessarily are mutually reinforcing. In well-functioning, connected neighborhoods, choice and opportunity go hand-in-hand.

Neighborhoods and regions thus define and need each other. A successful region offers an array of neighborhood choices to attract different segments of its population, and ensures that its neighborhoods are connected, deploying their assets into the regional economy. A successful neighborhood creates opportunity for its residents and businesses by developing and deploying these assets into the regional economy, and provides the amenities to serve the population segment that chooses to live there.

This understanding of the dynamic interdependence of neighborhoods and regions, particularly in today's economy, suggests a new approach to neighborhood economic development. It also highlights the importance of middle neighborhoods, given that regions in this economy need healthy places that attract middle class residents and enable them to prosper.

PRINCIPLES FOR NEIGHBORHOOD GROWTH PLANNING

Economic growth planning requires a different approach in today's economy than it did in the old economy, at both regional and neighborhood levels.

REGIONWIDE PRINCIPLES

At the regional level, today's economic realities imply several principles for guiding effective practice, which can be applied at the neighborhood level as well:

> **Leverage regional assets.** "Grow to compete" rather than competing to grow. The focus must be on building from existing assets and becoming a place where people and firms can be most productive and efficient[6] (rather than, for example, paying firms to come to the region only to lose them later to other locations better suited to their fundamental needs).[7] Many, if not most, of these existing assets are located in or near neighborhoods.

> **Compete on value added, not low cost.** Long-term economic growth requires investment in infrastructure, workforce, technology, innovation, entrepreneurship, and other resources that enhance the productivity and efficiency of the economy for firms and workers. Rather than competing on low cost (via, for example, lax zoning or labor regulations), the goal should be creating economic growth policies and actions that make the region an attractive and "sticky" place for the most productive firms.

---

[6]   This focus starts at the level of the economic system, not the individual firms: It is economic development, not business development.

[7]   Deal-level incentives for firm attraction—the main traditional regional economic development practice—then become a subservient tactic, targeting firms that enhance strategies focused on the intersection of particular clusters, technologies, and human capital.

Align poverty alleviation with economic growth. Inclusive growth moves people and places into the economic mainstream[8] rather than creating alternative poverty programs. The increasing focus on creating a more nimble, demand-driven workforce development system is a good example of this more effective approach.

Design for synergies. Housing, workforce development, infrastructure, industry cluster, innovation, and other activities all succeed or fail in the context of each other. Programs that are currently fragmented must be integrated and tailored to reinforce each other in particular places and activities.

Create collaborations based on economic, not political, geography. Regional economic growth planners must collaborate across the true market geography of a particular economic activity, rather than competing across jurisdictional borders.

Act through public-private partnerships. Successful regional economic growth needs a market-based orientation that creates new cross-sector networks and leverages private resources, rather than a top- down, government-driven approach.

NEIGHBORHOOD-SPECIFIC PRINCIPLES

A few additional growth-planning principles, specific to neighborhood-level practice, are implied by the two functions of neighborhoods in the regional context, and by the inherently place-specific nature of neighborhoods' assets, challenges, and opportunities.

Engage a broad, inclusive set of neighborhood and regional stakeholders. For both planning and implementation, ensure that the work is of, by, and for the community. At the same time, other key stakeholders beyond neighborhood residents must be engaged. These include employers, developers, firms whose suppliers are in the neighborhood, regional growth institutions, program partners, government, and others who invest in, hire, buy from or otherwise have a stake in the neighborhood—or will, as the neighborhood reconnects. Regions have a huge stake in their neighborhoods, and regional stakeholders must be principal partners in neighborhood development.

Tailor programs to align neighborhood assets with regional opportunities. Those involved in neighborhood revitalization need to customize and adapt neighborhood initiatives specifically and directly to better connect unique neighborhood assets with regional economic opportunities. In Milwaukee, for example, city government efforts to improve the 30th Street Corridor and Century City, a 45-acre vacant former industrial site, are targeting growth clusters in the region, working to get companies on the site that will be part of regional growth, and connecting job training and placement for nearby residents with the growth opportunities.

---

[8]   See Weissbourd, *Into the Economic Mainstream: Bipartisan Policies for Inclusive Economic Growth* (Philadelphia: Opportunity Finance Network; Washington, DC: CFED, 2006), available at http://www.rw-ventures.com/publications/downloads/Distribution%20Draft%20IEM%20Paper%208-6-06%20rw.pdf

Coordinate and integrate programs in place. Designing for synergies (a regional principle mentioned above) is particularly fruitful for neighborhoods. Organizations can work together to tailor their respective programs to neighborhood conditions and to the mix of other programs within a particular local area. For example, the Greater Chatham Initiative Comprehensive Plan for Economic Growth and Neighborhood Vitality—a neighborhood business plan—establishes 16 linked strategies, and leadership has specified over 30 complementary initiatives to implement them.[9]

Drivers of Neighborhood Growth. The two functions neighborhoods play in the regional economy make two sets of factors important to economic growth planning at the neighborhood level. The community of opportunity (or "connectedness") function requires an understanding of the growth trajectory of the regional economy, the levers driving its growth, and the ways that neighborhood assets can connect to regional economic growth and prosperity. The community of choice function requires an understanding of the type of neighborhood, the way it is performing for particular segments of the regional population, its trajectory for the future, and how its position might be improved.

CONNECTING INCLUSIVE GROWTH PLANNING TO OTHER DEVELOPMENT ACTIVITIES

The integrated, market-based approach to comprehensive neighborhood growth in the regional context described in this chapter builds from a long and vital legacy of community practice. Three primary and interrelated fields of practice relate to strengthening neighborhoods:

Community development. Internal focus on neighborhoods as good places to live.
Economic development. Focus on creating wealth for community residents.
Economic growth. Focus on improving economic performance and market functioning, particularly by addressing the drivers of productivity and economic output.

Inclusive economic growth seeks to understand and align these dynamics among communities, people, businesses, and regional markets to create communities with prosperous residents and businesses that participate in and constitute a vital and prosperous region.

---

[9]   The Greater Chatham Initiative, http://www.greaterchathaminitiative.org.

Figure 2. Inclusive Growth Planning and Other Development Activity

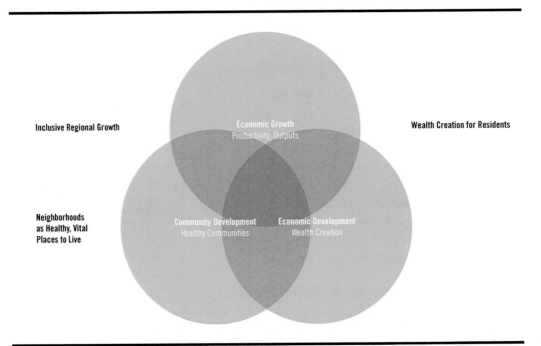

The remainder of this essay offers a high-level view of these factors.

MARKET LEVERS THAT DRIVE NEIGHBORHOODS OF OPPORTUNITY

Metropolitan economies grow by increasing the total value of goods and services produced by local firms. Firm creation and growth, as well as businesses' movement into and out of the region, are determined by regional characteristics that affect the efficiency and productivity of various types of firms and markets.

In the twenty-first-century economy, five market levers account for the efficiency and productivity of firms and markets. Together, they provide a framework for understanding a region's economic assets, challenges, and opportunities, and the ways a given neighborhood's assets can contribute to regional growth (see Figure 2).

CLUSTERS

Clusters are industry-based concentrations of closely interacting firms and related institutions.[10] Firms in a cluster benefit from relationships that improve efficiency and productivity by reducing transaction costs among buyers, suppliers, and customers; enabling shared labor and other inputs across firms; facilitating the exchange of knowledge; and enhancing the cluster's innovative capacity.

---

10   Clusters can also be based on concentrating economic functions, rather than industries, such as business services and headquarters.

The prospects of neighborhood (nonretail) businesses depend on the extent of their participation in high-growth regional clusters, enabling growth, investment, and job creation for local residents.

HUMAN CAPITAL

Human capital is the single most important factor in economic growth, particularly in the knowledge economy. To have an impact, however, workers must be properly deployed into jobs that best match their skills and education. Getting this match right requires attention not just to education and training, but also to job creation in growing clusters, the alignment of labor supply and demand, and enhanced labor market efficiency through better mechanisms for matching workers with firms.

In neighborhoods, workers can be productively deployed by ensuring residents have ready access to education and training resources for in-demand occupations, as well as direct access to employers who are participating in high-growth regional clusters. Effectively deploying human capital into the regional economy brings assets (i.e., income) into the neighborhood, creating demand for amenities and further contributing to a virtuous cycle of neighborhood growth and development.

INNOVATION, ENTREPRENEURSHIP, AND SMALL BUSINESS

The ability to innovate is the core driver of increasing productivity. A knowledge-based economy, heightened competition in globalized markets, and the quickening pace of change make continual innovation, commercialization, and business creation imperative for economic success.

Figure 3. Market Levers for Economic Growth

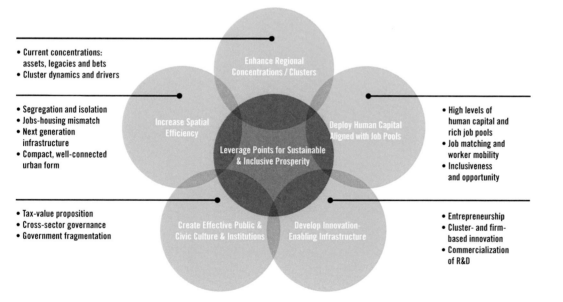

Neighborhoods can enhance their innovation and entrepreneurial environments by connecting to regional networks and resources, and reducing barriers to small business creation and growth— particularly in the supply chains of high-growth regional clusters. Neighborhoods benefit through increased income via business ownership, job creation opportunities, and improved resident access to new products and services.

SPATIAL EFFICIENCY

The proximity of businesses, suppliers, workers, and consumers within a region, and the physical and virtual infrastructure that connects them, is a key determinant of efficiency and productivity. These two features of the built environment—co-location and connecting infrastructure—determine transportation and transaction costs for the movement of goods, people, and ideas—magnifying or diminishing many economic benefits of agglomeration, such as shared labor pools and knowledge spillovers. Mixed-use communities with excellent transportation connections are best positioned to flourish in today's economy.

Within neighborhoods, spatial efficiency determines the most appropriate mix of economic uses and associated infrastructure. This will vary from one neighborhood to another depending on the characteristics of each one's land assets, proximity to other uses, transportation connections, and other elements of the built environment. The synergies that result from co-location in the knowledge economy present particular opportunities for neighborhood development. They result in people and firms embracing urban density, creating possibilities for attraction of new firms and residents, reusing abandoned industrial land, and creating innovation districts as well as other "economic place making."

GOVERNANCE

Government shapes and enables market activity and provides critical public goods, from roads to education, which enhance firms' productivity and efficiency. Civic, private-sector, and cross-sector institutions constitute the institutional environment—or governance—that fosters economic networks, innovation, and other activity. In neighborhoods, new forms of governance must be developed to simultaneously represent local stakeholders' interests, foster market connections between local assets and regional economic opportunities, and implement an integrated set of strategic activities to drive growth.

AMENITIES THAT CREATE NEIGHBORHOODS OF CHOICE

HOUSING

Neighborhood housing markets (each of which is a submarket within the broader regional market) affect and reflect a neighborhood's status as a community of choice for particular populations within the region. The characteristics of the housing stock (including size, quality, amenities, cost) and its potential to appreciate are significant factors in determining a neighborhood's competitiveness relative to other communities. This bundle of housing characteristics makes a given neighborhood more or less attractive to specific segments of the regional population, affecting individuals' and households' decisions to stay in place, move in, or move out of the neighborhood.

RETAIL

A neighborhood's commercial environment serves as an amenity for local residents, interacting closely with housing market dynamics to make a community more or less attractive. These businesses offer further benefits for neighborhood residents by creating accessible jobs and providing wealth-creation opportunities through entrepreneurship and small-business development.

PUBLIC SAFETY

Residents choose to stay in, and move to, neighborhoods that offer a safe and secure environment. At the same time, providing economic opportunity and well-being is one of the strongest paths to improving public safety. More immediately, enhancing public safety requires "collective efficacy," engaging all of the community's stakeholders, and strong communication and coordination between the community and the police.

OTHER AMENITIES AND SUPPORT SERVICES

A host of other local amenities influences the attractiveness of a neighborhood and also must be tailored to the needs of present and desired residents. These include public, civic, and private services such as libraries, schools, parks, and police stations; recreational facilities; community centers; support services for youth, seniors, and the formerly incarcerated; health services; and social and cultural institutions.

As discussed above, all the factors in neighborhood growth are iterative, acting as drivers of one another. More important, most of them iterate with and are heavily influenced by the drivers of regional connectedness. For this reason, even leading public safety, housing, and retail programs emphasize the critical importance of jobs and income. Retail demand depends on households, while housing demand depends on regional employment but also public safety, which in turn is influenced by employment, retail presence, and social services, and so forth. Neighborhoods, in essence, are complex adaptive systems that arise and continually change as a result of these neighborhood factors interacting with one another, and with systems (particularly markets) that extend beyond the neighborhood.

IMPLICATIONS, APPLICATIONS, AND CONCLUSIONS

The functions and factors that define neighborhoods and influence their well-being are undeniably complex—but focusing on the underlying economics, particularly in the twenty-first century economy, reveals that regions need their neighborhoods to succeed, and vice versa. That focus also implies an approach to neighborhood development that engages regional stakeholders, and starts with strengthening the connections of neighborhood assets to the trajectory of the regional economy. Detailed neighborhood business plans analyze regional markets as they relate to the assets of neighborhoods to create these connections. In addition, they identify a particular neighborhood's role, aspirations, and potential trajectory as a community of choice—addressing housing, retail, and amenities tailored to the realistic, desired neighborhood type. For a complete neighborhood business plan illustrating a detailed application of the approach outlined here, see the Greater Chatham Initiative Comprehensive Plan for Economic Growth and Neighborhood Vitality.

The message to regional growth planners is clear: regional prosperity depends on strategically investing in your neighborhoods—making them places of opportunity whose assets serve the regional economy, and places of choice to attract the varied populations that drive the regional economy. The corollary message applies to neighborhoods, which must develop through participating in and driving their regional economies. Given the underlying asset and market-based approach, the obvious place to start is in middle market neighborhoods, which by definition have more market-ready assets and nascent market connections.

Robert Weissbourd is president of RW Ventures, LLC, an economic development firm that applies sophisticated market analysis and business planning to develop products and enterprises to drive inclusive growth in neighborhoods, industries, and regions. He serves or has served in executive positions at Shorebank Corporation, as an adjunct professor at the University of Chicago Harris School of Public Policy, a nonresident senior fellow at the Brookings Institution Metropolitan Policy Center, chair of the Obama Campaign Urban Policy Committee, and on the Obama Transition HUD Agency Review Team. He brings over 30 years of experience leading economic development work in dozens of cities and scores of neighborhoods. He is also a frequent author, public speaker, and lecturer on a broad range of urban markets, housing, business, and economic development issues. He has testified on these issues before federal, state, and local legislatures as well.

X. REBUILDING FROM STRENGTH AS A STRATEGY TO SAFEGUARD MIDDLE NEIGHBORHOODS IN DETROIT: A PHILANTHROPIC PERSPECTIVE

By Wendy Jackson, The Kresge Foundation

There is perhaps no other topic that evokes more passion about Detroit's long-term potential for revitalization than the future direction of its neighborhoods. As beacons for those seeking an improved quality of life in a growing city, Detroit neighborhoods were designed with early twentieth century prosperity in mind. Detroit's streets once featured block after block of well-constructed and well-kept brick, single-family homes buttressed by thriving commercial corridors and stately tree-lined boulevards. For Detroit, neighborhoods have always been a source of pride and a symbolic gateway to middle class opportunity. They provide the city its character and definition, but more important, neighborhoods are the places where generations of Detroiters have placed their bet on the future and made an investment for the long term.

For these reasons, the brutal erosion of neighborhood quality of life in Detroit—exacerbated by the Great Recession and foreclosure crisis—has been particularly difficult to witness. Between 2000 and 2010, more than 750,000 manufacturing jobs vanished from Michigan. In the same decade, 241,000 mostly middle-income residents moved out of Detroit. Mortgage and tax foreclosures combined to worsen physical decline and, as a result, no neighborhood has been immune to the effects of the economic downturn. By late 2007, the telltale signs of blight and vacancy were evident in a handful of Detroit neighborhoods. But by 2011, mortgage foreclosure had touched one in every four habitable houses in the city, more than 63,000 of them. The devastation in the wake of the foreclosure crisis is almost unfathomable. The city lost almost $500 million in tax revenue during the crisis.[1]

Even in Detroit's strongest neighborhoods, the economic shock waves from structural unemployment and the crash of the housing market left blocks riddled with blight and burdened with a persistent public safety crisis. These combined effects have been devastating to Detroit's neighborhoods.

The rapidly deteriorating neighborhood conditions required an abrupt shift from the optimism toward revitalizing distressed areas that had started to take root citywide a few years earlier. Suddenly, public and private partners had to adopt a pragmatically defensive posture that required

---

[1] Christine McDonald and Joel Kurth, "Foreclosures Fuel Detroit Blight, Cost the City $500 Million," *Detroit News Special Report*, June 24, 2015, available at http://www.detroitnews.com/story/news/special-reports/2015/06/03/detroit-foreclosures-risky-mortgages-cost-taxpayers/27236605/.

preserving the strength that remained in communities by deploying stabilization strategies to keep pivotal neighborhoods on the cusp from tipping into decline.

It was at this critical juncture that The Kresge Foundation adopted its Reimagining Detroit 2020 program as the guiding vision for the foundation's investments and work in Detroit. Since then, we have partnered with local and national philanthropies in a series of investments and initiatives that have stabilized and strengthened the city's physical, economic, and social fabric and increased the likelihood that Detroit will move on to a more positive path for the future. Through this framework, Kresge began to develop a "complete neighborhoods" strategy to foster environmental sustainability, increase economic opportunity, and stabilize property values. The Foundation decided to invest primarily in middle market neighborhoods that had traditionally competed exceptionally well in holding and attracting residents, but whose future was threatened by the economic damage of the 2000s.

The strategy, very simply, was to create a concentrated set of investments that were stacked and aligned to: (1) retain and attract residents; (2) preserve market strength and the city's tax base wherever possible; and (3) build the capacity of neighborhood leaders and organizations to address quality of life. These 2007–2012 investments in the acquisition and rehab of vacant properties, environmentally conscious strategies for blight removal, neighborhood beautification, and community engagement represented the first wave in what ultimately became a much larger public-private agenda to revitalize Detroit neighborhoods. That larger strategy was the Detroit Future City Strategic Framework.

The Foundation's approach had as its core an understanding that scarce philanthropic resources could be most effective where immediate intervention had the greatest likelihood of preserving neighborhood stability and laying the groundwork to attract new investment. Spurred on by Kresge CEO Rip Rapson, the Detroit Neighborhood Forum (DNF) became the city's primary philanthropic vehicle to understand and respond to the challenges facing Detroit neighborhoods. The roughly 75-member forum is composed of foundations, corporate funders, financial institutions, intermediaries, and key public officials. The DNF amplified its leadership role when it hosted a 2008 meeting with the board of Living Cities to identify effective long-term strategies for the revitalization of Detroit. It was during that meeting when the underpinnings for the Woodward Corridor Initiative, Detroit Future City Strategic Framework, and a host of other transformative initiatives were established. The DNF also provided stability and continuity of focus for neighborhood efforts during the collapse of the housing market and foreclosure crisis.

The investments in these middle neighborhoods had a twofold impact. They helped many neighborhoods remain relatively stable by engaging residents until the Detroit Future City Strategic Framework was complete, and they taught public and private partners valuable lessons about what works to improve quality of opportunity within neighborhoods and how to bring those innovations to scale when the environment is ready for action and investment.

THE MENU OF INTERVENTIONS FOR THESE NEIGHBORHOODS INCLUDED:

Arts and culture: collaboration between the Skillman and Kresge foundations launched the Community+Public Arts: Detroit program, engaging local artists and youth in public arts projects to beautify and animate Detroit neighborhoods.

Blight remediation: Before launching the Detroit Blight Task Force in 2014 and expanding the citywide blight remediation strategy, The Kresge Foundation sponsored several pilot projects to develop key lessons about the best approaches for safe and environmentally secure demolition and deconstruction. These included the Community Property and Preservation Mini-Grants (now known as the SAFE mini-grant program) and administered by Michigan Community Resources, which engaged neighborhood leaders through funded activities to improve basic neighborhood safety, appearance, and quality of life by targeting security, maintenance, and beautification projects for vacant property. In addition, neighborhood vacant property planning engaged residents in a process to transform vacant land and property into uses that improve the quality of life in neighborhoods.

Environmental Stewardship: With support from the U.S. Environmental Protection Agency, the Fred A. and Barbara M. Erb Family Foundation, and The Kresge Foundation, neighborhood green infrastructure projects became a tool for stabilizing neighborhoods and repurposing vacant land.

Middle market acquisition and rehab: A collaboration between the Ford and Kresge foundations tested neighborhood stabilization strategies through a partnership of the Grandmont Rosedale Development Corporation and Detroit Development Fund to acquire, renovate, and resell up to 500 vacant houses in five northwest Detroit neighborhoods. The Detroit Green and Healthy Homes Program also brought together 50 partner organizations dedicated to creating green, healthy, and safe homes for children and families.

Neighborhood placemaking: Support from the Kresge and W.K. Kellogg foundations launched efforts by the Project for Public Spaces to involve the community in imagining "lighter, quicker, cheaper" improvements to the streets and public spaces around two neighborhood farmers' markets and identify the 10 destinations that could serve as focal points for neighborhood renewal.

Neighborhood small-business development: This component strengthened small-business development along key commercial corridors, including fostering neighborhood grocery stores and streetscape improvements.

Public safety initiatives: The AmeriCorps Urban Safety Program based at Wayne State University, Center for Urban Studies worked in several key neighborhoods. The program fosters collaboration between law enforcement and community residents to combine crime mapping and data analysis with greater neighborhood guardianship.

Although the interventions slowed the impact of foreclosures in a handful of Detroit middle market neighborhoods, they were more significant for their ability to tap the creative energy of residents—particularly at a time when it was easy for them to lose confidence in speedy neighborhood recovery. Detroiters will have to live with the effects of the housing market collapse for a long time. These investments helped to strengthen community identity and build resilience and social cohesion.

On January 9, 2013, Detroit reached an important milestone with the launch of Detroit Future City Strategic Framework, a world-class, citywide strategic framework that delineates a broad range of actionable and innovative tactics to improve core economic, physical, and social conditions in Detroit. The framework builds much-needed citywide capacity for neighborhood redevelopment and is reinforced by Kresge's commitment to fully align all of its Detroit investments over the next five years with the recommendations of a framework plan.

And now we are at the moment to move forward. The Detroit Future City Strategic Framework provides a tremendous opportunity to align our philanthropic support with an innovative, effective, and comprehensive set of recommendations for neighborhood transformation. As the city rationalizes its services and stabilizes its fiscal health, Detroit has an opportunity to forge stronger public-private partnerships with local, federal, and state government in support of neighborhood redevelopment.

Wendy Lewis Jackson is co-managing director for the Detroit Program. She co-leads The Kresge Foundation's efforts to revitalize Detroit and to strengthen its social and economic fabric. Her work supports organizations providing economic opportunity for low-income people and addresses the needs of vulnerable children and families. Prior to joining Kresge in 2008, she was a program director for Children and Family Initiatives and executive director for education initiatives at the Grand Rapids Community Foundation in Grand Rapids, Michigan. She taught at Grand Valley State University in Allendale, Michigan, and has co-authored and assisted in the publication of several reports and publications that address community needs and problem solving. She is an American Marshall Memorial Fellow of the German Marshall Fund of the United States; the Association of Black Foundation Executives named her an Emerging Leader in 2008. She earned a B.A. in political science and communications from the University of Michigan. She also holds an M.S.W. in social work from U-M, with a concentration in community organization and social policy and planning.

XI. PRESERVATION IN MIDDLE NEIGHBORHOODS: PROMISING RESULTS IN OHIO

By Cara Bertron, Preservation Rightsizing Network
and Nicholas Hamilton, The American Assembly, Columbia University

At its heart, historic preservation is about recognizing and valuing what was created in the past. It offers a lens for recognizing the value of neighborhoods and telling the stories of the people who have shaped and continue to shape them. This chapter articulates the case for a community-oriented preservation model that supports longtime residents, creates pathways for newcomers, and strengthens neighborhoods for all. The idea that there is economic, social, and environmental value worth preserving in existing buildings, neighborhoods, and communities is an essential theme in stabilizing middle neighborhoods. Stabilization is often discussed in theoretical terms, but it has very practical effects on neighborhood real estate values, as the other chapters in this book attest. Reinvesting in buildings can boost property values. When the process of reinvestment includes and honors local communities and their ongoing stories—their heritage—preservation can be a powerful tool for significant and sustainable change in neighborhood dynamics.

Preservation offers an approach to and set of strategies for thoughtfully managing change in areas with high development or demolition pressures. The most obvious tools for managing change are zoning and other local regulations—particularly in designated historic districts—and financial tools, such as historic tax credits and tax abatements.[1] However, this chapter focuses on strategies and tools that are not tied to historic designation and thus are more broadly applicable in middle neighborhoods and elsewhere. These tools help to stabilize and strengthen real estate markets in older neighborhoods and, in a related benefit, provide an avenue for active community stewardship of places. As will be discussed below, preserving older housing in middle neighborhoods serves sustainability, health, and social equity objectives in addition to providing market stabilization benefits.

America's legacy cities are uniquely positioned to innovate across a slate of policy areas, including preservation, as the immediacy of physical, economic, and social challenges demands new thinking

---

[1] Historic tax credits are available federally for designated historic buildings that are also income-producing; the credit comprises 20 percent of qualified rehabilitation expenditures and requires rehabilitation work to comply with the Secretary of the Interior's Standards for Rehabilitation. More than 30 states and many more cities offer historic tax credits that can be layered with the federal tax credits. A lesser-known 10 percent federal historic tax credit is available for nonresidential buildings constructed before 1936 that retain a substantial amount of their original structure and walls. There is no formal review process for work completed using this credit. Many states also have tax credits for restoration of historic structures.

on complex challenges. The first section of this chapter describes how a growing network of actors has redefined preservation in legacy cities. The second section explores the multiple value propositions that preservation can bring to holistic neighborhood stabilization and preservation. The chapter concludes with case studies of three Ohio coalitions that are implementing effective preservation strategies in stabilizing middle neighborhoods, as well as a discussion of ways forward.

REDEFINING PRESERVATION

To be clear, we advocate for a type of preservation that is not Thomas Jefferson's Monticello, New York's Grand Central Terminal, or the gracious Lower Peninsula in Charleston. It is about neighborhoods with buildings where siding has been patched and windows replaced, where vacant lots and buildings sit between occupied homes. It is about people, their stories, and the collective heritage of neighbors and families. In short, it is about individual and community investment rooted in a passion for a specific place. This approach represents a pragmatic preservation ethos: one that recognizes that not every building can or should be saved and embraces instead a holistic view that prioritizes actions—from mothballing to demolition to rehabilitation—based on realistic assessments of neighborhood conditions and likely short- to medium-term changes.

The earliest preservation advocates in the United States saw their work in the context of community. Beginning in 1853 with a campaign to save George Washington's home, the fledgling movement looked to the past to shape a more virtuous future. Subsequent efforts have often been motivated by a "civic patriotism" that uses the tangible past to define a common identity. When New Yorkers rallied to try to save Penn Station in 1963, they were in part reacting to larger autocratic decisions around demolition, freeways, and the shape of their city. Although the building was lost, it catalyzed a broad-based preservation movement that saw the urban landscape as a more democratic endeavor.

Too often, preservation has been perceived as an elite discipline dominated by monuments and wealthy, typically white, neighborhoods. The situation is more complex than that, of course, but it holds truth. The stories most often recorded and celebrated are those of privileged groups, and the buildings that typically receive attention are grand buildings built for and occupied by the same groups. Even as preservationists and community advocates have expanded the conception of multilayered, multicultural histories, the historic designation required for powerful historic tax credits and other incentives has historic integrity as a core requirement. That limits eligibility to buildings or neighborhoods that remain largely unchanged, a quality virtually impossible in long-disinvested low-income neighborhoods and communities of color that have faced—and are still facing—pervasive structural discrimination and underinvestment. Although not all middle neighborhoods share this particular history, most have faced decades of struggle.

It can be argued that the current iteration of preservation has goals similar to the earliest movements, but with equity and sustainability as driving forces and a much larger view of what should be preserved. Preservationists point to sturdy houses and commercial districts with "good bones" and unique architecture as the basis for neighborhood revitalization. They see incentives for reinvesting in buildings as tools that help build wealth for longtime homeowners. They promote mixed-use buildings and neighborhoods with a mix of unit sizes as opportunities to start businesses, foster socioeconomic diversity, and preserve informal affordable housing—as with the "Older, Smaller, Better" work of the Preservation Green Lab at the National Trust for Historic Preservation.[2] They emphasize that reoccupying a vacant house keeps it from being demolished and its remains dumped in a landfill. Finally, they value building community capacity through deep public engagement, while new technologies create opportunities for more inclusive planning—such as the Austin Historical Wiki Project and the Detroit Historic Resource Survey. While these ideas are rooted in the preservation movement's origins, their traction and application within the field has been limited. Renewed attention to middle neighborhoods and legacy cities is a fresh opportunity to promote these ideas; to examine how preservation frameworks and tools can be more equitable and useful; and to be taken seriously by other stakeholders, including politicians, planners, land bank officials, financial institutions, and community members.

PRESERVATION'S "TRIPLE BOTTOM LINE" VALUE PROPOSITION

The physical fabric of most middle neighborhoods offers many desirable characteristics aligned to advance complementary goals of sustainability and health, social equity, and economic prosperity. This triple bottom line payoff for middle neighborhood stabilization is rooted in the fact that the existing physical inventory of middle neighborhoods is relatively dense.[3] Although the age of the building stock may often require substantial system upgrades, the compact urban form of many middle neighborhoods offers increased walkability and decreased vehicle miles traveled compared with newer developments. These characteristics—similar to those aligned with smart growth principles—are associated with lower rates of asthma, obesity, and heart disease, as well as lower incidence of car crash fatalities.[4] Moreover, reduced dependence on private cars, increased rates of walking, and greater use of public transportation result in a smaller carbon footprint.[5] Finally, when comparing buildings of equivalent size and function, building reuse almost always offers environmental savings over demolition and new construction.[6] In other words, keeping a relatively dense neighborhood as dense as possible has all the positive benefits associated with smart growth—notwithstanding the challenges placed on the real estate market by low demand or other negative effects of high numbers of vacant buildings.

With respect to economic mobility, density, a variety of sizes and price points, homeownership, and property values found in older neighborhoods offer toeholds that are generally absent from newer

---

[2] Preservation Green Lab, National Trust for *Historic Preservation, Older, Smaller, Better: Measuring How the Character of Buildings and Blocks Influences Urban Vitality* (Washington, DC: author, 2014), available at http://www.preservationnation.org/information-center/sustainable-communities/green-lab/oldersmallerbetter/report/NTHP_PGL_OlderSmallerBetter_ReportOnly.pdf.

[3] For Youngstown neighborhood density, see Youngstown Neighborhood Development Corporation, *City of Youngstown, Neighborhood Conditions Report* (Youngstown: author, 2013), p. 13; Cuyahoga County municipal population densities are available at http://planning.co.cuyahoga.oh.us/census/2010land.html.

[4] Reid Ewing and Shima Hamidi, *Measuring Urban Sprawl and Validating Sprawl Measures* (Salt Lake City: Metropolitan Research Center at the University of Utah for the National Cancer Institute, the Brookings Institution, and Smart Growth America, 2014), p. 43.

[5] Ibid.

[6] Preservation Green Lab, *The Greenest Building: Quantifying the Environmental Value of Building Reuse* (Washington, DC: National Trust for Historic Preservation, 2011). The study found that it takes "10 to 80 years for a new building that is 30 percent more efficient than an average-performing existing building to overcome, through efficient operations, the negative climate change impacts related to the construction process" (p. vii).

developments. In his 2009 book, *Place, Race, and Story*, Ned Kaufman cites Donovan Rypkema's research, writing, "A thriving local economy will include 'small businesses, nonprofit organizations, start-up firms, bootstrap entrepreneurs' who cannot pay the high rents commanded by new construction. Old buildings provide ecological niches for essential activities. Without them, settled communities cannot thrive."[7]

Although stabilizing the real estate markets of middle neighborhoods is of primary import to city governments and community residents, other complementary factors are advanced through successful neighborhood preservation. Preservation's intangible values of community character, social equity, quality of life, memory, and beauty are generally the most lasting and important arguments for saving buildings and community heritage.[8] These intangible benefits often underpin demand by owner occupiers and investors in homes. They can also serve as common ground to build new relationships required for the broadly based partnerships necessary to achieve outcomes. Moreover, existing civic capacity around historic preservation provides valuable partners, influence, and constituencies in place-based stabilization efforts. Indeed, as the following case studies demonstrate, preservation groups can be an early force in convening and furthering neighborhood stabilization initiatives.

In neighborhoods facing substantial change, one social equity concern is very often voiced: Will current residents benefit from the changes that are coming? In addition to the environmental outcomes and opportunities for investment, neighborhood-based preservation strategies and tools lean heavily on incremental improvements—as opposed to wholesale redevelopment—and are much more likely to be helpful for current residents than new development. Small repairs can help make an older home safe, habitable, and high quality for years to come. These are also repairs and tools that can be undertaken and obtained by homeowners, in contrast with the professionalized technical and financing requirements of new construction. Painting, repairing windows, and taking some energy efficiency measures can be completed by homeowners with minimal training. Many homeowners in middle neighborhoods can afford to make these upkeep repairs. For those who cannot, public or subsidized resources are often available for weatherization and improvements to increase energy and water efficiency. Unlike complex, large-scale financing tools for new development (e.g., New Markets Tax Credits), the paperwork for these small home improvement grants can be handled between homeowners and program administrators such as city staff, utility companies, or privately run programs like the Heritage Home Program discussed later in this chapter.

On the community action side, preservation offers a way to organize local residents and other stakeholders around collective concerns and goals using the tangible built environment. Stories are one of the most fundamental ways to connect with other people and the heritage of a place. This may take the form of collecting oral histories about local places and people; organizing to save a building with local ties or distinctive (or typical) architecture; or discussing how to guide

---

[7]   Ned Kaufman, *Place, Race, and Story* (New York: Routledge, 2009), p. 400.
[8]   Ibid., p. 396.

rehabilitation, new development, or demolition in a way that preserves the built character of a block or neighborhood.

Community members can take tangible actions through preservation, too. Demolition is appropriate for many vacant and abandoned buildings, but it must be done by professionals at a per-building cost ranging from $10,000 for a detached house to $50,000 or more for a row house with occupied neighbors. Boarding up buildings, on the other hand, can be completed by neighbors at a weekend work party with hand-held drills and low-cost or donated materials. As shown by community-led board-ups in Youngstown, Ohio, this "mothballing" helps people to be active participants in combating blight—to feel that they are taking back their neighborhood and contributing to a positive upward trend. It also allows breathing room to see if the market will rebound, while ensuring that vacant buildings are secured from illegal squatting or other criminal activities.

This last opportunity is a particularly important one in middle neighborhoods, where decline in demand sometimes leads to lower housing values and higher rates of abandonment and demolition. Out-of-town investors are often major landholders in these areas and they are difficult to hold accountable for property maintenance. Taking a careful look at the building stock and allowing local residents to weigh in on appropriate strategies help to reclaim a neighborhood in spirit—and, more practically, galvanize public pressure to invest in rehabilitations, board up vacant houses, complete strategic demolitions, and hold inattentive building owners accountable through targeted code enforcement and tax liens where applicable. The community-based planning work of the Youngstown Neighborhood Development Corporation (YNDC), a case study in this chapter, offers a model for inclusive processes that invites people to shape their place. Although preserving buildings is not always an outcome of this process, residents' motivation for participating often comes from a connection to the neighborhood's built environment, and a feeling that the place is distinctive enough to merit a personal investment of time and energy.

BUILDING EFFECTIVE PLACE-BASED PARTNERSHIPS

As discussed, preservation dovetails with many other disciplines shaping place, building community capacity, and improving local social networks. Collaboration between these disciplines and the community is critical. This is especially true in middle neighborhoods, where resources are limited, community needs may be significant and multifaceted, and residents have historically been disempowered from decision making about their own neighborhoods. Particularly in legacy cities, middle neighborhoods face myriad challenges. Vacant buildings and lots punctuate occupied homes, a downward trend in middle-income jobs creates a highly uneven patchwork of income levels, and public education quality can be hit or miss. These challenges are fundamentally interconnected and place-based, with a multiplicity of players making decisions. Everyone has something at stake, and everyone should have a place at the table in developing strategies and tools.

A broader definition of preservation creates many collaborative opportunities and expands the list of stakeholders and partners. Preservation shares goals with many groups, including:

- Advocates for quality affordable housing and commercial space.
- Programs that seek to increase and maintain homeownership.
- Community wealth-building advocates.
- Community members seeking to improve their neighborhoods in tangible ways.
- Community organizers with the goal of increasing community engagement and developing capacity for direct involvement and political action.
- Local historians looking to preserve community heritage and stories.
- City and neighborhood champions hoping to retain and attract new residents via unique built character.[9]
- Sustainability advocates.

The three case studies that follow highlight Ohio organizations working to address most of these priorities in some way. The case studies represent a range of on-the-ground initiatives with exceptional track records—not the only work happening in this arena, but some of the strongest. The programs explored in these case studies are conducted by nonprofit organizations, county land banks, and private partners using public, private, and self-generated funding. One program hews to traditional preservation standards; the others simply aim to keep buildings standing and return them to productive parts of the neighborhood that are valued both in the economic and community senses.

YOUNGSTOWN NEIGHBORHOOD DEVELOPMENT CORPORATION

The Youngstown 2010 plan made national headlines when it was adopted in 2005. Youngstown was the first legacy city to acknowledge that its decades-long population loss was permanent and would continue unless drastic changes were made.[10] It would not regain the 51 percent of its population that departed between 1960 and 2000. But the plan was optimistic, citing an opportunity to "change the status quo." "Many difficult choices will have to be made as Youngstown recreates itself as a sustainable mid-sized city," read the first point in the plan's framework. Presidential candidate John Edwards called the plan "visionary" during a 2007 campaign stop in Youngstown, and media in other legacy cities like Detroit looked to Youngstown's pragmatic, forward-looking approach as a potential model.[11]

Youngstown residents accepted the forecast and recommendations for a smaller city. In fact, they had shaped them as part of a broad-based community engagement process. More than 5,000 people participated in the plan's development via community and neighborhood meetings. Significantly, more than 150 people had a hands-on role in creating the plan via working groups that articulated how to realize an overall vision for the city. The American Planning Association recognized

---

9   See Marcia Nedland's chapter in this volume.
10 City of Youngstown and Youngstown State University, *Youngstown 2010* (Youngstown: City of Youngstown, 2003).
11 David Skolnik, "Edwards Called City's 2010 Plan 'Visionary,'" *The Vindicator*, July 18, 2007, available at http://www.vindy.com/news/2007/jul/18/edwards-called-city8217s-2010-plan/; Terry Parris, Jr., "Youngstown 2010: What Shrinkage Looks Like, What Detroit Could Learn," *Model D*, May 4, 2010, available at http://modeldmedia.com/features/ytownplan5022010.aspx.

Youngstown 2010 with its Public Outreach Award in 2007, and in 2010 the *The New York Times* featured "civic energy" as a bright spot in Youngstown's ongoing struggle with vacancies.[12]

STARTING SMALL: IDORA

The Youngstown Neighborhood Development Corporation (YNDC) was established in 2009 with a focus on Idora, a residential, predominantly single-family neighborhood on the city's southside. In many ways, Idora was typical of Youngstown as a whole. Established as an early streetcar suburb in the early twentieth century, the neighborhood prospered until the collapse of the steel industry in the late 1970s.[13] In the next three decades, the neighborhood lost 36 percent of its population: less than the citywide population decline of roughly 50 percent, but still substantial.

As one of Youngstown's more viable neighborhoods, Idora was an early target for stabilization.[14] Youngstown 2010 prioritized the stabilization of viable neighborhoods as one of its four guiding themes: "a starting point from which to reclaim some of the adjacent neighborhoods that have not so successfully withstood the test of time." In 2009, a report from the National Vacant Properties Campaign (now the Center for Community Progress) underscored the importance of focusing comprehensive strategies on viable neighborhoods like Idora.[15] It also noted an issue not uncommon in legacy city neighborhoods: Even though 27 percent of buildings in the neighborhood were vacant at the time, according to Ian Beniston, the executive director of YNDC, the report pointed out that "the same problem...is likely to be true in other neighborhoods in the city which are still potentially viable."

A 2008 neighborhood plan for Idora cited an 86 percent occupancy rate and 67 percent homeownership rate—both roughly proportional to the city as a whole.[16] However, the neighborhood had higher rates of poverty, lower education, and a median home value of just $33,767—nearly 20 percent lower than the citywide median of $40,900. More than one-quarter of buildings and 15 percent of parcels in the neighborhood were vacant; Youngstown had a combined vacancy rate of 40 percent.[17]

The Idora Comprehensive Neighborhood Plan named six goals: increasing safety, increasing pride, revitalizing the neighborhood's commercial corridor, preserving existing housing, reclaiming vacant land and structures, and cleaning and greening the neighborhood. Youngstown Neighborhood Development Corporation tackled most of these goals, with the overall aim of catalyzing

[12]   Sabrina Tavernise, "Trying to Overcome the Stubborn Blight of Vacancies," *The New York Times*, December 19, 2010, available at http://www.nytimes.com/2010/12/20/us/20youngstown.html.

[13]   City of Youngstown Planning Department and Ohio State University, *Idora Neighborhood Comprehensive Neighborhood Plan* (Youngstown: City of Youngstown, 2008), available at http://www.cityofyoungstownoh.org/about_youngstown/ youngstown_2010/neighborhoods/south/idora/idora.aspx.

[14]   Youngstown uses the terms "constrained" and "functional" markets to refer to middle neighborhoods.

[15]   Dan Kildee, Jonathan Logan, Alan Mallach, and Joseph Schilling, *Regenerating Youngstown and Mahoning County through Vacant Property Reclamation: Reforming Systems and Right-sizing Markets* (Washington, DC: National Vacant Properties Campaign, 2009).

[16]   Data from U.S. Census, Census 2000, (Washington, DC: U.S. Census Bureau); *Idora Neighborhood Comprehensive Neighborhood Plan*.

[17]   Sabrina Tavernise, "Trying to Overcome the Stubborn Blight of Vacancies," *The New York Times*, December 19, 2010. Youngstown had 4,500 vacant buildings and more than 23,000 vacant parcels.

reinvestment in the neighborhood. From the beginning, the organization took a multipronged approach to neighborhood stabilization and revitalization, with tactics including demolition, greening, and reuse of vacant lots; partnerships with code enforcement; home repairs, rehabilitation, and sales; public art; and the development of community gardens and an urban farm in the neighborhood.

By 2012, four years after work began, YNDC had demolished 93 houses, rehabilitated 43 vacant and owner-occupied houses and completed minor repairs to 30 more, boarded up 40 houses, and cleaned and repurposed more than 150 vacant lots composing more than 17 acres into uses such as community gardens, native planting sites, and side yard expansions.[18] It had launched a Community Loan Fund to provide mortgages in target neighborhoods, financial training for homebuyers, and repair funds. It had also completed homeownership training for 36 people and developed job training for city residents.

COMMUNITY-POWERED

YNDC's work in Idora and other middle neighborhoods has built on and expanded the focus in Youngstown 2010 of engaging community members. "REVITALIZE" is emblazoned on YNDC annual reports and materials. The houses that YNDC rehabilitates are frequently advertised as "revitalized" instead of "renovated." The word is "a call to action," says Tom Hetrick, YNDC's neighborhood planner. "It gets different groups involved in helping to improve the community."

YNDC's website highlights the need for "a renewed sense of ownership and community among residents. We must leverage the most important asset in our neighborhoods: the time, energy and resources of existing residents." Even more directly, many YNDC plans, T-shirts, vehicles, and even a storage facility bear the slogan "STAND UP—FIGHT BLIGHT." The responsibility is clear.

Although YNDC staff and City of Youngstown planners develop each Neighborhood Action Plan, public meetings give neighborhood stakeholders the opportunity to identify local priorities and assets at the beginning of the planning process, and offer feedback on specific strategies during the process. When each plan is completed, Neighborhood Action Teams composed of local leaders and residents are charged with implementation. Beniston says that each team plays a central role as "the infrastructure to communicate and implement the plans." It meets quarterly to update a list of priority properties and provides a local communication network for YNDC and the City to better connect with residents. In turn, YNDC staff track the work of Neighborhood Action Teams and report back on impact at the end of each year.

Neighborhood residents also have the opportunity to roll up their sleeves at community workdays held in each of YNDC's 10 target neighborhoods. More than 1,200 volunteers showed up to 26 workdays in 2015 to clean vacant lots, clear debris from vacant houses and lots, board up 553 houses, and help with basic rehabilitation tasks. Volunteers cleaned and secured more than 200

---

[18]   Ian J. Beniston, "Idora: Creating a Smaller Stronger Neighborhood." Presentation at the Thriving Communities Ohio Land Bank Conference, November 28, 2012, available at http://www.wrlandconservancy.org/documents/F2-Idora-Crea tingaSmallerStrongerNeighborhood.pdf.

vacant buildings. A robust AmeriCorps volunteer program also provides on-the-job construction training for city residents—13 local residents worked across 25 neighborhoods in 2015 as part of the program. If neighborhood groups want to do board-ups on their own, they can look to the YNDC's "Board-Up Manual" for guidance.

Whether completed by one-time volunteers, returning volunteers, or AmeriCorps members, hands-on work helps people see what is happening in their neighborhood. In the short run, says Beniston, "They want to become a part of it so they can get more done." And in the long run, "It helps instill pride in their neighborhoods."

ON-THE-GROUND REVITALIZATION

YNDC's work advances parcel by parcel. When it completes a Neighborhood Action Plan, YNDC makes recommendations for all buildings in the area that are vacant or have code violations. The recommendations are based largely on field surveys, but also incorporate data on ownership, including absentee owners; how recently the property has been transferred; and delinquent taxes. To provide tangible items for immediate actions, 25 "priority properties" are identified on the basis of factors such as code violations, severity of deterioration, public safety, and proximity to assets and otherwise stable areas. Community members adjust this list as needed, and it is updated as properties are demolished or rehabilitated or code violations are brought into compliance.

In a recently completed Neighborhood Action Plan for the Wick Park neighborhood, the majority of properties were recommended for code enforcement (Table 1). Of the 25 priority properties identified for immediate action by the Neighborhood Action Team, just under one-half were recommended for near-term demolition by the City, with the remaining properties recommended for code enforcement and boarding up. (As used in the table, "preservation" denotes long-term board-ups of buildings that have architectural value, but whose size, rehab cost, and/or surrounding market conditions may preclude immediate rehab and resale.)

Table 1. Wick Park Neighborhood Housing and Property Strategies

	All properties	Priority properties*
Demolition by City	17	11
Needs code enforcement	89	14
Board up/clean up	18	13
Preservation	9	9

*Some priority properties are included in more than one strategy.

Because much of YNDC's rehabilitation work is unsubsidized, most decisions about vacant buildings come down to whether YNDC can rehab and resell them at a profit or at least without significant loss. The Mahoning County Land Bank partners with YNDC to transfer tax-foreclosed buildings at no cost, but a typical rehabilitation costs $20-$30 per square foot—between $30,000 and $80,000 for recent projects, according to Beniston. AmeriCorps volunteers and YNDC construction crews complete the work, with community members providing assistance on unskilled tasks such as cleaning out debris and painting.

If the local market will absorb a rehabilitated house at or near the rehab cost, YNDC says it is worth the work. In addition to providing jobs and job training, renovated houses help repopulate a neighborhood with owner-occupants, increase the value of the property and adjacent houses, and build the city's property tax base. A vacant lot is worth $250; a rehabbed house is worth $60,000, and saving it preserves neighborhood character. "The homes that we're rehabilitating have more character than all the similar product in the suburbs, and they're totally updated," says Beniston.

Residents often champion rehabilitation of vacant houses rather than demolition. "Most people want the houses reoccupied," says Beniston. "They don't want their whole neighborhood torn down." Community members push back against some recommended demolitions during the Neighborhood Action Plan process or in subsequent Action Team meetings, where proposed parcel-level strategies are examined in detail. Some go further. One local group is hiring an intern to market rehabbed houses in its neighborhood. In select cases when vacant buildings have significant architectural or other value and community members advocate for rehabilitation, but near-term sales are unlikely, YNDC assigns a "preservation" strategy to the buildings and boards them up.

YNDC's rehab work is not limited to vacant buildings. The organization's Community Loan Fund offers long-term financial counseling coupled with mortgages to homebuyers who have been denied an affordable loan by traditional lending institutions. This "high accountability, character-based approach" allows community members to purchase YNDC-rehabilitated houses and complete minor repairs, even with imperfect credit in a conservative lending market.[19] The program is offered in partnership with the city, state, a local foundation, a local bank, HUD-certified counseling agencies, and others. For owner-occupied houses, the Paint Youngstown program provides free external repairs to avoid potential code violations and improve the overall image of the neighborhood.

IMPACTS

As any legacy city resident knows, stabilizing a neighborhood market takes time and requires much more than just fixing one house. Since work began in Idora in 2009, vacancy rates have dropped roughly 8 percent and average sales prices have risen nearly 80 percent. In those seven years, YNDC has rehabilitated and resold 31 vacant homes, repaired 84 additional homes for low-income homeowners, boarded up 46 vacant houses, and provided loans to 19 homeowners through its Community Loan Fund.[20] Nearly 130 buildings have been demolished, and close to 200 vacant lots have been repurposed as gardens, parks, recreation, events, and an urban farm. All this has bolstered market confidence: More than 160 property owners have made significant investments in their homes since 2009. And the organization's work continues in the neighborhood.

---

[19]   Ian Beniston, email to the authors, 3/16/2016.
[20]   Youngstown Neighborhood Development Corporation, *Evidence-based Neighborhood Revitalization: The Idora Neighborhood in Youngstown, Ohio* (Youngstown: Youngstown Neighborhood Development Corporation, 2015).

Figure 1. Home Price and Vacancy Rates in the Idora Neighborhood of Youngstown, Ohio

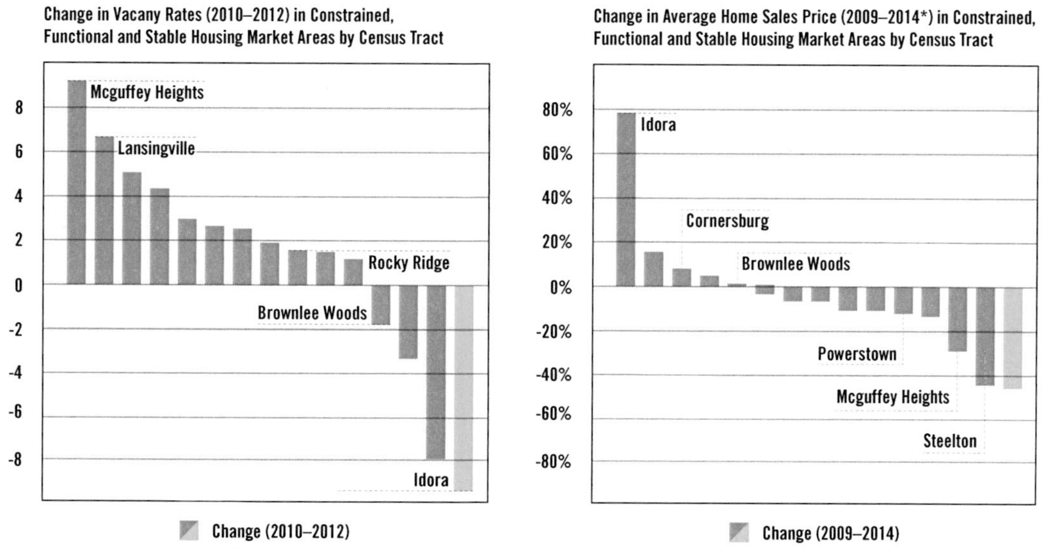

Change in Vacany Rates (2010–2012) in Constrained, Functional and Stable Housing Market Areas by Census Tract

Change in Average Home Sales Price (2009–2014*) in Constrained, Functional and Stable Housing Market Areas by Census Tract

Mcguffey Heights
Lansingville
Rocky Ridge
Brownlee Woods
Idora

Change (2010–2012)

Idora
Cornersburg
Brownlee Woods
Powerstown
Mcguffey Heights
Steelton

Change (2009–2014)

Reproduced with permission from Youngstown Neighborhood Development Corporation.

YNDC expanded its focus beyond Idora to other middle neighborhoods in Youngstown, guided by a 2014 *Neighborhood Conditions Report* that classified neighborhoods by market strength, from extremely weak to stable. YNDC is now working in nine other constrained and functional neighborhoods using Neighborhood Action Plans and Neighborhood Action Teams. In 2015, the organization completed two owner-occupied rehabilitations, 27 limited repair projects for homeowners, brought 41 properties into code compliance, rehabbed 45 properties, cleaned up or boarded up 228 houses, and worked with the City and the land bank to prioritize demolitions of 220 houses.

The change, according to Beniston, goes well beyond the numbers: "We can look at the data all we want, and we know that's critical, but another piece is that these are neighborhoods that people live in…. We value what people think of their neighborhoods and their priorities for buildings."

OHIO'S HERITAGE HOME PROGRAM—PIONEERED BY CLEVELAND RESTORATION SOCIETY

The Heritage Home ProgramSM supports preservation projects across 42 communities in northeast Ohio, but it does so by almost any other name than "historic preservation." Low-interest loans are available to "older houses," while "old house experts" provide technical advice. Any residential building with three or fewer units qualifies if it was constructed more than 50 years ago—no historic designation required.

Yet preservation it is. All exterior work must comply with the gold standard for preservation projects, the Secretary of the Interior's Standards for Rehabilitation, and loan funds cannot be used for historically incompatible alterations such as vinyl siding or vinyl windows. Participating property owners—largely homeowners—are required to consult with program staff while planning their project. The same staff members inspect the finished project to ensure that it complies with the program's "master specifications," a detailed set of technical standards.

Initially, the program was limited to houses in historic districts. But by 2012, foreclosures during the Great Recession continued to decimate residential neighborhoods in and around Cleveland. The Cleveland Restoration Society (CRS), the 44-year-old preservation organization that initiated the Heritage Home Program in 1992 and continues to operate it, saw a need for action. "It became not just fixing up historic homes, but about keeping people in their homes and their neighborhoods," said Margaret Lann, the Heritage Home Program associate at CRS. There was also, she added, a bigger question, how to extend the program to people in older homes so they can improve their homes and remain in them? Consequently, CRS made some significant changes by:

- Opening up the program to any house more than 50 years old;
- Expanding loan-eligible projects to include all forms of general rehabilitation, so long as the project is consistent with the architectural style of the house;
- Aggressively marketing the program to additional communities; and
- Reducing program fees and interest rates to attract more participants.

These changes were in line with CRS's progressive preservation ethos, which sees preservation as a powerful tool to advance the goals of community revitalization, a stronger regional economy, and higher quality of life.[21]

The Heritage Home Program remains available to any older house, but it incentivizes preservation-friendly decisions via inexpensive loan funds (with fixed-rate financing as low as 1.4 percent); education; and technical assistance. It also effectively addresses three of the top objections to buying older houses: the cost of maintenance, the specialized knowledge required of homeowners, and the functional obsolescence of kitchens and bathrooms in older houses. (Heritage Home Program loans can be used to fund those interior improvements with no historic standards or review.)

The program's low-interest loans are enabled by a "buy-down" of interest rates from two local banks. Public funds from the Cuyahoga County and the Ohio Housing Finance Agency (OHFA) provide capital to subsidize the difference between at-market interest rates and the lower subsidized rate.[22] Loan amounts are determined by an after-rehab appraisal that estimates the post-rehabilitation home value to establish equity. The loan terms are for 7 to 10 years, with no prepayment penalty. The CRS banking partner can hold the first or second lien on the property.

21 Cleveland Restoration Society, *Mission, Vision & Strategy* (Cleveland: author, 2015), available at http://www.clevelandrestoration.org/about/vision.php.
22 Heritage Home Educational Society, *Heritage Home Program: Loan Subsidy Application* (Cleveland: author), available at http://www.heritagehomeprogram.org/assets/pdf_files/Heritage%20Home%20Program%20Application.pdf.

Borrowers must meet participating banks' standard lending requirements, Lann notes. This includes income sufficient to pay back the loans, though loans subsidized by OHFA dollars are restricted to low- and moderate-income households earning up to approximately $76,000 per year. Program staff estimate that, over the life of the program, it has made more than 300 loans worth $11 million to low- and moderate-income homeowners in northeast Ohio. (Loans subsidized by Cuyahoga County are unrestricted.)

The Heritage Home Program has become a national model in its nearly 25 years of operation. According to its website, it has made more than 1,200 low-interest loans for more than $46 million and provided technical assistance to more than 9,000 homeowners on projects valued at a total of $200 million. Loans range from $3,000 to $200,000, with an average loan of $25,000. A Cleveland State University study showed that the loans benefited the surrounding neighborhoods as well; assessed values and sales prices of homes surrounding the participating properties increased.[23]

The Heritage Home Program is open to any age-eligible house in participating communities, but some communities market the program in targeted ways. The city of Cleveland Heights is currently planning to focus its marketing efforts to areas hard-hit by the recession, where homeowners have been hesitant to reinvest in their homes, and the city of Bay Village has done targeted outreach to low- and moderate-income census tracts. The Lucas County Land Bank (Land Bank) is also taking a focused approach in several neighborhoods in and around Toledo, as will be discussed later.

TECHNICAL ASSISTANCE

Technical assistance, or "home improvement advice," is the heart and soul of the Heritage Home Program. Program staff offer consultations at no charge to owners of older residential properties in participating communities; homeowners outside those areas and owners of other building types are charged a small fee. Services include site visits; recommendations on maintenance, repair, rehab, additions, energy efficiency, and modernization of kitchens and bathrooms; and construction advice. In addition, staff help evaluate contractor bids and estimates and provide advice on materials and supplies.

"Not everybody is going to want a program loan, but they want to get the job done in one way or another," says Lann. Technical assistance "helps to get those projects done, hopefully with a preservation approach" that maintains the quality of local architecture and neighborhood character. Last year, program staff provided free advice to more than 1,500 homeowners.[24] In the past 10 years, 8,000 homeowners have used the program's technical assistance, including 5,200 site visits.

Although most technical assistance is requested, some is required for loan recipients. Staff members go on a site visit with prospective borrowers and review the proposed scope of the project prior to the application's submission. Before work begins, staff members develop exterior project specifications in collaboration with the property owner; these are referred to again during a final inspection.

---

[23] Brian Mikelbank, *Does Preservation Pay? Assessing Cleveland Restoration Society's Home Improvement Program* (Cleveland: Cleveland State University, n.d.).

[24] Heritage Home Educational Society, *Heritage Home Program*, Loan Subsidy Application.

Program involvement extends to the funding itself. The homeowner is the borrower, but the lending institution deposits loan funds into an escrow account held by CRS, which disburses them directly to the contractor as work is completed. According to Lann, CRS sees the escrow process as added value for multiple parties: It removes the hassle of managing payouts and contractors for the homeowner, assures the contractor they will get paid, and provides trusted quality control that reassures banks that the completed project will add value, which helps them take small risks with lending.

CRS also organizes public workshops on home maintenance and rehabilitation, and an online preservation toolbox rounds out the program's technical assistance. Practical topics are the focus of both programs: painting and color advice, maintenance basics, weatherization, roof repair, etc.

IMPACTS

Put simply, houses in the program achieve results. Between 2000 and 2006, the assessed values of Cleveland properties in the Heritage Home Program rose roughly 8 percent above the values of comparable properties.[25] Between 1994 and 2000, the assessed values appreciated 43 percent on average, compared with 28 percent for similar properties. The results were similar in communities outside Cleveland that adopted the program after 2001. There, nearly 100 properties saw a median appreciation of 28 percent compared with 21 percent for comparable properties.

Figure 2. Estimated Market Value Appreciation Associated With the Heritage Home Program

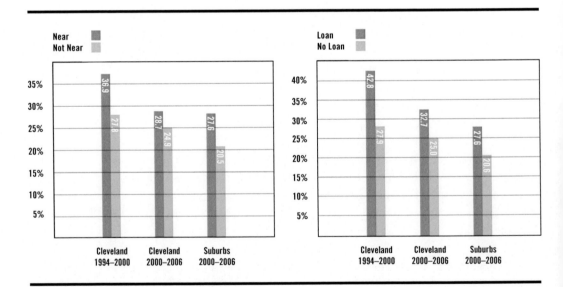

Reproduced with permission from Biran Mikelbank, Cleveland State University "Does Preservation Pay? Assessing Cleveland Restoration Society's Home Improvement Program.

---

[25]   Mikelbank, *Does Preservation Pay?*

Program participation is also correlated with lower rates of foreclosure, a broad indicator of neighborhood stability. A study of Heritage Home Program loan properties from 2006 to 2013 found that foreclosure rates for the sample track countywide trends, reflecting difficult market conditions.[26] However, the rate of foreclosure among program participants was 2.9 times (in 2008) to 11.1 times (in 2010) lower than the countywide foreclosure rate. Foreclosure rates for program participants were also lower than those in their surrounding communities, both within Cleveland and in inner- and outer-ring suburbs.[27]

Mikelbank's "Does Preservation Pay?" study established that the impacts for property values extend beyond the houses in the program—a particularly important point for middle neighborhoods where stabilizing and strengthening housing markets may be a priority. The spillover benefits were measured for houses within one-tenth of a mile of properties that had received CRS loans. In Cleveland, the sale price of the nearby houses had risen by 10 percent, compared with a 6 percent increase for other houses. In the surrounding communities, sale prices appreciated by 14 to 50 percent more than sale prices of other houses. Assessed values also rose more for nearby houses. In Cleveland between 1994 and 2000, assessed values for nearby houses had appreciated 9 percent more than other houses (37 percent vs. 28 percent); between 2000 and 2006, the difference was 4 percent higher (29 percent vs. 25 percent). Outside Cleveland, houses in the tenth of a mile radius were assessed at values roughly 7 percent higher than those outside it (28 percent vs. 21 percent).

The same study also suggested that the loan programs had nonmonetary benefits for the neighborhood. Few houses in the CRS loan programs sold between 1994 and 2006. Mikelbank thought that perhaps homeowners who had thoughtfully invested in their homes were less likely to sell them. If this were the case, the loan program could help encourage lower turnover and more stability. Lann at CRS noted that the program encourages a shift in attitude, from regarding a house as an investment—one that will eventually be sold—to seeing it as an asset that shapes the quality of daily life. "When people do a project that makes their day-to-day living better and know they've invested in their house, they tend to stay in it longer," she said.

LUCAS COUNTY LAND BANK

In 2014, CRS licensed the Heritage Home Program to the Lucas County Land Bank, which was established in 2010 to work in Toledo and surrounding communities in northwest Ohio. Through this move, and by making the program available for licensing to other land banks, CRS sought to make rehabilitation a stronger, easier tool for land banks to use.[28] According to Lann, licensing also allowed the program to grow beyond CRS's geographic area—a key move, given the importance of onsite technical assistance.

---

[26] Brian A. Mikelbank, "In Search of Stability: Adding Residential Preservation to the Planner's Toolkit," (unpublished manuscript, 2015), 15–16.
[27] Ibid., p. 17, 20.
[28] Heritage Home Educational Society, *Licensing the HPP: A Tool for County Landbanks* (Cleveland: author, 2015), available at http://www. heritagehomeprogram.org/joinus/licensing.php.

The Lucas County Land Bank ("Land Bank") was no stranger to rehabilitation, with a track record that included acquisition and resale of 329 houses in its first five years.[29] It does not rehabilitate homes itself, but resells the houses with the condition of renovation to leverage private dollars. For houses that do not require extensive renovation, offers from prospective owner-occupants are prioritized. The Land Bank has also worked with local immigrants to repurpose vacant buildings as part of the Welcome Toledo–Lucas County initiative. The Land Bank's *Five Year Progress Report* framed the work in terms of preserving "the fabric of our neighborhoods": "Each vacant property that is renovated helps stabilize surrounding properties by increasing values, eliminating blight, and generating new energy in our neighborhoods and commercial corridors."[30] This includes partnerships with immigrants.

According to David Mann, the Land Bank's executive director, the agency sees the Heritage Home Program as a proactive way to stabilize properties before they deteriorate, encourage upkeep of surrounding properties, and preclude more substantial Land Bank involvement—in the long run, achieving its mission to strengthen neighborhoods and preserve property values. According to the *Five Year Progress Report*, a recent survey of every parcel in Toledo yielded encouraging results about the condition of the housing stock—88 percent of houses were in good or very good condition. At the same time, it noted, "too many homeowners cannot keep up with major exterior maintenance": nearly 16,000 properties, or 17 percent of all buildings in the city, had missing siding and peeling paint.

Yet the challenging regional real estate market has significant repercussions for property owners who seek to repair their homes. The foreclosure crisis sent local property values into a downward spiral, with a 25 to 30 percent reduction in most Toledo neighborhoods, and home values have remained flat or climbed only slightly in subsequent years, according to Mann. Combined with banks' conservative approaches to calculating potential loans, this means that many homeowners have too little equity in their houses to qualify for a loan, even with the after-rehab assessments offered by the Heritage Home Program. They are not able to sell either. This is true even in Toledo's most stable neighborhoods, says Kathleen Kovacs, the Heritage Home Program director for the Land Bank.

As a result, technical assistance has by far been the largest component of the Heritage Home Program in Lucas County. In the 18 months since the program began there, approximately 120 homeowners have taken advantage of the free technical assistance offered by the program, compared to just two loans made. As in Cleveland and Cuyahoga County, program staff conduct site visits, help homeowners evaluate and prioritize needed work, determine what they can do themselves, and review contractor quotes when needed.

---

[29] Homes acquired for rehabilitation made up 30 percent of residential building acquisitions; the other 70 percent of houses were acquired for demolition. Lucas County Land Bank, *Five Year Progress Report: 2010–2015* (Toledo: author, 2015), 6, available at http://co.lucas.oh.us/DocumentCenter/View/55765.

[30] Ibid.

"It's about knowledge-sharing and education," says Kovacs. "If you leave a homeowner a little more educated about what they need to do to maintain their home, that leaves the community better off." Mann agrees: "If someone has gained real knowledge—or gained real knowledge and been able to make those improvements—that's a benefit to the community." Both see the Land Bank as a neighborhood resource with a long-term view, and the Heritage Home Program as a relatively inexpensive investment in—and toolkit for—early preventive intervention.

The program is open to all age-eligible houses in Lucas County, as in Cleveland, but the Land Bank has targeted its initial outreach to four neighborhoods in Toledo and one neighborhood in a suburban community. Kovacs noted that they chose stable and middle neighborhoods with the goal of preventing the need for other, more intensive land bank services. They began with two historic districts—one in a stable neighborhood and one in a middle neighborhood—working intensively with local partners. The program then expanded to two middle neighborhoods with historic housing stock in Toledo and a suburban neighborhood. In the four Toledo neighborhoods, technical assistance was in high demand. When it came to making improvements, most property owners in two of the higher-income neighborhoods preferred to use their own funds, while some homeowners in the other neighborhoods had insufficient equity to qualify for loans.

The Land Bank is currently exploring other tools to enable homeowners to complete necessary work. It just started the Rebuild, Invest, Stabilize, and Engage (RISE) program, a targeted effort being piloted in Toledo's character-rich Library Village neighborhood to layer multiple Land Bank programs and maximize impact. The Land Bank is also considering whether an existing program to fund energy-efficiency improvements in commercial buildings can be adapted for use with residential properties.[31]

In the meantime, the Heritage Home Program is aligned with other Land Bank programs: home sales for renovation, acquisition and resale of commercial buildings for renovation, and more. The Land Bank actively demolishes vacant houses—with an anticipated 1,800 demolitions by the end of 2016—but it also aims to help maintain neighborhood character and provide homeowners with strong tools for success, according to its *Five-Year Progress Report*. "By making direct investments, partnering on renovation projects, and offering the Heritage Home Program," says Mann on the Heritage Home Program website, "we hope we are setting an example for other land banks across the country that balance is key—and it's not an either/or."[32]

For example, $1.4 million from a Wells Fargo settlement provided partial funding for a Land Bank roof replacement grant program in 2014–2015.[33] The program was targeted to low- and moderate-income homeowners in three concentrations of majority-minority census tracts and included elements similar to the Heritage Home Program: homeowner education through credit counseling

---

[31]   The Property Assessed Clean Energy program (PACE) is administered through the Toledo Port Authority. It allows property owners to borrow money to make energy-efficiency improvements such as windows, insulation, and boilers. Debt is assessed directly to property taxes and paid in installments and is transferable to a new owner.

[32]   Heritage Home Educational Society, *Licensing the HPP*.

[33]   Lucas County Land Bank, *Five Year Progress Report*.

and wealth-building classes; technical assistance, with a home inspection by land bank staff and comprehensive repair list; and funds to replace roofs.[34] The program replaced 145 roofs, but the education and assistance had other lasting impacts. "The homeowners understood that we were going to invest in them in the long term, not the short term," Kovacs noted.

CONCLUSIONS

Evidence is growing for the positive impact that short-term investment programs—preservation and otherwise—have when they take a holistic, long-range view of neighborhood stabilization in middle market neighborhoods. These targeted, incremental improvements both benefit current residents and pave the way for much-needed newcomers. A more expansive view of historic preservation in middle neighborhoods provides neighborhood stabilization benefits along the equity, health, and environmental axes and encourages more robust real estate markets. Preservation tools such as those discussed in this chapter, and others yet to be tried, deserve careful attention by those seeking to stabilize middle neighborhoods.

This is particularly true because, when owner-occupied, the houses that make up middle neighborhoods are tremendously important concentrations of wealth for a large proportion of families.[35] Finding ways to stabilize and build market value (and restore market functionality for fair transactions) of these homes is an essential part of this volume. Underlying these strategies is an understanding that the historic character, the walkability, the sustainability, and the feel of these neighborhoods are both valued and an underused source of market demand.

Although it is true that each city, neighborhood, and block is unique, we can draw three conclusions about the importance of creating deep partnerships, fostering long-term community engagement, and targeting limited resources.

The value of strong partnerships cannot be understated. When preservation has been an effective tool in bringing a community and many external stakeholders together to achieve tangible results in a neighborhood, it has been rooted in partnerships between many actors, many of whom may have never previously worked closely together. It is precisely because different groups bring different experience, connections, and expertise to the table that their collaborative efforts are far greater than the sum of their parts.

Meaningful community engagement and long-term commitment to a specific community were also hallmarks of these programs' success. The Youngstown Neighborhood Development Corporation has not only conducted community engagement activities in Idora—it also supports the activities of Neighborhood Action Teams and tracks progress toward community goals. The result is more proactive and engaged representatives from the local community. The Heritage Home Program in Lucas County is joined by other land bank initiatives to build homeowners' financial acumen and practical know-how. These programs fall outside traditional land bank activities, but they meet larger

---

34   Ibid.; Lucas County Land Bank, *Neighborhood Roof Replacement Program Application Packet* (Toledo: author, n.d.).
35   See Mallach in this volume, "Homeownership and the Stability of the Middle Market Neighborhoods."

goals of neighborhood stabilization and help community members see the land bank as a long-term partner and resource.

For cities with a high proportion of middle neighborhoods, resources available for investment strategies are stretched extremely thin. The programs in Slavic Village and Idora have taken the approach that neighborhood investment strategies should be tailored to neighborhood conditions to achieve the highest likelihood of results. In Cleveland and Lucas County, the Cleveland Restoration Society and partners have made more financial resources available via after-rehab appraisals and lower interest rates. The simultaneous strategy of considering technical knowledge an important resource adds another dimension of value.

Because they could quickly turn up or down, middle neighborhoods in legacy cities offer unique opportunities for program innovation, and substantial returns on limited investments. We see an economic, equity, and environmental case for substantial increases in the strategic deployment in middle neighborhoods of programs that increase neighborhood curb appeal characteristics, such as (relatively) small-scale facade improvement grant and loan programs. This volatile context also makes it challenging to evaluate programs that intervene and underscores the need for careful research.

It is worth noting that those seeking to stabilize middle neighborhoods through preservation strategies often point to an absence of compelling quantitative research to share with stakeholders, funders, and regulators around the benefits of neighborhood-scale preservation programs. Future research that would be helpful in this arena would analyze a broad range of neighborhood stabilization tactics (e.g., occupant support, rehab, stabilization, mothballing, demolition, and vacant property uses) with regard to impacts on foreclosures, property values, and other demographic effects.

In the short term, we will be eying a few emerging programs, including the Healthy Rowhouse Project in Philadelphia; Rehabbed and Ready, a public-private partnership to renovate and auction homes in Detroit; and the Detroit Neighborhood Initiative—all oriented around furthering affordable homeownership in older neighborhoods. The Lucas County Land Bank's RISE program in Toledo (to be launched in 2016) and the Slavic Village Recovery Project in Cleveland also merit observation and full evaluation over the next few years.

Programs such as those in Youngstown's Idora neighborhood and the Heritage Home Program around Cleveland and in Lucas County reflect a new paradigm of holistic and broadly based historic preservation. With a practical orientation to contemporary community needs, historic preservation can help ensure that the older building stock of a neighborhood can effectively meet the triple bottom line goals of economics, equity, and the environment for future residents and those who, for a very long time, have called these neighborhoods home.

Cara Bertron is the chair of the Preservation Rightsizing Network, which works in legacy cities to preserve local heritage and revitalize the built environment. She has completed preservation-based planning and revitalization projects in numerous cities, including Seattle, Philadelphia, San Francisco, Cincinnati, and Charleston. Her work includes innovative historic resource scans, citywide preservation plans, and neighborhood community development projects with a focus on equity and data-driven decision making. She was the principal author of the Action Agenda for Historic Preservation in Legacy Cities.

Nicholas Hamilton is director of Urban Policy at The American Assembly, Columbia University's bipartisan policy institute. There, Hamilton leads the Legacy Cities Partnership, a national coalition working to revitalize America's legacy cities. His work focuses on economic development, governance, and civic engagement. Mr. Hamilton's previous architectural and urban design work for the firm Davis Brody Bond included the master planning and design of U.S. diplomatic facilities abroad as well as laboratory and teaching facilities for Columbia and Princeton Universities.

XII. LOCAL PUBLIC POLICY AND MIDDLE NEIGHBORHOODS

By Henry S. Webber, Brown School of Social Work and Washington University

Middle neighborhoods have traditionally been the heart of American cities. They are the neighborhoods where working- and middle class citizens live; raise families; pay taxes; send their children to school; go to church, synagogue, or mosque; and shop at the local grocer. They are home to the police officers, fire fighters, school teachers, and office workers who make up the civil service of American cities, as well as much of the private workforce. Middle neighborhoods rarely appear on lists of "must see" places in city guidebooks, and they are not the subjects of newspaper articles on urban decay, but they make up much of the residential housing stock and population of American cities and towns. Every American city, regardless of size, has numerous middle neighborhoods. Despite middle neighborhoods' ubiquity, their number is declining in urban America. This trend poses a serious threat to American cities and should be an area of focus for local governments.

THREE TYPES OF MIDDLE NEIGHBORHOODS

Middle neighborhoods can be categorized as stable, descending, or ascending. Stable middle neighborhoods have modest or moderate housing that was built for residents ranging from working class to middle income. In most cities, the housing stock is primarily single- or two-family homes—although in very large cities such as New York and Chicago, apartments are common. Often the housing stock is quite repetitive. In Chicago, for example, many middle neighborhoods contain block after block of bungalows, one-and-a-half-story brick homes on small lots. Built in the early part of the twentieth century, they represent approximately one-third of the city's single-family housing stock.[1] Middle neighborhoods rarely have homes of great size or historic value. They are generally family neighborhoods where children attend public or parochial school. Few residents are wealthy enough to send their children to private schools. Retail and other amenities usually serve local residents, not the broader region. These are the neighborhoods of diners and ethnic restaurants, not culinary palaces. Populations are often, but not always, relatively homogenous. Although many middle neighborhoods are primarily white, that is not always the case. Chatham, on Chicago's South Side, for example, is a longtime black middle neighborhood. Hispanics now dominate the once Eastern European middle neighborhoods at the west edge of the city adjacent to Midway Airport and in the inner-ring suburbs.

---

[1]   Historic Chicago Bungalow Association, 2015. http://www.chicagobungalow.org

The second type of middle neighborhood is the descending middle neighborhood; formerly upper-class neighborhoods that, owing to declines in demand for residential housing, have become middle class despite excellent housing stock. Such neighborhoods are much more common in weak housing markets. Detroit is a good example of a city with a number of middle neighborhoods that once were the homes of executives and professionals. When whites and then upper middle class blacks left the city and the negative cycle of disinvestment from public services began, these neighborhoods became home to a less wealthy population.

The third and final model is the ascending middle neighborhood. Ascending middle neighborhoods are neighborhoods that were traditionally poor, but because of rapid increases in demand for urban living have become popular with new residents, usually young adults. Such neighborhoods are disproportionately found in strong housing market cities and are often the sites of significant new housing designed to meet new demand. The South Loop in Chicago is a good example of such a neighborhood. Once the home of skid row and very low-quality housing, the South Loop has been transformed by the development of new housing. Such a transformation is only possible with strong market conditions and a very good location. For the South Loop, the proximity to downtown Chicago's massive employment center, high housing prices in many surrounding neighborhoods, and proximity to Lake Michigan combined to fuel redevelopment.

For the past several years, my colleagues and I have been conducting an in-depth analysis of neighborhood change from 1970 to the present in the urban core of the St. Louis region. For that study, we have defined the urban core as the region that was settled before 1950, which roughly equates to the current city of St. Louis and all inner-ring suburbs. Within this area, we identified nine unusually stable census tracks in middle neighborhoods. All of these census tracks had a population of between 90 percent and 110 percent of area median per capita income in 1970, 1990, and 2010. Of these neighborhoods, five are in the city proper, three are in the suburbs, and one is a smaller city located at the eastern edge of the St. Louis metropolitan area. All of these census tracks were almost all white in 1970. By 2010, between 52 percent and 93 percent of the population was white. Only one of these census tracks or its surrounding neighborhood has elegant housing stock. Almost all of the housing is primarily single-family homes. Only one of these census tracks is a "destination," frequently visited by nonlocal residents. These stable neighborhoods all have a sizable population of children. In 2010, the percentage of children under age 18 in these neighborhoods ranged from 15.4 percent to 26.7 percent. In the city's 2010 high-income tracts (defined as having per capita income greater than 125 percent of the study area median), the percentage of children under 18 is only 13.6 percent of the population.

Our analysis explored the change in the number of middle-income neighborhoods during the past 40 years. The results show a clear decline in the number and percentage of such neighborhoods. In 1970, 59 percent of the census tracks in the urban core had a median per capita income between 75 percent and 125 percent of the area median per capita income. By 2010, only 34 percent did (see Table 1). During the same period, the number of poor and wealthy neighborhoods both increased. Overall, the urban core of St. Louis has shifted from a region characterized by middle neighborhoods to a region with an even split between poor, middle-income, and wealthy neighborhoods. Stanford sociologists Sean F. Reardon and Cornell's Kendra Bischoff recently found that this change has occurred in urban centers across the country.[2] According to their research, from 1970 to 2007, the share of metropolitan-area residents living in neighborhoods with a median income of 80–120 percent of the metro median decreased from 65 percent to 44 percent.

Table 1. Census Tracts by Income in Urban Core of the St. Louis Region: 1970–2010

Number of census tracts with per capita median income:	1970	1990	2010
Less than 75% median per capita income ("Poor")	47 (22%)	69 (32%)	75 (34%)
75–125% median per capita income ("Middle")	129 (59%)	95 (43%)	75 (34%)
More than 125% median per capita income ("Wealthy")	42 (19%)	54 (25%)	68 (31%)
Total census tracts	218	218	218

The decline in the number of middle-income neighborhoods is particularly pronounced in central cities. In the city of St. Louis proper, for example, the number of middle-income census tracts declined steeply from 52 percent in 1970 to 28 percent in 2010. The city, even more than the region, has experienced a widening chasm between neighborhood types—with an increase in upper- and lower-income neighborhoods, and a large decrease in middle class neighborhoods. In a recent study of Chicago, journalist Whet Moser found similar results. In 1970, much of the city was lower middle class; many of these neighborhoods have since been replaced with rich neighborhoods and poor neighborhoods. Anecdotal evidence suggests the same phenomenon is occurring in most American cities.

Figure 1: Percent "Poor," "Middle," and "Wealthy" Neighborhoods in the City of St. Louis: 1970 and 2010

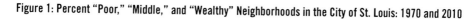

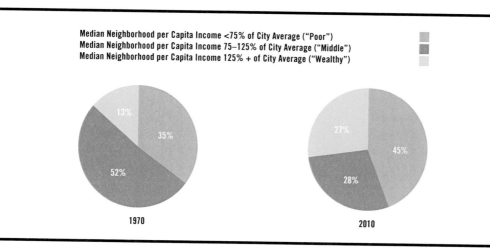

Median Neighborhood per Capita Income <75% of City Average ("Poor")
Median Neighborhood per Capita Income 75–125% of City Average ("Middle")
Median Neighborhood per Capita Income 125% + of City Average ("Wealthy")

1970

2010

2   S. Reardon and K. Bischoff, "Income Inequality and Income Segregation," *American Journal of Sociology*, 116, no. 4 (2011): 1092–1153.

REASONS FOR THE DECLINE IN MIDDLE NEIGHBORHOODS

The decreasing number of middle-income neighborhoods in America has many causes. First is the change in the distribution of American income.[3] As a nation, more of us are rich and more of us are poor, with fewer families in the middle. Changing employment patterns— particularly the loss of nearby manufacturing employment—have reduced the demand for housing in many urban core neighborhoods, leading to urban decline. Some suburban middle neighborhoods composed of small, ranch-style houses built after World War II have suffered from changes in consumer tastes. Many middle-income families, the backbone of most urban working-class neighborhoods, have reacted to the weakness of urban public school systems and the loss of parochial school choices by moving to the suburbs. Perhaps the least recognized cause of the decline in middle-income neighborhoods is the change in average household composition, from larger families to smaller households, many without children. This change has created a mismatch between the supply of housing in many older cities and the demand for housing designed for smaller families. Although these trends have led many middle neighborhoods to decline into poor neighborhoods, there is a contrary trend as well. Some middle neighborhoods—particularly those located near large and growing employers such as universities or medical centers or that have a particularly attractive historic housing stock— have become very attractive to professionals, leading to gentrification. The South End of Boston and Lincoln Park in Chicago are notable examples.

CAUSE FOR CONCERN

The shrinking number of middle neighborhoods in America is challenging for cities and a cause for deep concern. Part of the reason is financial. As neighborhoods become poorer, city revenue—which in America depends primarily on property taxes—has declined. As city revenue declines, the ability for cities to offer quality services also decreases. Unchecked, these trends lead to a self-perpetuating cycle of decline—decreased services leading to further loss of population leading to lower property values. Distressed areas of cities that depend heavily on public services are particularly affected by this cycle of decline. If a city cannot attract and hold middle class residents, it will not have the resources to help the poor. The rise in wealthy city neighborhoods from gentrification has no such negative financial effects on cities. Increasing property values improve the financial capacity of cities. However, except in a very few cities, gentrification is not widespread enough to counter the forces of decline. As John Landis has reported, the analysis of the 70 largest U.S. metro areas reveals that decline, not upgrading, was the dominant form of neighborhood socioeconomic change between 1990 and 2010. As of 1990, roughly 20 percent of the residents of these large metro areas lived in census tracts that would subsequently decline. By contrast, only 6 percent lived in tracts that subsequently upgraded, and only 3 percent lived in pre-gentrifying neighborhoods.[4]

The concerns about the decline of middle neighborhoods are more than financial. One of the key values of cities is that they are centers of opportunity, where new industries grow, new ways

---

[3]   See, for example, S. Reardon and K. Bischoff, *No Neighborhood is an Island. The Dream Revisited Series* (New York: Furman Center, New York University, November 2014).

[4]   http://www.penniur.upenn.edu/publications/the-reality-of-neighborhood-change-planners-should-worry-about-decline

of life develop, and individuals can pursue their dreams of economic improvement. As Edward Glaeser argues so persuasively—in *Triumph of the City: How Our Greatest Invention Makes Us Richer, Smarter, Greener, Healthier and Happier*—the mixing of people from different places and social classes makes cities the great forces for economic growth. The ballet of the street that Jane Jacobs describes in *The Death and Life of Great American Cities* is not just an attractive way to live; it contributes to upward mobility and economic growth. Numerous studies of the past few decades document the negative effects on the poor of social isolation.[5] We need cities that bring all of us together. No mayor wants his or her city to become home to only the poor or only the rich. All want to see cities become productive homes to a diverse population, including a large number of middle class residents and immigrants. The declining number of middle neighborhoods threatens the viability of this goal.

THE PUBLIC POLICY CHALLENGE

The public policy challenge for most cities in the United States is to preserve and grow the number of middle neighborhoods. The focus of this article is on the role of local government in meeting this challenge. By focusing on local government, I do not wish to ignore the importance of state and federal governments. The latter are important sources of revenue for cities and can be important assets. But the public services that most affect neighborhood improvement—services such as police, public schools, and parks—are managed, and to a great extent funded, locally. Local government selects the leadership of police forces and public school systems, invests in parks and afterschool programs, decides how to allocate resources to neighborhoods, and makes key policy decisions. States and the federal government can help and provide financial assistance, but they are rarely the key decision makers.

My fundamental argument is that it is appropriate and important for local governments to invest in middle neighborhoods, particularly stable and declining middle neighborhoods. Without this assistance, many middle neighborhoods will decline and cities will be increasingly challenged. As the data above illustrate, middle neighborhoods are far less stable than they may appear. They are declining across the country, and the threat of much greater decline is real. The likely largest cause of decline in middle neighborhoods, the hollowing out of the middle of the American income distribution, is unlikely to change in the short term. The decentralization of jobs within metropolitan areas has reduced the number of workers who can significantly reduce commuting time by living in urban middle neighborhoods. The public believes, with some justification, that suburban communities are safer and suburban public schools are better. To preserve middle neighborhoods will require that cities and regions craft strategies of neighborhood preservation and improve services.

Arguing for a focus on middle neighborhoods does not require the neglect of poor neighborhoods. Cities must direct federal and local resources toward neighborhoods with high poverty rates, weak schools, and high crime. Justice and human needs require such investments.

---

[5]   See, for example, P. Dreier, J. Mollenkopf, and T. Swanstrom, *Place Matters: Metropolitics for the Twenty-First Century*, 3rd ed. (Lawrence: University Press of Kansas, 2014).

What is often surprising, however, is how much cities invest in high-income neighborhoods and in downtowns. There are reasons for this; these neighborhoods are often centers for jobs, recreation, tourism, and culture that benefit the entire city or region. A weak Central Park in the 1970s was very bad for New York City and the region. Government support for Central Park, while disproportionately benefiting high-income surrounding neighborhoods, attracted residents and tourists back to the region for the long-term benefit of all New Yorkers. The dynamics of real estate development also favor high-income neighborhoods. High-income or rapidly ascending neighborhoods are the focus of most market-based real estate development in American cities, but securing these developments often requires public subsidies. It is not surprising that a city would grant $5 million in subsidies to obtain $40 million in development. But what is often lost is that the $5 million in subsidies exceeds what is provided to any middle neighborhood. Finally, high-income neighborhoods are a focus because the wealthy make political contributions, serve on city boards and committees, are politically active, and vote. Nonetheless, redirecting some of these funds is a likely pool of resources for middle neighborhoods.

The right approach is a balanced investment in low, middle, and high-income neighborhoods. Cities must focus on their jewels—such as Central Park and Golden Gate Park—and on the play lots that are the only safe places for kids to play in very disadvantaged neighborhoods. But they also need to focus on the soccer fields and baseball diamonds of middle neighborhoods. Spending only at the top and bottom is the wrong strategy over the long run.

BUILDING A MIDDLE NEIGHBORHOODS STRATEGY

Before getting into specifics of a smart strategy, it is critical to understand the dynamics of housing markets. All but the very poorest neighborhoods are made up of consumers who make choices about where they and their families want to live. These choices are shaped by family income— few of us can live in the most expensive neighborhoods—but most of us have many other choices. As other authors in this volume have described in considerable detail, most residents of any given middle neighborhood could choose to live in other neighborhoods, either in central cities or in surrounding suburbs. For a middle neighborhood to prosper, it must induce new residents to move to a particular neighborhood. These newcomers replace those who will inevitably leave owing to job relocations, aging, or other reasons. The challenge for neighborhoods is to compete for new families so that property values are maintained or improved.

Consumer choice in neighborhoods, as in any product, is about tangible and intangible factors. Better schools, safe streets, and good retail will all make a neighborhood more attractive, as will new housing that meets the needs of modern families. But intangible factors also matter. Buyers must first know of a neighborhoods to choose it. Neighborhoods can generate a buzz or identity that draws certain segments of the population. The job of shaping consumer choice can be led by a community development corporation, neighborhood improvement organization, or a local government. Regardless of the organizer, however, local government must be a full partner. Only local government can improve schools, reduce crime, or invest in parks. All stable and descending middle neighborhoods depend on government to improve services. In some ascending middle neighborhoods, a key local government task is preserving housing affordability to ensure that the benefits of new development and residents help longtime residents so they can remain in the neighborhood. This may require ceilings on property tax increases, assistance in home renovation, and affordable housing development and rehab if the neighborhood market is turning hot.

There is no silver bullet; all neighborhood strategies must consider neighborhood conditions, the regional housing market, and neighborhood strengths and weaknesses. The key is to develop a strategy that is right for a particular neighborhood at a particular time. Although strategies vary, the process of developing and implementing a middle-neighborhoods strategy has four distinct steps: (1) strengthening and empowering local organizations; (2) using data to drive programs; (3) focusing on drivers of consumer choice; and (4) marketing to key audiences.

STRENGTHENING AND EMPOWERING LOCAL ORGANIZATIONS

The rise of the asset-based community development movement has focused the community development field on the realization that all neighborhoods, even the poorest, have assets to build on.[6] Even the most devastated neighborhoods have strong leaders, organizations, people, and groups dedicated to neighborhood improvement. But if very poor neighborhoods have assets, middle neighborhoods have far more. Common assets include anchor institutions, such as local banks, churches, and businesses as well as local organizations, such as block clubs, citizen groups, and business organizations.

Local organizations are critical to neighborhoods. They provide essential local input for decisions that affect neighborhood life, advocate for neighborhoods with government agencies to ensure the flow of essential resources, and provide a vehicle for citizens to engage in their community and form bonds with other citizens. Neighborhood involvement strengthens neighborhood cohesion, as do local activities such as festivals, local youth organizations, and neighborhood beautification. The presence of an active citizens' group should be a goal for all of our neighborhoods, and enlightened city officials should see strong neighborhood groups as their strongest allies in improving neighborhoods.

The challenge is for neighborhood actors to work together to improve and promote their neighborhood. The most common technique for neighborhood organization is forming a private nonprofit Community Development Corporation (CDC) that unites many groups and interests for a common purpose. Throughout the country, CDCs have proved effective in organizing internal neighborhood groups and external parties interested in neighborhood improvement to achieve lasting success. Local organizations such as CDCs are positioned to actively involve citizens in the future of their neighborhood, strengthen neighborhood cohesion, make relocation less likely, and make neighborhoods more attractive to residents and potential residents.

---

[6]   J. Kretzmann and J. McKnight, *Building Communities from the Inside Out: A Path toward Finding and Mobilizing a Community's Assets* (Evanston, IL: Institute for Policy Research, 1993).

Local organizations require partners to implement neighborhood change. In almost all cases, the most important outside partner is local government. Part of the reason is financial; the internal resources of neighborhoods are usually insufficient to fund even local community-building activities. The number of neighborhood festivals in Chicago, for example, changed dramatically when the City began funding such efforts. Most important, however, is the control that government has over the key aspects of community life. Local CDCs can design housing redevelopment or public safety improvement programs, but implementing these programs through land use controls or local police is a local government responsibility. True progress requires partnership between local citizens, local organizations, and government.

USING DATA TO DRIVE PROGRAMS AND STRATEGY

Developing effective strategies for improving middle neighborhoods requires up-to-date and accurate data. Those seeking to influence residents' choice of middle-income neighborhoods must understand trends in a particular neighborhood and its competitor neighborhoods—and, when necessary, take corrective action. A crime wave, a rise in housing abandonment, or a growing number of residents who do not shovel the snow in the winter or maintain their yards in the summer—any of these factors may cause potential new residents to look elsewhere or long-term residents who might be experiencing a change in family circumstance to move away. On the other hand, a good new charter school, a reinvigorated public school, or a new high-quality day care center can make a neighborhood far more attractive to potential residents. Some important changes are apparent even to casual observers. Retail trends, for example, are often obvious. But other trends are more difficult to characterize. Is the rise in neighborhood crime, for example, the same or different from regional trends? Is the increase concentrated on a few blocks or widespread? Does it appear that the same perpetrators are responsible for all of the crimes? Without the answers to these questions—answers that require data—appropriate action is impossible.

Getting the right data to develop neighborhood strategies is not simple. Easily available national data are usually too rough grained and outdated to be helpful. Ten-year census data, while very detailed, are likely to be out-of-date. Fortunately, great progress has been made. A leader in this effort is the National Neighborhood Indicators Partnership (http://www.neighborhoodindicators.org), a collaboration of the Urban Institute and local partners. Another is The Reinvestment Fund's Market Value Analysis, described in the third essay of this volume. Common practice is for local groups to track public school, property, crime, social service, housing, and health statistics on an annual basis. Housing data—including asking and sales prices, days on the market, and rental and retail vacancy rates—and crime patterns are often updated weekly. Some groups combine quantitative data with local resident surveys of attitudes and concerns. The best data systems combine hard data with interpretation by skilled local observers. A rise in vacancy rates for rental housing, for example, may indicate a problem of slack demand or result from the emptying out of buildings for major rehabilitation or a condominium conversion.

The most sophisticated data systems provide not only neighborhood data but also detailed data on surrounding neighborhoods and citywide or regional trends.[7] It is far easier for a target neighborhood to improve if nearby neighborhoods are improving; maintaining neighborhood strength in the midst of deterioration is an uphill climb. Citywide or regional trends allow for comparative analysis, helping to determine when problems can be attacked by the neighborhood and when regional solutions are necessary. Cleveland and Minneapolis are examples of cities that have developed particularly strong systems of neighborhood data.

FOCUSING ON DRIVERS OF CONSUMER CHOICE

Strengthening local organizations, increasing neighborhood cohesion, and using data are all steps in developing a neighborhood strategy that will attract and retain residents. But effective neighborhood strategies, like strategies for other products, must be targeted. The quality of public schools, for example, is very important to families with school-aged children, but much less important to those without children. Those without children, on the other hand, are more likely to want local restaurants and nightlife. All neighborhoods are packages of attributes, of housing stock, retail offerings, parks and recreation options, crime rates, and the like. Neighborhood strategies must examine a neighborhood's strengths, compare it with other neighborhoods' strengths, analyze where improvement is possible, and then decide which groups of potential residents should be targeted.

Some issues, however, must be addressed regardless of a neighborhood's particular strategy, however. Evidence suggests that even a very small number of abandoned properties have a major effect on the attractiveness and desirability of entire blocks. Neighborhoods with abandoned buildings have crime rates that are twice as high as those in neighborhoods with no abandoned buildings. Crime is a universal issue. Although parents with children and single females may be particularly concerned about crime, a basic level of security is important for any successful neighborhood. Getting to know your neighbors, participating in civic life, and using local retail and recreation are all influenced by the perception and reality of crime. Beyond these essentials, however, neighborhoods can offer many different packages of amenities.

Those implementing neighborhood strategies should remember several key lessons. First is the importance of focusing on what can be changed by local or municipal action in a reasonable period of time. Regional economic performance, the quality of housing stock in fully built out neighborhoods, and, in most cases, local employment are not amenable to change by community actors and hence should usually not be the focus of neighborhood strategies. The quality of local parks and schools, the fate of abandoned and derelict property, and crime trends are far more appropriate issues for local action. All of these can be changed with local government action.

A second lesson is that competition between neighborhoods precludes certain strategies. For much of the first decade of the 2000s, I was deeply involved in developing neighborhood

---

[7]   For an example, see R. Sampson, *Great American City: Chicago and the Enduring Neighborhood Effect* (Chicago: University of Chicago Press, 2012).

strategies for communities on the mid-South Side of Chicago that were hoping to move from poor to middle neighborhoods. After decades of disinvestment, the South Side was improving and had the potential to improve more—fueled by the growth of the Chicago central business district (popularly known as the Loop) and the increase in the number of middle class African Americans wanting to return to the city. One key question was which potential residents could these neighborhoods successfully attract? I, and many of my colleagues, concluded that although neighborhoods on the South Side could successfully attract families if public schools were improved, these neighborhoods could not draw large numbers of young professionals. The clubs, restaurants, and culture of the North Side were too attractive to young professionals.

Third is to pay attention to what might appear to be modest programs. Traditional analyses of the quality of neighborhoods as places for children, for example, focus on the quality of public schools. There is no doubt that quality public schools are a key factor, but they are not the only factor. A set of strong summer programs, afterschool activities, and weekend activities can balance weak school choices. A great ballet program, or great Little League and soccer leagues can anchor families to a neighborhood. Few cities have recognized the importance of these activities, particularly in an era when both parents are often working full-time.

The final lesson is the importance of balancing attention between sharpening neighborhood strengths and alleviating neighborhood problems. The strengths of neighborhoods entice citizens to rent an apartment or buy a house. Neighborhood weaknesses can cause them to leave. The recent college graduate who buys a fixer-upper in a middle neighborhood is seeking value appreciation and excitement and may not be greatly concerned about crime. The same person may leave the neighborhood if the house is broken into several times.

MARKETING TO KEY AUDIENCES

Middle neighborhoods are often unknown to many potential residents. Lacking tourist attractions and regional amenities, middle neighborhoods must take affirmative steps to make themselves known. There is no magic to the process of making a neighborhood visible. Offering tours of neighborhoods to real estate agents and potential new residents are staples. But creativity can lead to better results. In St. Louis, a south city neighborhood is home to a major festival each year. The festival is on one of the great streets of the city and located in a wealthy neighborhood. But the middle neighborhood immediately to the north buys a booth at the festival, advertises the assets of the middle neighborhood, organizes tours and shows very attractive pictures of homes for sale or rent.

Most successful neighborhood marketing campaigns depend on a mix of three kinds of strategies. The first strategy is to establish a sense of neighborhood identity that is perceptible to current and prospective residents. Sometimes this sense is already present. At other times it is helped by visual cues such as street banners or special lighting or painting. Coordinated strategies of plantings or house painting are also common. Second is publicity. Events that bring potential residents to the neighborhood—such as home or garden tours and neighborhood festivals—are options. Some neighborhoods create special promotions for which all retail establishments in a neighborhood offer special discounts. Third is the use of incentives. Large employers have used Employer Housing Assistance Programs to encourage employees to live in selected neighborhoods. Although these incentives are usually relatively modest, they can be effective in encouraging first-time homebuyers and others with limited equity.

CONCLUSION

Middle neighborhoods are the lynchpin of the success of most American cities. They are also relatively ignored by academics and policymakers, who have focused on the problems of concentrated poverty, gentrification, and the need for downtown revitalization. Although understandable, such oversight is not in the long-term interests of cities or their citizens. Middle neighborhoods are the core of most American cities and are increasingly threatened. Local governments must be prepared to invest in middle neighborhoods and join with local citizens to develop and implement neighborhood strategies that strengthen and empower local organizations, use data to drive programs and strategy, focus on drivers of consumer choice, and market to key audiences. Strategic investments in middle neighborhoods will do much to improve urban America and city residents.

Henry S. Webber is the executive vice chancellor for Administration and Professor of Practice at the Brown School of Social Work and Sam Fox School of Design & Visual Arts at Washington University in St. Louis. He has been a leader in equitable regional development and neighborhood improvement efforts in Chicago and St. Louis. He writes widely on issues of neighborhood change, the role of anchor institutions in community development, and segregation.

APPENDIX

THE AMERICAN ASSEMBLY
COLUMBIA UNIVERSITY

ABOUT

Founded by Dwight D. Eisenhower in 1950, The American Assembly is a national, nonpartisan public affairs institute that illuminates issues of public policy by commissioning research, issuing publications, and sponsoring meetings.

The American Assembly's projects bring together leading authorities representing a broad spectrum of views and interests. American Assembly reports and other publications are used by government, community, civic leaders, and public officials. American Assembly topics concern a wide variety of domestic and foreign policy issues. The American Assembly is an affiliate of Columbia University.

HISTORY

When Dwight D. Eisenhower became president of Columbia University in 1948, he believed that American democracy was facing external as well as internal threats to its continued existence. He saw a need for thorough and reasoned dialogue in the crucial issues affecting U.S. interests, and he envisioned an organization that would bring citizens together to examine these major problems and arrive at workable solutions. It was out of this concept that, in 1950, The American Assembly was created. It remains Eisenhower's principal legacy from his tenure as president of Columbia University.

Please visit our website for more information on the history of The American Assembly, or see *Dwight D. Eisenhower and the Founding of The American Assembly*, by Travis Beal Jacobs.

CURRENT PROGRAMS

The American Assembly has developed projects and held assemblies on a wide range of issues. Current work focuses on two broad themes—cities and knowledge economies—and provides a framework for an array of convening, publication, and research activities.

THE FEDERAL RESERVE BANK OF SAN FRANCISCO
THE COMMUNITY DEVELOPMENT DEPARTMENT

The Community Development Department of the Federal Reserve Bank of San Francisco created the Center for Community Development Investments to research and disseminate best practices in providing capital to low- and moderate-income communities. Part of this mission is accomplished by publishing the *Community Development Investment Review*. The *Review* brings together experts to write about various community development investment topics, including:

- Finance—new tools, techniques, or approaches that increase the volume, lower the cost, lower the risk, or in any way make investments in low-income communities more attractive;
- Collaborations—ways in which different groups can pool resources and expertise to address the capital needs of low-income communities;
- Public Policy—analysis of how government and public policy influence community development finance options;
- Best Practices—a showcase of innovative projects, people, or institutions that are improving the investment opportunities in low-income areas.

The goal of the *Review* is to bridge the gap between theory and practice and enlist as many viewpoints as possible—government, nonprofits, financial institutions, and beneficiaries. As a leading economist in the community development field describes it, the *Review* provides "ideas for people who get things done."

CENTER FOR COMMUNITY DEVELOPMENT INVESTMENTS
Scott Turner, Vice President
David Erickson, Director, Center for Community Development Investments
Laura Choi, Senior Research Associate
Naomi Cytron, Senior Research Associate
Ian Galloway, Senior Research Associate
William Dowling, Research Associate

ABOUT THE EDITOR

Paul C. Brophy is a principal with Brophy & Reilly, LLC. This consulting firm specializes in inclusive economic development and neighborhood improvement in legacy cities, the management of complex urban redevelopment projects, and the development of mixed-income housing communities. Brophy also is a senior advisor to Enterprise Community Partners and the chair of the Legacy Cities Partnership. Previously, Brophy was a non-resident senior fellow at the Brookings Institution, a senior advisor to the Center for Community Progress, and a senior scholar at the George Warren Brown School at Washington University in St. Louis, Missouri. Prior to the formation of Brophy and Reilly, LLC, Brophy was the co-CEO of Enterprise Community Partners.

From 1977–1986, Brophy worked for the city government in Pittsburgh, Pennsylvania, where he was director of housing and then executive director of the Urban Redevelopment Authority. A leader in the Renaissance II initiatives of Mayor Richard S. Caliguiri, Brophy worked on such projects as downtown revitalization, the reuse of vacant steel mill sites, and the strengthening of the city's neighborhoods. For his work in Pittsburgh, Brophy was named one of the "savviest municipal issuers" by *Institutional Investor* and "The Best of the New Generation" by *Esquire*.

Brophy has directed three projects for the prestigious American Assembly: In 1997, Brophy led a project that resulted in a widely read report, *Community Capitalism: Rediscovering the Markets of America's Urban Neighborhoods*. In 2007, he conducted a project that produced the report, *Retooling for Growth: Building a Twenty-First Century Economy in America's Older Industrial Areas*. In 2011, Brophy codirected a meeting that led to the report, *Reinventing America's Legacy Cities: Strategies for Cities Losing Population*.

In early 2009, Brophy codirected a project that The University of Pennsylvania's Institute for Urban Research sponsored. The resulting report—*Retooling HUD for a Catalytic Federal Government: A Report to Secretary Shaun Donovan*—provided recommendations to reframe the U.S. Department of Housing and Urban Development's approach to housing, cities, and metropolitan areas.

Brophy holds degrees from La Salle University and The University of Pennsylvania. He also is coauthor of three books: *Neighborhood Revitalization: Theory and Practice* (1975); *Housing and Local Government* (1982); and *A Guide to Careers in Community Development* (2001).

Made in the USA
San Bernardino, CA
08 August 2017